INTELLI 2017

The Sixth International Conference on Intelligent Systems and Applications

InManEnt 2017

International Symposium on Intelligent Manufacturing Environments

July 23 - 27, 2017

Nice, France

INTELLI 2017 Editors

Leo van Moergestel, HU Utrecht University of Applied Sciences, the Netherlands

Gil Goncalves, Instituto de Sistamas Robotica,University of Porto, Portugal

Sungshin Kim, Pusan National University, Korea

Carlos Leon, Universidad de Sevilla, Spain

Printed from e-media with permission by:

Curran Associates, Inc.
57 Morehouse Lane
Red Hook, NY 12571

Some format issues inherent in the e-media version may also appear in this print version.

Printed by Curran Associates, Inc. (2017)

International Academy, Research, and Industry Association (IARIA)
412 Derby Way
Wilmington, DE 19810

Phone: (408) 893-6407
Fax: (408) 527-6351

petre@iaria.org

Additional copies of this publication are available from:

Curran Associates, Inc.
57 Morehouse Lane
Red Hook, NY 12571 USA
Phone: 845-758-0400
Fax: 845-758-2633
Email: curran@proceedings.com
Web: www.proceedings.com

Table of Contents

INTELLI 2017

Foreword

The Sixth International Conference on Intelligent Systems and Applications (INTELLI 2017), held between July 23 - 27, 2017 - Nice, France, was an inaugural event on advances towards fundamental, as well as practical and experimental aspects of intelligent and applications.

The information surrounding us is not only overwhelming but also subject to limitations of systems and applications, including specialized devices. The diversity of systems and the spectrum of situations make it almost impossible for an end-user to handle the complexity of the challenges. Embedding intelligence in systems and applications seems to be a reasonable way to move some complex tasks form user duty. However, this approach requires fundamental changes in designing the systems and applications, in designing their interfaces and requires using specific cognitive and collaborative mechanisms. Intelligence became a key paradigm and its specific use takes various forms according to the technology or the domain a system or an application belongs to.

INTELLI 2017 also featured the following Symposium:

- InManEnt 2017, The International Symposium on Intelligent Manufacturing Environments

We take here the opportunity to warmly thank all the members of the INTELLI 2017 Technical Program Committee, as well as the numerous reviewers. The creation of such a high quality conference program would not have been possible without their involvement. We also kindly thank all the authors who dedicated much of their time and efforts to contribute to INTELLI 2017. We truly believe that, thanks to all these efforts, the final conference program consisted of top quality contributions.

Also, this event could not have been a reality without the support of many individuals, organizations, and sponsors. We are grateful to the members of the INTELLI 2017 organizing committee for their help in handling the logistics and for their work to make this professional meeting a success.

We hope that INTELLI 2017 was a successful international forum for the exchange of ideas and results between academia and industry and for the promotion of progress in the field of intelligent systems and applications.

We are convinced that the participants found the event useful and communications very open. We also hope that Nice provided a pleasant environment during the conference and everyone saved some time for exploring this beautiful city.

INTELLI 2017 Chairs:

INTELLI Steering Committee

Lars Braubach, Hochschule Bremen, Germany
Leo van Moergestel, HU University of Applied Sciences Utrecht, Netherlands
Sungshin Kim, Pusan National University, Korea
Maiga Chang, Athabasca University, Canada
Sérgio Gorender, Federal University of Bahia (UFBA) & Federal University of the South of Bahia (UFSB), Brazil
Chin-Chen Chang, Feng Chia University, Taiwan
Stefano Berretti, University of Florence, Italy
Antonio Martin, Universidad de Sevilla, Spain

INTELLI Industry/Research Advisory Committee

David Greenhalgh, University of Strathclyde, Glasgow, UK
Carsten Behn, Technische Universität Ilmenau, Germany
Paolo Spagnolo, National Research Council, Italy
Luca Santinelli, ONERA Toulouse, France
Sourav Dutta, Bell Labs, Dublin, Ireland
Floriana Gargiulo, Gemass - CNRS | University of Paris Sorbonne, Paris, France

InManEnt Advisory Committee

Ingo Schwab, University of Applied Sciences Karlsruhe, Germany
Gil Gonçalves, University of Porto, Portugal
Juha Röning, University of Oulu, Finland
Grzegorz Redlarski, Gdansk University of Technology, Poland
Jerry Chun-Wei Lin, Harbin Institute of Technology - Shenzhen Graduate School, China
Marcello Pellicciari, University of Modena and Reggio Emilia, Italy

INTELLI 2017

Committee

INTELLI Steering Committee

Lars Braubach, Hochschule Bremen, Germany
Leo van Moergestel, HU University of Applied Sciences Utrecht, Netherlands
Sungshin Kim, Pusan National University, Korea
Maiga Chang, Athabasca University, Canada
Sérgio Gorender, Federal University of Bahia (UFBA) & Federal University of the South of Bahia (UFSB), Brazil
Chin-Chen Chang, Feng Chia University, Taiwan
Stefano Berretti, University of Florence, Italy
Antonio Martin, Universidad de Sevilla, Spain

INTELLI Industry/Research Advisory Committee

David Greenhalgh, University of Strathclyde, Glasgow, UK
Carsten Behn, Technische Universität Ilmenau, Germany
Paolo Spagnolo, National Research Council, Italy
Luca Santinelli, ONERA Toulouse, France
Sourav Dutta, Bell Labs, Dublin, Ireland
Floriana Gargiulo, Gemass - CNRS | University of Paris Sorbonne, Paris, France

INTELLI 2017 Technical Program Committee

Azizi Ab Aziz, Universiti Utara Malaysia, Malaysia
Witold Abramowicz, Poznan University of Economics and Business, Poland
Zaher Al Aghbari, University of Sharjah, UAE
Gábor Alberti, University of Pécs, Hungary
Rachid Anane, Coventry University, UK
Mohammadamin Barekatain, Technical University of Munich, Germany
Daniela Barreiro Claro, Federal University of Bahia, Brazil
Ana Isabel Barros, TNO, Netherlands
Carmelo J. A. Bastos-Filho, University of Pernambuco, Brazil
Carsten Behn, Technische Universität Ilmenau, Germany
Giuseppe Berio, IRISA | Université de Bretagne Sud, France
Stefano Berretti, University of Florence, Italy
Jonathan Bonnet, IRT Saint Exupery, Toulouse, France
Lars Braubach, Hochschule Bremen, Germany
Simeon C. Calvert, Delft University of Technology, Netherlands
Carlos Carrascosa, Universidad Politécnica de Valencia, Spain
Chin-Chen Chang, Feng Chia University, Taiwan
Maiga Chang, Athabasca University, Canada

Chanjuan Liu, Dalian University of Technology, China
Prabhat Mahanti, University of New Brunswick, Canada
Mohammad Saeid Mahdavinejad, University of Isfahan, Iran
Giuseppe Mangioni, University of Catania, Italy
Francesco Marcelloni, University of Pisa, Italy
Antonio Martín-Montes, University of Sevilla, Spain
René Meier, Hochschule Luzern, Germany
Michele Melchiori, University of Brescia, Italy
John-Jules Charles Meyer, Utrecht University, The Netherlands
Angelos Michalas, TEI of Western Macedonia, Kastoria, Greece
Dusmanta Kumar Mohanta, Birla Institute of Technology, India
Fernando Moreira, Universidade Portucalense - Porto, Portugal
Debajyoti Mukhopadhyay, Maharashtra Institute of Technology, India
Kenric Nelson, Boston University, USA
Filippo Neri, University of Napoli "Federico II", Italy
Cyrus F. Nourani, akdmkrd.tripod.com, USA
Kenneth S. Nwizege, Swansea University, UK
Gregory O'Hare, University College Dublin (UCD), Ireland
José Angel Olivas Varela, UCLM Universidad de Castilla-La Mancha, Spain
Joanna Isabelle Olszewska, University of Gloucestershire, UK
Sanjeevikumar Padmanaban, University of Johannesburg, Auckland Park, South Africa
Endre Pap, University Singidunum, Serbia
Marcin Paprzycki, Systems Research Institute / Polish Academy of Sciences - Warsaw, Poland
Luigi Patrono, University of Salento, Lecce, Italy
Joao Paulo Carvalho, INESC-ID /Instituto Superior Técnico | Universidade de Lisboa, Portugal
Miltos Petridis, University of Brighton, UK
Agostino Poggi, Università degli Studi di Parma, Italy
Marco Polignano, University of Bari "Aldo Moro", Italy
Dilip Kumar Pratihar, Indian Institute of Technology Kharagpur, India
Radu-Emil Precup, Politehnica University of Timisoara, Romania
José Raúl Romero, University of Córdoba, Spain
Mohammadreza Rezvan, University of Isfahan, Iran
Daniel Rodriguez, University of Alcalá, Spain
Alexander Ryjov, Lomonosov Moscow State University | Russian Presidential Academy of National Economy and Public Administration, Russia
Fariba Sadri, Imperial College London, UK
Ozgur Koray Sahingoz, Turkish Air Force Academy, Turkey
Abdel-Badeeh M. Salem, Ain Shams University, Cairo, Egypt
Demetrios Sampson, Curtin University, Australia
Luca Santinelli, ONERA Toulouse, France
Florence Sèdes, Université Toulouse 3, France
Hirosato Seki, Osaka University, Japan
Wen Shen, University of California, Irvine, USA
Kuei-Ping Shih, Tamkang University, Taiwan
Marius Silaghi, Florida Institute of Technology, USA
Paolo Spagnolo, National Research Council, Italy
Pei-Wei Tsai, Swinburne University of Technology, Australia
José Valente de Oliveira, Universidade do Algarve, Portugal

Sergi Valverde, Universitat Pompeu Fabra (UPF), Spain
Leo van Moergestel, HU University of Applied Sciences Utrecht, Netherlands
Jan Vascak, Technical University of Kosice, Slovakia
Jose Luis Vazquez-Poletti, Universidad Complutense de Madrid, Spain
Susana M. Vieira, IDMEC - Instituto Superior Tecnico - Universidade de Lisboa, Portugal
Longzhi Yang, Northumbria University, Newcastle upon Tyne, UK
George Yee, Carleton University & Aptusinnova Inc., Ottawa, Canada
Katharina Anna Zweig, TU Kaiserslautern, Germany

InManEnt Advisory Committee

Ingo Schwab, University of Applied Sciences Karlsruhe, Germany
Gil Gonçalves, University of Porto, Portugal
Juha Röning, University of Oulu, Finland
Grzegorz Redlarski, Gdansk University of Technology, Poland
Jerry Chun-Wei Lin, Harbin Institute of Technology - Shenzhen Graduate School, China
Marcello Pellicciari, University of Modena and Reggio Emilia, Italy

Program Committee Members

Lars Braubach, Hochschule Bremen, Germany
Bayram Deviren, Nevsehir Hacı Bektas Veli University, Turkey
Francesco Fontanella, Università di Cassino e del Lazio Meridionale, Italy
Luigi Fortuna, University of Catania, Italy
Gil Gonçalves, University of Porto, Portugal
Richard Jiang, Northumbria University, UK
Dilip Kumar Pratihar, Indian Institute of Technology Kharagpur, India
Jerry Chun-Wei Lin, Harbin Institute of Technology - Shenzhen Graduate School, China
Prabhat Mahanti, University of New Brunswick, Canada
Joao Paulo Carvalho, INESC-ID /Instituto Superior Técnico | Universidade de Lisboa, Portugal
Marcello Pellicciari, University of Modena and Reggio Emilia, Italy
Grzegorz Redlarski, Gdansk University of Technology, Poland
Juha Röning, University of Oulu, Finland
Fariba Sadri, Imperial College London, UK
Ingo Schwab, University of Applied Sciences Karlsruhe, Germany
Alessandra Scotto di Freca, Università di Cassino e del Lazio Meridionale, Italy
Leo van Moergestel, HU University of Applied Sciences Utrecht, Netherlands

A Model of Pulsation for Evolutive Formalizing Incomplete Intelligent Systems

Marta Franova, Yves Kodratoff
LRI, UMR8623 du CNRS & INRIA Saclay
Bât. 660, Orsay, France
e-mail: mf@lri.fr, yvkod@gmail.com

Abstract— **The notion of pulsation concerns a possibility of a particular kind of intelligent controlled and secured evolution in dynamic real-world systems. It is related to fundamentals in intelligent systems and applications as well as to the topic of intelligence by design. In this paper we present a model of pulsation based on Ackermann's function. This brings more clarity to understanding Symbiotic Recursive Pulsative Systems that are important, for instance, for designing and implementing intelligent security systems or for automating robots' programming in incomplete domains and unknown environments. One particular application for these systems is our Constructive Matching Methodology for automating program synthesis from formal specifications in incomplete domains.**

Keywords-pulsation; Symbiotic Recursive Pulsative Systems; intelligent systems; intelligence by design; Ackermann's function; control; security; progress; practical completeness.

I. INTRODUCTION

For more than three decades now, we worked on automation of programs synthesis in incomplete domains via inductive theorem proving [2] [8]. Our approach differs from standard computer science approaches based on modularity of developed parts. This standard is called Newtonian Science in contrast to Cartesian Intuitionism [6] that provides a basis for Symbiotic Recursive Pulsative Systems (SRPS) roughly described in [6].

The notion of SRPS is very rich and complex. In our latest work [4] [5], we are trying to progressively disentangle this symbiotic complexity by presenting notions individually (as much as possible for symbiotic parts of a whole). Such a disentangling is important for perceiving the usefulness of working on particular SRPS for real-world applications where Newtonian Science has shown its limitations.

In this paper we focus on a model for the notion of pulsation. Such a systemic approach influences the overall perception, the guidelines for research and development and elaboration of details of SRPS. We will show in this paper that meta and fundamental levels in SPRS are symbiotic. In other words, their separation leads to a non-sense or an irrecoverable mutilation. This is important for understanding our work on Constructive Matching Methodology (*CMM*) for automating program synthesis from formal specifications in incomplete domains via inductive theorem proving.

The paper is organized as follows. In Section II, we recall the definition of symbiosis we work with and we present an example illustrating symbiosis of information that is present in recursive representations. In Section III, we present a way to construct Ackermann's function and to replace, for given two numbers *a* and *b*, its non-primitive recursive computation by a computation via an on-purpose generated sequence of primitive recursive functions that has to be used for *a* and *b*. In Section IV, we show that prevention and control can be modeled by Ackermann's function. Section V shows that even pulsative systems can be modeled by Ackermann's function. In Section VI, we speak about pulsative development of our Constructive Matching Methodology. Section VII presents an example of a technological vision for which the work presented in this paper is important.

II. SYMBIOSIS OF INFORMATION IN RECURSION

As specified in [6], by symbiosis we understand a particular composition of two or several parts that make an indivisible whole. In other words, a separation of one sole part is a reason for extinction or for irrecoverable mutilation of the all other parts as well as the whole.

Let us point out that we speak here of symbiotic information and not of symbiotic computation.

Let us consider the following simple problem. On a sufficiently big table consider a stack of blocs a, b, c, d and e as shown in Figure 1.

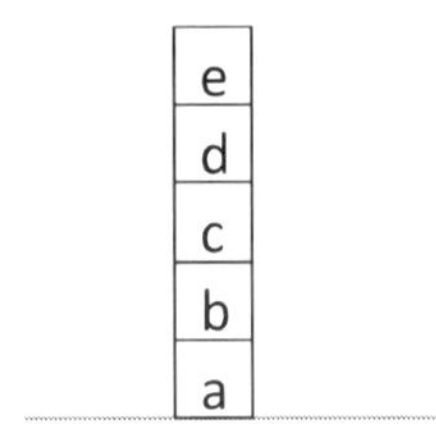

Figure 1. The stack of blocks before the intended action is taken

We say that a bloc m is clear if there is no other bloc on m. (In Figure 1, the bloc e is clear.) There can be at most one bloc on the top of the other. If n is on the top of m we say that n is top of m written as: n = top(m). Let us consider the primitive recursive procedure "put on table" as being hardware defined in the robot that will execute the following informal primitive recursive program makeclear:

```
makeclear(x) =
  if  x is clear then procedure ends
  else
    if     top(x) is clear
    then   put(top(x)) on table
    else   first makeclear(top(x)) and
           then     put(top(x)) on table
```

It can easily be checked that makeclear(b) results not only in clearing bloc b but also in the situation where blocs c, d and e are on the table. This means that the procedure makeclear contains in its description not only its direct effects (such as: the bloc b is cleared) but also the full description of all the secondary effects of any action performed. In Figure 2, these secondary effects are that the blocks c, d and e are on the table.

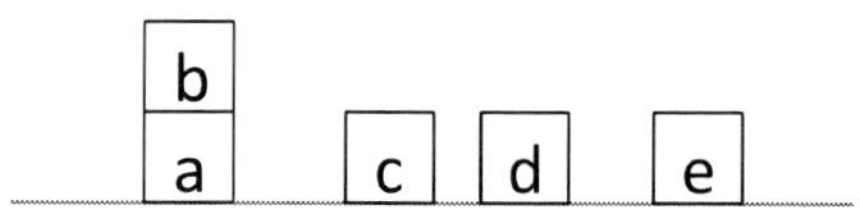

Figure 2. The stack of blocks after the action 'makeclear' is taken

For some other primitive recursive procedures the secondary effects do not modify the environment, but this should not be a barrier for general perception of primitive recursive procedures to be seen as invisible procedural 'seeds' containing symbiotically related the effects (i.e., the results of the computations) and the secondary effects (i.e., the consequences of the computation of a particular value). Therefore, implementing recursive procedures is interesting in all the environments where the control over the secondary effects is important.

The above procedure makeclear is an example of primitive recursion. A recursion that is not primitive goes even further in representing symbiotically information that concerns control, rigor and reproducibility. Ackermann's function is a suitable representative for explaining how non-primitive recursion modelizes a particular kind of pulsation in SRPS.

In the following sections, we shall give a formalized presentation of the pulsation starting by a presentation of a construction procedure that results in Ackermann's function. It will become clear how this construction and the notion of pulsation are linked together. Then, we shall present a practical application of this notion.

III. Ackermann's Function

The idea to model pulsation by Ackermann's function comes from the understanding how this function can be constructed. The practical use of this function becomes then exploitable by a particular 'simplifying' the computation of its values.

A. *A Construction*

Let ack be Ackermann's function defined by its standard definition, i.e.,

$$ack(0,n) = n+1$$
$$ack(m+1,0) = ack(m,1)$$
$$ack(m+1,n+1) = ack(m,ack(m+1,n)).$$

We shall show here how this function can be constructed.

By definition, each primitive recursive function f is a composition of a finite number of primitive recursive functions and of f itself.

Since ack is a non-primitive recursive function (see a proof in [12]), by definition of non-primitive recursion, it is a particular composition of an infinite sequence of primitive recursive functions. We shall build a function ack' as a particular composition of an infinite sequence of primitive recursive functions built so that the definitions for ack and for ack' (defined below) are identical.

Let us construct such an infinite sequence of primitive recursive functions f_0, f_1, f_2, …, f_n, f_{n+1}, …. respecting the following relationships

$$f_0(n) = n+1$$
$$f_{i+1}(n+1) = f_i(f_{i+1}(n))$$

for each i from 0, 1, 2 …. We are thus able to define a new function ack' as follows:

$$ack'(0,n) = f_0(n) \text{ and}$$

$$ack'(m+1,n+1) = f_{m+1}(n+1).$$

This definition is still incomplete since the value for ack'(m+1,0) is not yet known.

Since we want ack' to be a non-primitive recursive function, we need to guarantee that it cannot be reduced to any of f_i. In order to do so, we shall simply perform a progressive diagonalization on this infinite sequence of functions by defining the value of $f_{i+1}(0)$ as being the value of f_i in 0+1, i.e.,

$$f_{i+1}(0) = f_i(1).$$

In other words, we define

$$ack'(m+1,0) = f_m(1).$$

By this construction we see that f_{i+1} is more complex than f_i for each i. It is obvious that

$$ack'(m,n) = ack(m, n) = f_m(n).$$

This construction is at the same time a guarantee that ack is not primitive recursive, since it is indeed a composition of an infinite sequence of primitive recursive functions each of them more complex than those before it and ack cannot be reduced to any one of them. As a by-product, we have thus simplified also the standard presentation of the non-primitive character of ack, which is usually done by a proof by a projection of Ackermann's function ack into a sequence of primitive recursive functions $a_m(n)$ = ack(m,n) and showing that ack grows more rapidly than any of these primitive recursive function (see [12]). The difference thus lies in our use of an indirect construction (instead of a projection) and relying on a particular diagonalization.

To our best knowledge, this construction with a use of progressive diagonalization was not presented so far. Note that the notion of pulsation that refers to this construction of Ackermann's function has no relation to measures of the computation complexity of a function, such as Ritchie's hierarchy [11].

B. A 'Simplification' of the Computation

The above construction of the Ackermann's function shows immediately that the computation of its values for given m and n using non-primitive recursive definition can be 'simplified' - or, rather, replaced - by a definition of m primitive recursive functions obtained by a suitable macro-procedure.

Our recursive macro-procedure will simply compute, step by step, each of the values $f_{i+1}(0)$ (for i < m) in advance and will define the whole f_{i+1} with this already computed value. This may not lead to a fast computation but we are not concerned now with computational efficiency of this way of proceeding, only by its practical feasibility and reproductiveness. In no way is our presentation an attempt to optimize Ackermann's function. On the other hand, computing in advance some values is a known technique, we have just adapted it here for our macro.

Note that there exists efficient algorithms that go further with the computation of the values of Ackermann's function than our macro-procedure, but these known algorithms are based on a relation of Ackermann's function with a kind of usual exponentiation function. Our way of proceeding is thus useful for practical applications that will be based on use of SRPS. Indeed, not many practical applications (such as security information system or robots programming themselves in unknown environments, for instance) can be modeled by exponential functions. Therefore, our macro, even though less efficient, aims at general use of different systemic non-primitive recursive functions in the framework of SRPS.

We define a macro-procedure, ack_macro, that uses a standard program of LISP which adds a text at the end of the file that will contain the programs generated by ack_macro. We thus create an auxiliary file F that stores the functions f_i generated by ack_macro. Our ack_macro uses thus the LISP procedures add_to_file and load_file. The procedure add_to_file(*text*,*F*) adds the *text* at the end of the file *F*. The procedure load_file(*F*) loads the file *F* in order to make computable the functions written in the file. Our macro-procedure ack_macro(m,n) uses the infinite sequence of functions defined above as being representative of Ackermann's function.

```
Step 1:
  text:= { f0(n) = n+1 }
Step 2:
  Create the file F (empty at start) and
  add_to_file(text,F)
  load_file(F)
Step 3:
  i:=0
  aux:= compute the value of fi(1)
Step 4:
  text := { fi+1(0)= aux and
            fi+1(n+1)= fi(fi+1(n))}
  add_to_file(text,F)
  load_file(F)
  aux := compute the value of fi+1(1)
  i:= i+1
  if i < m
  then Go to step 4
  else stop
```

Figure 3. A macro-procedure for computing particular values of ack

ack_macro(m,n) is now completed and file F collects the definitions of m primitive recursive functions. We are now able to compute ack(m,n) = $f_m(n)$.

In the next section, we shall explain how prevention and control are modeled by Ackermann's function.

IV. Prevention and Control In Recursion

We have seen above in the example of the program makeclear that primitive recursion captures the effects (computation) and the secondary effects (consequences of the computation). We have also seen that the non-primitive recursive Ackermann's function is obtained using a diagonalization procedure. This diagonalization brings forward complementary information about the process of this symbiotic information in the recursion. Since diagonalization is a meta-level procedure, we understand this complementary information as a kind of meta-level prevention. In particular, we interpret it as a prevention factor simply because diagonalization prevents ack to be reduced to computation and consequences of computations of functions from which it is constructed.

It is interesting to note that some scientists may intuitively 'feel' that Ackermann's function provides a model of human thinking of 'everything' for a particular situation. The makeclear program mentioned shows that this intuition can be presented in terms of symbiosis of the information included in a particular situation. Note that the above macro-procedure (Figure 3) simplifies only the computation of thinking of 'everything'. In order to illustrate this particular 'simplification' of the computation we may mention that, as it can be checked, the trace of the computation of the value for ack(3,2) using the standard definition shows (see [3]) that the value ack(1,1) is computed twenty-two times for obtaining the result of ack(3,2). This is not the case for the computation of simplified $f_3(2)$. However, it is necessary to understand that the overall complexity of this situation remains the same since, in order to be able to 'simplify' (i.e., to define the above macro-procedure), we already need to have available Ackermann's function equivalent to the constructed sequence of f_i. In other words, the principle and effectiveness of 'thinking of everything' remain on the global level. The simplification concerns only focusing on one particular local level defined by the two values *a* and *b* instantiating Ackerman's variables. Of course, the macro-procedure is general, but for *a* and *b* given, it generates only the finite sequence of primitive functions $f_0, f_1, \ldots, f_a$.

This makes explicit that 'thinking of everything' keeps its theoretical order of complexity after presented simplification. It is only the computational complexity that is simplified. Systems requiring a simultaneous handling the prevention and control factors such as information flow security systems [7] [10] are practical examples of a problem requesting to think of 'everything'.

V. PULSATIVE SYSTEMS

The above sections will help us explaining how Ackermann's function enables us to formally specify the notion of the **pulsation**. This is interesting not only from the point of view of building particular formal theories for unknown domains, but also for understanding the difference between revolution, innovation and evolutive improvement in this building process.

In the context of program synthesis, we have defined the notion of oscillation in [5] and [6]. Since the notion of oscillation provides an informal background for the notion of pulsation, we shall recall this notion here.

In scientific fields, the obvious basic paradigm is, for a given problem, to find an idea leading to a solution. For instance, in program synthesis, for a given problem one tries to find a *heuristic* that solves the problem. This can, in general, be expressed by the formula

$$\forall \text{ Problem } \exists \text{ Idea Leads\_to\_a\_solution(Idea,Problem)}.$$

We shall call this formulation: "first paradigm."

However, another and rather unusual (except in Physics) paradigm is to find an idea that provides a solution for all problems. We shall show how Ackermann's function provides a model for this last paradigm. First, however, let us express this second paradigm by the formula

$$\exists \text{ Idea } \forall \text{ Problem Leads\_to\_a\_solution(Idea,Problem)}.$$

We shall call this formulation: "second paradigm."

The difference between these two formulas lies in the fact that in this second case the 'Idea' obtained is unique, while in the first formula each problem can use its own Idea.

We have explained in [6] that the goal of *CMM* is to build a program synthesis system (Idea) that solves the problem of program construction in incomplete theories (e.g., unknown environments in space). We thus globally work with the second paradigm. However, in our everyday research (which means to acquire fruitful experiences enabling to build relevant knowledge), we work locally with the first paradigm while keeping in mind the second paradigm. This means that we *mentally oscillate* between two paradigms. The second paradigm presents a global vision and the direction of the solution we seek and, to make this goal achievable, we perform our everyday work in the framework of the first paradigm following nevertheless the direction imposed by the second paradigm. We call **oscillation** this approach of *symbiotic* switching between the two above paradigms. We speak here about symbiotic switching, since both paradigms are in reality considered simultaneously and cannot be separated.

Let us consider now a potentially infinitely incomplete theory. In unknown environments that may be seen as a framework for potentially infinitely incomplete theories, building a formal theory becomes then a process of *suitable completions* of a particular initial theory T_0. We shall say that this theory T_0 is **practically complete** when it formalizes solutions for the problems met so far. Since the theory is potentially incomplete, sooner or later we shall meet a problem that cannot be solved in the framework of T_0. In the vocabulary of scientific discoveries we may say that we need a conceptual switch (a new axiom or a set of axioms) that *completes* T_0. Note that we speak here about *completion* and

- not about a *revolution* - which would mean in a sense rejecting T_0
- not about a *innovation* - which would simply mean a particular reformulating T_0.

Thus, in fact this completion T_1 contains T_0 and it is coherent with T_0. However, since a new conceptual switch guarantees that T_1 is more powerful than T_0, we consider this particular kind of completion as a suitable model for one step of *improvement*, or pulsation, in our search for suitable completions. Since we consider here a potentially infinitely incomplete theory, we can then see the **pulsation** (particular improvement) as an infinite sequence of theories $T_0, T_1, \ldots, T_n, \ldots$. In this sequence, T_{i+1} completes and thus is coherent with T_i for all $i = 0, 1, 2, \ldots$

We have seen that, in the infinite sequence from which Ackermann's function is built, the function f_1 relies on (is coherent with) f_0, and f_{i+1} relies on f_i for each i. It means that Ackermann's function really provides a model for evolutive improvement (or progress in Bacon's sense [1]). We understand it different from revolution and innovation.

Let us now come back to our notion of pulsation. We have seen that, in the informally specified notion of oscillation, we switch coherently between two paradigms. In our interpretation, the second paradigm, i.e.,

$$\exists \text{ Idea } \forall \text{ Problem Leads\_to\_a\_solution(Idea,Problem)}$$

represents the idea of Ackermann's function and the first paradigm, i.e.,

$$\forall \text{ Problem } \exists \text{ Idea Leads\_to\_a\_solution(Idea,Problem)}.$$

represents particular primitive recursive functions from which Ackermann's function is constructed. In the definition of Ackermann's function we have seen that

$$f_{i+1}(0) = f_i(1).$$

Analogously, we shall state that the sequence of completing theories can be written as:

$$T_{i+1} = T_i + A_{i+1},$$

where A_{i+1} is an axiom (or a set of axioms) representing the conceptual switch that enables solving the problem unsolvable in T_i. Let us stress the fact that by pulsation we understand an infinite sequence of theories T_0, T_1, ..., T_n, T_{n+1}, ... with the just mentioned property and not only one particular step in this sequence. This means that pulsative systems are systems that are formalized progressively and potentially indefinitely.

We have seen above that Ackermann's function is also a model for symbiotic consideration of prevention and control. We could see that f_0 must be defined in a way that guarantees the non-primitive recursion of the constructed infinite sequence. We could see that, with respect to our requirement, f_0 must be defined in a way that guarantees the non-primitive recursion of the constructed infinite sequence. Indeed, if f_0 were a constant, for instance 3 (which would mean that f $f_0(n) = 3$ for all n), the resulting infinite composition would also be the constant 3. This means that, even though f_0 is the first function of this infinite construction, since it must be defined as a symbiotic part of the final composition, the prevention and control factors must be taken into account in this function.

So, we can see that Ackermann's function provides in fact a model for the ***improvement*** that guarantees symbiotic handling prevention and control already from the start.

VI. On Pulsative Development of *CMM*

Roughly speaking, *CMM* is developed as a methodology for automation of program synthesis in incomplete domains via inductive theorem proving (ITP). It represents an experimental work that illustrates this paper. For understanding this section it is not necessary to present a formalization of this particular application (it can be found in [5]). However, it is useful that we describe what we understand by a methodology.

Given a non-trivial goal, its methodology is a full formalized description of all the problems that arise in achieving this goal and, of course, of the complete solutions for these problems. In other words, a methodology is a full 'know-how' of a successful achieving the given goal.

Automating program synthesis in incomplete domains via ITP is far from a simple problem. This is because a unified know-how is not available even for by-hand construction of inductive proofs that are necessary for program synthesis. This means that a unified know-how must first be found. This is the goal of our *CMM*.

It is important to note that we are still at the level 0 of pulsative development of *CMM*. In other words, we work on defining a powerful primitive recursive f_0 with respect to the overall goal of resulting non-primitive recursive SRPS for *CMM*. This means that already level 0 has required several decades of research and many useful results not known in automation of ITP were obtained so far. A full bibliography of these results can be found in [9]. We have described above the process of building f_0 by oscillating between two above mentioned paradigms. However, we still need to work on transmission of the technical details of this oscillation. We have explained in [6] that Cartesian Intuitionism, and thus *CMM* as well, cannot use tools developed by Newtonian approaches.

Understanding the process of oscillation between the two paradigms described above is very important for the development of SRPS (namely the systems on level 0) in various domains. However, a detailed illustration in the framework of program synthesis would be too much complex for readers that are not expert in this particular topic. We intend to present a compact but detailed illustration on an example that concerns a 'safe' transmission of relevant scientific knowledge. This problem was already pointed out by Francis Bacon. By a 'safe' transmission of knowledge we understand a transmission that guarantees that no mutilation is possible during such a transmission and that all the creative potential of the knowledge and know-how to be transferred is preserved. Our book [3] is an example of such a safe transmission. We shall tackle this topic also in one of our future papers.

VII. A Pulsative Technological Vision

It is interesting to be focused on the topic of SRPS in general and of *CMM* in particular because, in long term consideration, this seems to be the only way how robots will be able to

- formalize recursively unknown domains (e.g., in space research) handling perfectly control, rigor and evolutive improvement;
- perform experiments necessary for finding such suitable formalizations;
- program themselves autonomously with the help of the formalizations found.

By formalizing an unknown domain we mean its progressive exploration and acquiring experiences – through experiments – that lead to facts enabling a progressive formalization of this domain.

Of course, a successful achievement of this technological vision will require not only *CMM* but also the tools developed in Machine Learning, Big Data, Computational Creativity and some other maybe not yet known scientific fields that will become known as soon as scientific community overcomes artificial human factors that are a barrier for seriously investigating this technological vision.

Let us recall once again that each unknown environment is potentially infinitely incomplete and thus the notion of pulsation really has an enormous importance for Science.

VIII. CONCLUSION

There are technological visions that need to be solved in the framework of Symbiotic Recursive Pulsative Systems and thus, they need to be tackled by Cartesian Intuitionism. This means that all the notions of SRPS and their algorithmic elaborations should become widely known so that really symbiotic long-term collaborations become possible. This need for symbiotic collaborations requires also a replacement of Newtonian management strategies by the management strategies that are proper to Cartesian Intuitionism. This paper extends thus our preliminary work on transmission of fundamental notions of Cartesian Intuitionism and SRPS by presenting the origin and the motivation for the model of pulsation inherent to SRPS. By its practical applications and already existing use mentioned in the paper this notion shows its importance for Science already now and not only for future technological visions. Indeed, this notion allows to consider progress as different from innovation for which a control of negative secondary effects appearing in future is not handled systematically. The Ackermann's function as a model for pulsation allows to provide such a control since the control of the secondary effects is built in SRPS themselves and already from the start of their design. This paper shows that Ackermann's function should not be considered as a simple abstract mathematical curiosity but as a legacy with a rich scientific potential.

ACKNOWLEDGMENT

We thank to Michèle Sebag and Yannis Manoussakis for a moral support. Anonymous referees of the submitted version provided a very useful feedback.

REFERENCES

[1] F. Bacon, The Advancement of Learning; Rarebooksclub, 2013.

[2] M. Franova, "CM-strategy: A Methodology for Inductive Theorem Proving or Constructive Well-Generalized Proofs"; in, A. K. Joshi, (ed), Proc. of the Ninth International Joint Conference on Artificial Intelligence, pp. 1214-1220, 1985.

[3] M. Franova, Formal Creativity: Method and Use – Conception of Complex "Informatics" Systems and Epistemological Patent (Créativité Formelle : Méthode et Pratique - Conception des systèmes « informatiques » complexes et Brevet Épistémologique); Publibook, 2008.

[4] M. Franova, "Cartesian Intuitionism for Program Synthesis"; in. S. Shimizu, T. Bosomaier (eds.) , Cognitive 2013, The Fifth International Conference on Advanced Cognitive Technologies and Applications ; pp. 102-107, 2013.

[5] M. Franova, "A Cartesian Methodology for an Autonomous Program Synthesis System"; in M.Jäntti, G. Weckman (eds)., proc. of ICONS 2014, The Ninth International Conference on Systems; ISBN, 978-1-61208-319-3, pp. 22-27, 2014.

[6] M. Franova, "Cartesian versus Newtonian Paradigms for Recursive Program Synthesis"; International Journal on Advances in Systems and Measurements, vol. 7, no 3&4, pp. 209-222, 2014.

[7] M. Franova, D. Hutter, and Y. Kodratoff, Algorithmic Conceptualization of Tools for Proving by Induction «Unwinding» Theorems – A Case Study; Rap. de Rech. N° 1587, L.R.I., Université de Paris-Sud, France, Mai 2016.

[8] M. Franova and Y. Kodratoff, "Cartesian Handling Informal Specifications in Incomplete Frameworks"; Proc. INTELLI 2016, The Fifth International Conference on Intelligent Systems and Applications, pp. 100-107, 2016.

[9] M. Franova, List of publications (retrieved 2017/05/17) https://sites.google.com/site/martafranovacnrs/publications

[10] H. Mantel, A Uniform Framework for the Formal Specification and Verification of Information Flow Security; PhD thesis, Universitty of Saarlandes, 2003.

[11] R. W. Ritchie, "Classes of predictably computable functions", Trans. Amer. Math. Soc. 106, pp. 139-173, 1963.

[12] A. Yasuhara, Recursive Function Theory and Logic; Academic Press, New York, 1971.

Intelligent Software Development Method by Model Driven Architecture

Keinosuke Matsumoto, Kimiaki Nakoshi, and Naoki Mori
Department of Computer Science and Intelligent Systems
Graduate School of Engineering, Osaka Prefecture University
Sakai, Osaka, Japan
email: {matsu, nakoshi, mori}@cs.osakafu-u.ac.jp

Abstract—**Recently, Model Driven Architecture (MDA) attracts attention in the field of software development. MDA is a software engineering approach that uses models to create products, such as source code. On the other hand, executable UML consists of activities, common behavior, and execution models. However, it has not been put to good use for transforming into source code. This paper proposes a method for transforming executable UML and class diagrams with their association into source code. Executable UML can detail system's behavior enough to execute, but it is very difficult for executable UML to handle system's data. Therefore, the proposed method uses class diagrams and executable UML to transform into source code. The method can make models independent from platform, such as program languages. The proposed method was applied to a system. Source code of Java and C# was generated from the same models of the system, and development cost was verified. As a result, it was confirmed that this method could reduce cost very much when models are reused.**

Keywords—executable UML; activity diagram; model driven architecture; UML.

I. INTRODUCTION

In today's software development, software reuse, modification, and migration of existing systems have increased rather than new development. According to an investigative report [1] of Information-Technology Promotion Agency (IPA), reuse, modification, and migration of existing systems account for about 59.4% of software development and new development for about 40.6%. Many software bugs enter at upper processes, such as requirement specification, system design, and software design. However, the bugs are mostly discovered at lower processes, such as testing process. The request to detect bugs at upstream is coming out. Under such a situation, software developers require development technique that is easy to reuse and deal with changes of implementation technique. Model driven architecture (MDA) [2] is attracting attention as an approach that generates source code automatically from models that are not influenced of implementation [3][4][5]. Its core data are models that serve as design diagrams of software. It includes a transformation to various types of models and an automatic source code generation from the models. Therefore, it can directly link software design and implementation.

The final goal of MDA is to generate automatically executable source code for multiple platforms. For that purpose, it is necessary to make architecture and behavior of a system independent from platforms. Platform Independent Model (PIM) that does not depend on platforms, such as a programming language. Executable UML [6][7] is advocated as this type of model. This expresses all actions for every kind of processing, and input and output data by a pin in an activity diagram, which is one of UML [8] diagrams. The source code for various platforms is generable from one model since processing and data are transformed for every platform if this executable UML is used.

In this study, a method is proposed that generates source code automatically from executable UML. It is very difficult for executable UML to handle system's data. To solve this problem, this paper proposes a modeling tool that associates an executable UML with class diagrams and acquires data from them. It can treat not only data, but can introduce the hierarchical structure of class diagrams in executable UML. If the platform of future systems, such a programing language, is changed, software developers could not reuse existing source code, but they can reuse UML models to generate automatically new source code of the new programming language.

The contents of this paper are as follows. In Section II, related work is described. In Section III, the proposed method is explained. In Section IV, the results of application experiments confirm the validity of the proposed method. Finally, in Section V, the conclusion and future work are presented.

II. RELATED WORK

This study uses related work called Acceleo and executable UML.

A. Acceleo

MDA's core data are models that serve as software design drawing. The models are divided into platform dependent and independent models. Specifically, Acceleo [9] transforms models from PIM to Platform Specific Model (PSM) that depends on a platform, and generates source code automatically. Transformation of PIM is important and it can generate source code of various platforms from PIM by replacing transformation rules to each platform. Acceleo is plug-in of integrated development environment Eclipse [10], and a code generator that translates MetaObject Facility (MOF) [11] type models into source code on the basis of the code transformation rules called a template. Acceleo can translate the models directly, but the template has many constraints. For example, it cannot hold and calculate data. Therefore, it cannot recognize what type of model elements have been read until now. It is impossible to search the connection between nodes by using graph theory. When branches and loops of activity diagrams are transformed, Acceleo has a problem that it cannot appropriately transform them because it does not understand the environment.

B. Executable UML

Executable UML is a model that based on activity diagrams, like shown in Fig. 1. It has the following features:

- An action is properly used for every type.
- Input and output data of each action are processed as a pin, and they are clearly separated from the action.
- Model library that describes the fundamental operation in the model is prepared.

Each type of action has respectively proper semantics, and transformation with respect to each action becomes possible by following the semantics. The type and its semantics of action used in executable UML are show in the following.

1) *ValueSpecificationAction:* It outputs a value of the primitive type data like an integer, real number, character string, and logical value.

2) *ReadStructuralFeatureAction:* It reads a certain structural characteristics. For example, it is used when the property of class diagrams is read.

3) *ReadSelfAction:* It reads itself.

4) *CallOperationAction:* It calls methods in class diagrams.

5) *CallBehaviorAction:* It calls behaviors in behavior diagrams.

6) *AddVariableValueAction:* It addes a value to the variable or replace the variable by the value.

7) *ReadVariableAction:* It reads a variable or generate it.

8) *CreatObjectAction:* It creates a new object.

The model library consists of Foundational Model Library, Collection Classes, and Collection Functions. The contents of the model library are shown below

1) *Foundational Model Library:* It offers primitive type of data, and their behavior (four arithmetic operations, comparison, etc.) and the input-output relations.

2) *Collection Classes:* It offers collection class of Set, Ordered Set, Bag, List, Queue, Dequeue, and Map.

3) *Collection Functions:* It offers the methods (add, delete, etc.) of the collection class.

The model library is used by calling CallOperationAction or CallBehaviorAction.

III. PROPOSED METHOD

This section explains the technique of transforming executable UML to source code. Although executable UML is useful, this model has not been put to good use for automatic generation of source code. Moreover, the handling of data is inadequate by using only executable UML. To solve this problem, a method is proposed for generating source code automatically from executable UML. The method utilizes a modeling tool that associates executable UML with class diagrams. If executable UML needs data, the method gets the data from associated class diagrams.

The outline of the proposed method is shown in Fig. 2. Skeleton code is transformed from class diagrams by using Acceleo templates [12] for classes. The skeleton code consists only of class names, field, and methods that do

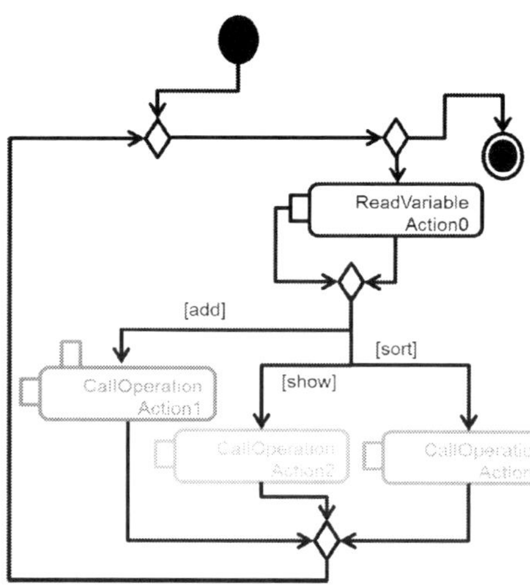

Figure 1. Example of executable UML.

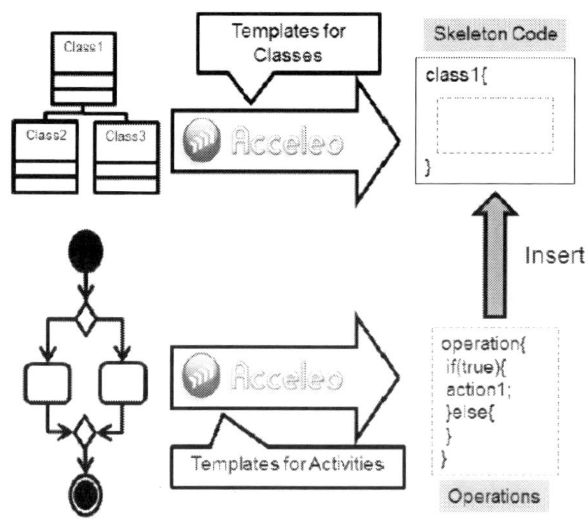

Figure 2. Schematic diagram of the proposed method.

not have specific values of data. Data and a method are automatically generated from executable UML afterwards. Since it is associated with class diagrams, other methods and data in the classes are acquirable using this association. Papyrus UML [13] was used for the association between these models.

A. Transformation from Class Diagrams to Skeleton Code

UML to Java Generator [14] was used as transformation rules from class diagrams to skeleton code. What are generated by these rules are shown below.

- Connection of inheritance or interface
- Field variables and methods like getter and setter
- Names and parameters of member functions

This is a template for Java. When transforming models to C#, it goes through several changes, such as deletion of constructors and addition of ":" to inheritance relationship.

B. Transformation from Executable UML to Source Code

Executable UML are based on activity diagrams. It consists of actions, data, and their flows. Although transform rules of actions and data differ from platform to platform, the flows are fundamentally common. Therefore, transformation of flows is separated from transformation of actions and data. Flows decide the order of transformation of actions and data. This separation can flexibly transform one model to source code of multiple platforms. The transformation flow of executable UML is described in the following.

1) Transformation of flows: A flow of executable UML is shown by connecting nodes, which include actions and data, with an edge. However, neither a branch nor loop is transformed only by connecting nodes along the flow. On transforming a decision or merge node that are used for a branch or loop, the proposed method searches a part of the executable UML near the node and gives an appropriate keyword to a connecting node and edge. The method transforms them according to the keywords. The keywords given to model elements are shown below.

a) finish: It means a node or edge whose processing are finished.

b) loop: It means a decision node in the entrance or exit of a loop.

c) endif: It means a merge node in the end of a branch.

d) read: It means an edge under searching.

The flow of search is shown in Fig. 3 and its algorithm is shown below.

(1) Follow an edge that is not searched in the reverse direction of its arrow.

(2) If an edge and node that are not searched, give the keyword of 'read'.

(3) If a node has the keyword of 'read', replace the keyword to 'loop'. If the node is a decision node, give the keyword of 'loop' to a searched edge going out from the decision node.

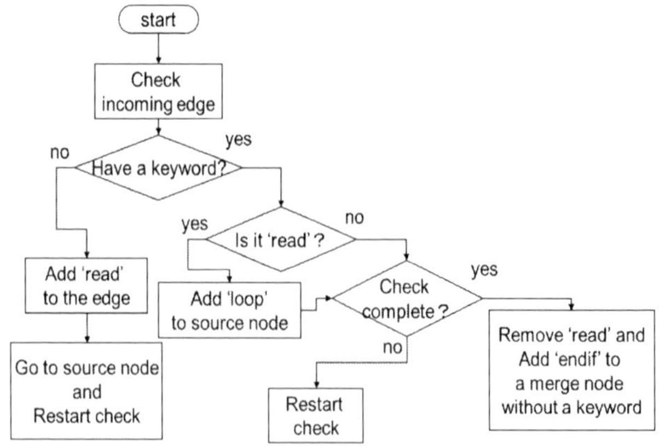

Figure 3. Search algorithm.

(4) Repeat the processing of (1) - (3) until there is no edge that can be searched.

(5) Remove 'read' at the last. If there is a merge node that does not have 'loop', 'endif' will be given to it.

2) Transformation of actions and data

Transformation rules of actions and data are prepared for every platform. In executable UML, an action is properly used for every type of processing, and a transformation rule may be defined per action. The flow of transformation processing is shown in the following.

(1) If a node is an action, it will be transformed and given keyword of finish. The processing will move to the next nodes. If the action has an input pin, its flow will be gone back and the objects and actions in the starting point of this flow will be transformed.

(2) If a node is a decision node and it has the keyword of loop, it will be transformed by rules for loop. If the decision node has no keyword, it will be transformed by rules for branch. In addition, the following nodes and conditional expressions are picked out from the connecting edges. Keywords of finish are given to these nodes and edges and the processing will move to the next nodes.

TABLE I. ACTIONS AND THEIR APPLICATIONS TO EACH LANGUAGE.

Action	Java	C#
CreateObjectAction	new *<object>*	new *<object>*
ReadSelfAction	this	this
ValueSpecification Action	*<value>*	*<value>*
ReadStructural FeatureAction	*<object>*.*<variable>* (*<resultType>*) *<object>*	*<object>*.*<variable>* *<resultType>*.Parse (*<object>*)
CallOperationAction	*<target>*.*<operation>* (*<parameter>*)	*<target>*.*<operation>* (*<parameter>*)
AddVariableValue Action	*<variable>*=*<value>*	*<variable>*=*<value>*

TABLE II. MODEL LIBRARY ELEMENTS AND THEIR APPLICATIONS.

Model Library	Java	C#
ReadLine	(new BufferedReader(new InputStreamReader(System. in))).readLine()	Console.ReadLine()
WriteLine	System.out.println(*value*)	Console.WriteLine(*value*)
List.size	<*target*>.size()	<*target*>.Count
List.get	<*target*>.get(<*index*>)	<*target*>[<*index*>]
List.add	<*target*>.add(<*data*>)	<*target*>.Add(<*data*>)
Primitive Functions	<*x*><*function*><*y*>	<*x*><*function*><*y*>

(3) If a keyword is given to a merge node, it will be transformed according to it.

Correspondence relation of actions with Java and C# is shown in Table I. The upper row of ReadStructural FeatureAction in Table I is the case where <variable> is specified, and the lower row is the case where it is not specified.

In addition, correspondence relation of model libraries with Java and C# is shown in Table II. ReadLine and WriteLine are model libraries for input and output. List.size, List.get, and List.add are prepared by Collection Functions, and they are used for output of list capacity, extraction of list element, and addition of list element, respectively. Primitive Functions are operations prepared in the primitive type. Collection Functions are used by calling CallOperationAction, and other functions except them are used by calling CallBehaviorAction. Variables inputted by pins and operators defined in the library are assigned in italics surrounded by <>.

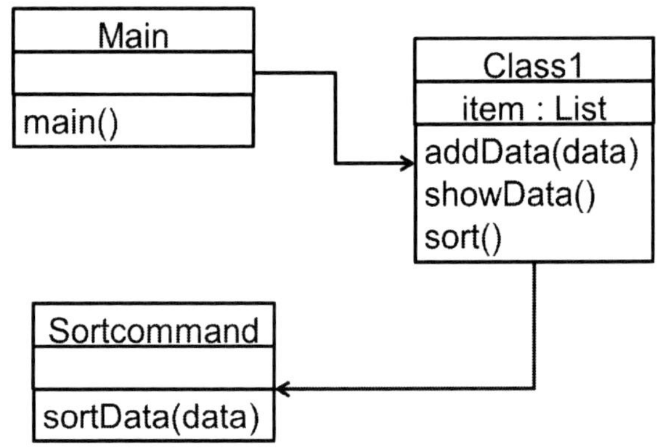

Figure 4. Class diagram of example system.

IV. APPLICATION EXPERIMENTS

As an experiment that verifies operation and development cost of created templates, a system shown below was developed by the proposed method. The system receives three commands of adding data to a list, sorting list elements, and outputting data. This system was described by executable UML and class diagrams. Source code of Java and C# was generated automatically. The same models were used for model transformation of both languages. Operations were checked by using the source code. Figures 4 and 5 show the class diagram and the behavior model of the system.

The generated source code of Java and C# is shown in Figures 6, 7, and 8, respectively. The development cost is

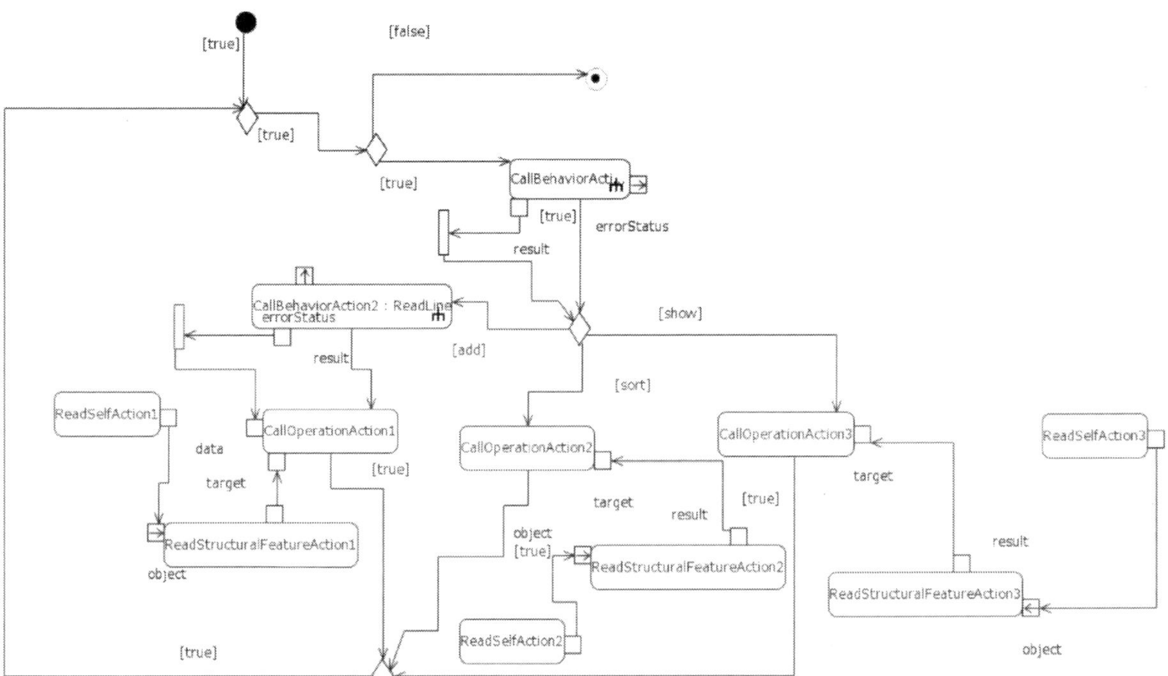

Figure 5. Total system behavior of example system.

evaluated according to [15]. It assumes that workload to add one node in UML diagrams equals to that to describe one line of source code. Table III shows the number of model nodes, the number of lines of added or modified lines, and finished source code of each language. The added and modified lines correspond to parts that cannot be expressed by executable UML like package, import, and so on. Table IV shows the rate of automatically generated code to the finished code. In addition, it shows the rate of cost of new development and reuse as compared with manual procedures from scratch to finish. The calculation formulas used in Table IV are shown below.

```java
package Package1;
import java.util.ArrayList;
public class Class1 {
    private Sortcommand sortcommand=new Sortcommand();
    private List item=new List();
    public Class1() {
        super();
    }
    public void addData(String data) {
        this.item.add(data);
    }
    public void showData() {
        System.out.println(this.item);
    }
    public void sort() {
        this.sortcommand.sortData(this.item);
    }
    public Sortcommand getSortcommand() {
        return this.sortcommand;
    }
    public void setSortcommand(Sortcommand newSortcommand) {
        this.sortcommand = newSortcommand;
    }
    public List getItem() {
        return this.item;
    }
    public void setItem(List newItem) {
        this.item = newItem;
    }
}
```

Figure 6. Generated Java code of Class1.

```csharp
using System;
using System.Collections.Generic;
namespace Package1
{
    public class Class1 {
        private Sortcommand sortcommand=new Sortcommand();
        private List item=new List();
        public  void sort() {
            this.sortcommand.sortData(this.item);
        }
        public  void showData() {
            Console.WriteLine(this.item);
        }
        public  void addData(String data) {
            this.item.Add(data);
        }
        public Sortcommand getSortcommand() {
            return this.sortcommand;
        }
        public void setSortcommand(Sortcommand newSortcommand) {
            this.sortcommand = newSortcommand;
        }
        public List getItem() {
            return this.item;
        }
        public void setItem(List newItem) {
            this.item = newItem;
        }
    }
}
```

Figure 7. Generated C# code of Class1.

Production rate = (finished code lines – added and modified lines) *100 / finished code lines (1)

New development cost rate = (model nodes + added and modified lines) *100 / finished code lines (2)

Reuse cost rate = (added and modified lines) *100 / finished code lines (3)

Cost by the proposed method is about 130 - 160% in developing new software, but it is held down to less than 10% in reusing them. According to the investigative report of IPA, about 60% of software development is reuse, modification, and migration of existing systems and new software development occupies about 40%. If a system is developed by the proposed method, the cost is

```java
package Package1;
import java.util.List;
public class Sortcommand {
    public Sortcommand() {
        super();
    }
    public void sortData(List<Integer> data) {
        int dumy = 0;
        int min = 0;
        int j = 0;
        int s = 0;
        int k = 0;
        while (k < data.size() == true) {
            min = (int) data.get(k);
            s = k;
            j = k + 1;
            while (j < data.size() == true) {
                if (min < (int) data.get(j) == true) {
                    min = (int) data.get(j);
                    s = j;
                } else
                if (min < (int) data.get(j) == false) {
                }
                j = j + 1;
            }
            dumy = (int) data.get(k);
            data.set(k, data.get(s));
            data.set(s,dumy);
            k = k + 1;
        }
    }
}
```

Figure 8. Generated Java code of Sortcommand.

TABLE III. COMPARISON OF MODEL NODES AND GENERATED LINES.

Number of model nodes	Languages	Number of added or modified lines	Number of finished lines
94	Java	3	74
	C#	5	65

TABLE IV. COMPARISON OF DEVELOPMENT COST.

Languages	Production rate	New development cost	Development cost by reusing
Java	96%	131%	4%
C#	92%	152%	8%

$$10*0.6+160*0.4=70(\%) \quad (4).$$

Although the proposed method is more expensive than manual procedures in new development, it can be less expensive in when it comes to reusing. Created templates can be diverted to other projects and the cost declines further by repeating reuse. In present software development with much reuse, a large effect can be expected. The systems can be hierarchically divided into several classes for every function.

V. CONCLUSION

Based on the situation where the rate of reuse, modification, and migration of existing systems is increasing in software development, a MDA method that uses executable UML jointly with class diagrams was proposed in this paper. The proposed method associates class operations with executable UML. Source code of Java and C# was generated from the same models of the system, and development cost was verified.

If the platform of future systems is changed, software developers could not reuse existing source code, but they can reuse UML models to generate automatically new source code of the new programming language. As a result, it was confirmed that this method could reduce cost very much when models are reused. The proposed method can transform models into source code written in any kinds of programming languages if there is an appropriate template. However, how to make models in the method is very vague.

As future work, it is necessary to decide a standard of model partitioning and a notation system of objects that are not defined by executable UML. In addition, important future task is investigating what type of problems will occur when models are changed.

ACKNOWLEDGMENT

This work was supported in part by JSPS KAKENHI Grant Number JP16K06424.

REFERENCES

[1] Information-Technology Promotion Agency, "Actual condition survey on software industry in the 2011 fiscal year," (in Japanese) [Online]. Available from: https://www.ipa.go.jp/files/000026799.pdf, 2017.06.06.

[2] S. J. Mellor, K. Scott, A.Uhl, and D.Weise, MDA distilled: Principle of model driven architecture. Addison-Wesley Longman Publishing Co., Inc. Redwood City, CA, 2004.

[3] T. Buchmann and A. Rimer, "Unifying modeling and programming with ALF," Proc. of the Second International Conference on Advances and Trends in Software Engineering, pp. 10-15, 2016.

[4] M Usman, N. Aamer, and T. H. Kim, "UJECTOR: A tool for executable code generation from UML models. In Advanced Software Engineering and Its Applications, ASEA 2008, pp. 165-170, 2008.

[5] Papyrus User Guide, [Online]. Available from: http: //wiki.eclipse.org/Papyrus_User_Guide#Code_Generation_Support, 2017.06.06.

[6] Object Management Group, "Semantics of a foundational subset for executable UML models," [Online]. Available from: http://www.omg.org/spec/FUML/1.1/, 2017.06.06.

[7] Object Management Group, "List of executable UML tools," [Online]. Available from: http://modeling-languages.com/list-of-executable-uml-tools/, 2017.06.06.

[8] Object Management Group, "Unified modeling language superstructure specification V2.1.2, " 2007.

[9] Acceleo: [Online]. Available from: http://www.eclipse.org/acceleo/, 2017.06.06.

[10] F. Budinsky, Eclipse modeling framework: A developer's guide. Addison-Wesley Professional, 2004.

[11] Object Management Group, "Metaobject facility," [Online]. Available from: http://www.omg.org/mof/, 2017.06.06.

[12] Acceleo template: [Online]. Available from: https://www.eclipse.org/home/search.php?q=template, 2017.06.06.

[13] A. Lanusse et al. "Papyrus UML: An open source toolset for MDA," Proc. of the Fifth European Conference on Model-Driven Architecture Foundations and Applications, pp. 1-4, 2009.

[14] UML to Java Generator [Online]. Available from: https://marketplace.eclipse.org/content/uml-java-generator, 2017.06.06.

[15] K. Matsumoto, T. Maruo, M. Murakami, and N. Mori, "A graphical development method for multiagent simulators," Modeling, Simulation and Optimization - Focus on Applications, Shkelzen Cakaj, Eds., pp. 147-157, INTECH, 2010.

A Professional Competency Development of Service Oriented Industry based SIA-NRM Approach

Chia-Li Lin
Department of Recreation Management
Shih Chien University
Kaohsiung, Taiwan
email:linchiali0704@yahoo.com.tw

Yen-Yen Chen
Department of Hospitality Management
Tajen University
Pingtung, Taiwan
email:yc0611@tajen.edu.tw

Abstract—**The development of service-oriented industries rely on not only the investment of equipments but also the large number of high-quality service personnel. Therefore, competition among service-oriented enterprises has gradually changed from facilities and store decoration investments to personnel training and education. This study attempts to analyze the competency need state for different job attributes in terms of "professional competence" and "working attitude" from the perspective of competency development and talent cultivation. This study also explores the relationship between the "professional competence" and "working attitude" for the practitioners in service-oriented industry. This study summarizes the two competency development aspects of "professional competence" and "working attitude" by literature review and expert interview and propose the competency development system of for service-oriented industry. This study proposes the concepts of professional competence and working attitude to evaluate the competency development needs and use the satisfaction-importance analysis (SIA) technique to determine the competency development state for service oriented industry. Besides, the study also analyzes the influence relation structure of competency development aspect based on the network relation map (NRM) technique. We hope that this research findings can aid decision makers understand competency development needs of different job attributes based on "professional competence" and "working attitude" for service-oriented industry. Therefore the study also propose the improvement strategies of competency development through the SIA-NRM (Network Relation Map), and aid decision maker to strengthen practitioners competency competitiveness by competency development and education and training.**

Keywords-Service-oriented industry; Professional competence; Working attitude; SIA (satisfaction-importance analysis); NRM(Network Relation Map).

I. INTRODUCTION

In the tourism and hospitality industry, the service personals must satisfy different customers' needs every day. We need to explore and compare service levels with other industries. In the tourism industry, the employee turnover rate is of a high proportion so it is necessary to determine what kind of people remain in this industry, what incentives can let the industry to retain employees, and what skills must be acquired so that employees still keep a high standard of service and motivation. In the course of our practice, we see each class stratum exhibit a work ethos, knowledge and ability that are not the same. The responsibility to make the managerial-level decisions means that when one has more power, he/she must deal effectively with the lower echelons of his/her team. Managers should know how to address things according to each person's emotions and attitudes, and how to further explore the changes in multiple sectors of the industry.

The staff who is working in different areas share a common responsibility to represent a positive work attitude. This demonstration tends to have great relevance within their work group, and some employees would like to advance and allow their work performance to improve. Many service staff does not mind staying in this so-called menial work for a long periods of time. This level will suffice due to a fundamental lack of ambition, educational opportunities, and minimal direction. Some may feel so good about their daily experience, there will be no consideration and no need to climb higher. Through this study, it will be possible to clearly know taxonomy of the various classes of personnel in the hotel and tourism industry. However, the need to find additional staff for the tourism and hotel industry keeps apace of the regular turn-over rate. The need to retain staff usually leads to an enhancement of their abilities to cultivate knowledge and to develop an attitude whereby a sense of accomplishment is engendered. As such, it is first important to understand the current state of corporate personnel career development and knowledge base used to develop an employee retention program that will address all levels, work attitudes, and industry knowledge. If staff and management are not aware of different changes, they may encounter people do not wish to continue to move forward. This makes work attitude frequently hostile and thus shows a poor quality of work leading to a declining service levels. When people become more motivated and possessing a positive attitude, the quality of finishing their work is greatly enhanced. In order to understand their own knowledge levels, service employees must learn to handle their own personal concerns in the face of customer appeals. The chief concern for employers is for such employees to give the best service response to make guests happy and to protect the corporate image. For the members of the workforce, there is a correct way how to teach service capability to new team members. These lessons may also be applied to travel & hospitality students prior to their entry into the workplace.

This study is divided into four sections: in the second section we discuss about the competency development of service oriented industry; the third part is research concept, in the fourth section we use service oriented industry as examples to evaluate; the fifth section is the conclusion. In the end, we would like to find the key success factor when developing competency.

II. LITTERATURE REVIEWS

McClelland [1] proposed the "iceberg model", where the competency includes the explicit competence (seen above water) and implicit competence (under water). A clinical competence study of pre-graduate nursing students point out that skills enhancement program can improve the clinical competence for pre-graduate nursing students. This study use the three-part survey (the respondent's rooftop, the Skills Enhancement Program Questionnaire, and the Clinical Competence Questionnaire) based on the sample of 245 pre-graduate nursing students. This study also adopts the Factor Analysis (FA) to explain the attributes of the skills enhancement program, and determine the network relation structure by the Structural Equation Modeling (SEM) and path analysis. The study proposed the clinical competency evaluation system which includes four aspects (supportive clinical instructor, comprehensive orientation, formative goals and objectives, and conductive learning environment) for pre-graduate nursing students. The research finding also point out that the aspect of supportive clinical instructor is the strongest aspect among the clinical competency aspects [2]. In order to develop the systematic competency evaluation system for operating room nurses (ORN), the study propose the competency evaluation system of operating room nurses based on the AHP approach. The proposed method integrated the three analytic techniques which include the in-depth interviews, the Delphi method and AHP (Analytic Hierarchy Process). The study explored ORN competencies and proposed the four aspects (specialized knowledge, professional ability, personality and self-motivation) and 32 criteria for ORN competency evaluation system. The research finding also point out that the aspects of specialized knowledge is the most important aspects and the aspect of self-motivation is the least important aspect in the ORN competency evaluation system [3].

III. RESEARCH CONCEPT

This section introduces the service improvement model based on SIA-NRM of online shopping. First, we need to define the critical decision problem of professional competency development and then identify the aspects/criteria that influence professional competency development of service oriented industry through literature review and expert interviews in the second stage. In the third stage, using SIA analysis, this study indicates that the aspects/ criteria that are still associated with low satisfaction and high importance are also linked to low professional competency development needs. The current study determines the relational structure of professional competency development system, and identifies the dominant aspects/criteria of the service system based on NRM analysis in the fourth stage. Finally, this study integrates the results of SIA analysis and NRM analysis to establish the improved strategy path and determine the effective service improvement strategy for professional competency development system. The analytic process includes five stages. (1) It clearly defines the critical decision problems of professional competency development system. (2) It establishes the aspects/ criteria of professional competency development system. (3) It measures the state of aspects/ criteria based on SIA analysis. (4) It measures the relational structure using network ration map (NRM). (5) It integrates the results of SIA analysis and NRM analysis to determine the improvement strategy and improvement path of professional competency development system. The analytic process uses the analytic techniques (SIA analysis, NRM analysis and SIA-NRM analysis) and five analytic stages as shown in Fig. 1.

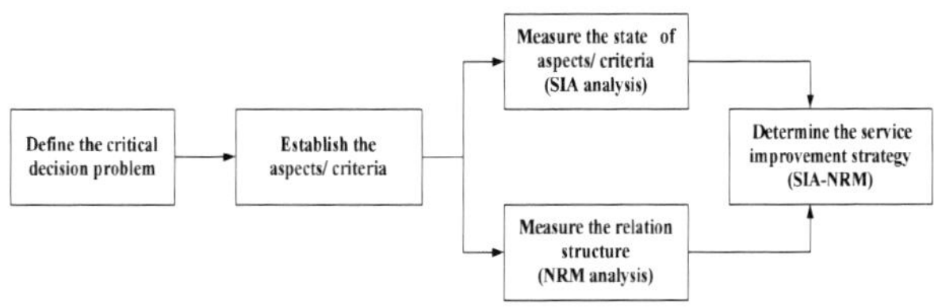

Figure 1. The analysis process of SIA-NRM

IV. THE EMPIRICAL STUDY

The analysis processes of SIA-NRM include two stages. The first stage is the satisfied importance analysis (SIA) and the second stage is the analysis of the Network Ration Map (NRM). The SIA analysis determines the satisfaction and importance degree of aspects/criteria for professional competency development system; the SIA analysis can help decision marking find criteria that should improved while the standard satisfied degree is less than the average satisfied degree. The three improvement strategies are presented in Table I. Improvement strategy A, which requires no further improvement, can be applied to the aspects of Working attitude (WA) (SS > 0). Improvement strategy C, which requires indirect improvements, can be applied to the aspect of Professional competence (PC). The SIA-NRM approach determines the criteria which should be improved based on SIA analysis and the suited improvement path using the network ration map (NRM). As shown in Fig. 2, we can determine that the aspect of PC should be improved, and the WA is the aspect that is the major dimension with net influence. So we can improve the PC aspect by the aspect of WA as shown in TABLE I and Fig. 2.

TABLE I. THE IMPROVEMENT STRATEGY TABLE OF SERVICE ORIENTED INDUSTRY

	SIA			NRM			Strategies
Aspects	SS	SI	(SS, SI)	*d+r*	*d-r*	(R, D)	
PC	-0.707	-0.707	▼ (L, L)	282.714	-1.000	ID (+,-)	C
WA	0.707	0.707	○ (H,H)	282.714	1.000	D (+,+)	A

Notes: The improvement strategies include three types: Improvement Strategy A (which requires no further improvement), Improvement Strategy B (which requires direct improvements) and Improvement Strategy C (which requires indirect improvements)

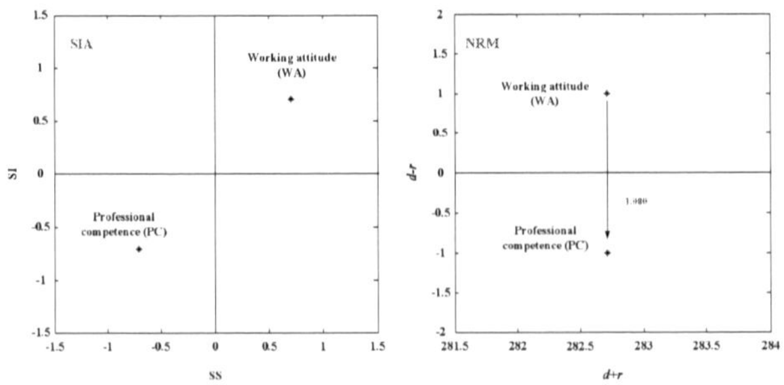

Figure 2. The improvement strategy map of service oriented industry

REFERENCES

[1] D. C. McClelland, "Testing for competence rather than for "intelligence."," *American Psychologist,* vol. 28, no. 1, pp. 1-14, 1973.

[2] M. C. D. R. Rebueno, D. D. D. Tiongco, and J. R. B. Macindo, "A structural equation model on the attributes of a skills enhancement program affecting clinical competence of pre-graduate nursing students," *Nurse Education Today,* vol. 49, pp. 180-186, 2017.

[3] Y. M. Wang, L. J. Xiong, Y. Ma, X. L. Gao, and W. F. Fu, "Construction of competency evaluation measures for operating room nurses," *Chinese Nursing Research,* vol. 3, no. 4, pp. 181-184, 2016.

Intelligent Media Format Conversion for Universal Multimedia Service over Heterogeneous Environments

Kwang-eun Won and Kwang-deok Seo
Yonsei University
Wonju, Gangwon, South Korea
e-mail: kdseo@yonsei.ac.kr

Jae-wook Lee
LG Electronics
Gasandong, Gurogu, Seoul, South Korea
e-mail: suance88@hanmail.net

***Abstract*—The rapidly growing Internet has come with an increasing heterogeneity and diversity in the network devices and connections used for information access. To guarantee the Quality of Service (QoS) to multimedia applications over heterogeneous networks and terminals, content adaptation is one of the most important technologies. The content adaptation can generally be classified into two different categories: 1) content scaling which controls the quality of the content according to the given constraints, 2) media format conversion which converts the given media format to a different one, such as video-to-image conversion. Although the content scaling approach can be employed to match the quality of the content to a worse condition of terminal and network resources, the resulting quality could be significantly deteriorated. In this case, media format conversion could be more preferable and better solution to guarantee the quality of the media service. In this paper, we specifically focus on converting video to image format. The effectiveness of the proposed media format conversion in terms of human perceptual aspect is verified through extensive simulations.**

Keywords-intelligent media format conversion; intelligent multimedia, universal multimedia service; multimedia access over heterogeneous environments, quality of service.

I. INTRODUCTION

In general, universal multimedia service deals with delivery of multimedia content (images, video, audio, and text) over different network conditions, user and publisher preferences, and capabilities of terminal devices. Recently Universal Multimedia Access (UMA) has become a new trend in multimedia communications [1]. In the UMA, the content adaptation is the important process to cope with various constraints of terminal and network. It can be commonly divided into two different categories as shown in Fig. 1: one is the content scaling technique, which controls the quality of the content according to the given constraints and the other is media format conversion, which converts one media format to another, such as video-to-image conversion.

Conventionally, the content scaling approach has been used to match the quality of the content to the corresponding constraints in terminal and network resources. However, media format conversion currently appears to take an important role in the evolution of UMA. In terms of human perceptual information, the quality of the content can be significantly destroyed although the content scaling is able to sufficiently reduce the rate. In this case, instead of the content scaling approach, media format conversion can be more preferable choice to guarantee the Quality of Service (QoS). MPEG-21 [2] provides the conversion preference, so that users can be able to customize the media format to the adapted resource. Besides, MPEG-21 also provides the AdaptationQoS descriptors to enable the adaptation engine to automatically scale the resource to cope with constraints of terminal/network.

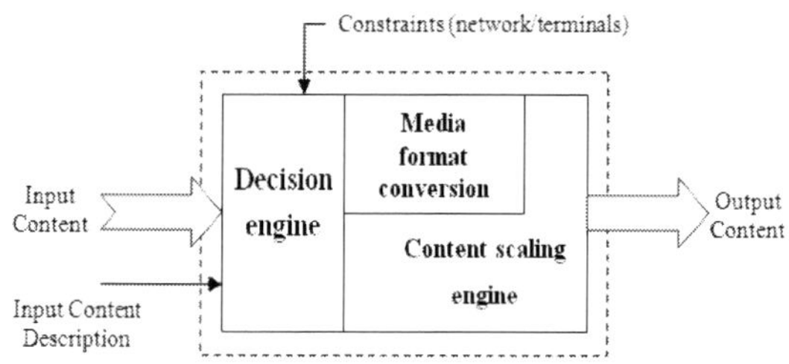

Figure 1. Content adaptation process.

In this paper, we propose an intelligent media format conversion technique, which converts video to image and guarantees the acceptable QoS under the obtained conversion boundary.

This paper is organized as follows. In Section II, we review related works including Overlapped Content Value (OCV) model. Section III describes the proposed intelligent video-to-image format conversion technique. In Section IV, we show the experimental results to verify the effectiveness of the proposed media format conversion in terms of human perceptual aspect. Finally, concluding remarks are presented in Section V.

II. REVIEW OF RELATED WORKS

Content adaptation can be performed either at the client, at an intermediate proxy side, or at the server [1]. Usually, most content adaptation systems [3]-[5] are proxy-based.

Client device requests Web pages. Then, the proxy catches client device's request for Web pages, brings the requested content, and adapts it. Finally, the proxy sends the adapted version to the client.

In the TranSend project [3], a proxy transcodes Web content on the fly. The adaptation which is also called as "distillation," is primarily limited to image compression and reduction of image size and color space. Video is also converted into different frame-rates and encodings using a video gateway.

Bickmore and Schilit [5] also propose a proxy based mechanism. They use a number of heuristics and a planner to perform outlining and elision of the content to fit the Web page on the client's screen. These transcoding proxies typically consider a few client devices and employ static content adaptation strategies. A common policy [3] [5] is to scale all images by a fixed factor. Therefore, these transcoding proxies fail to address the variation in the resource requirements of different Web documents. The set of client devices will also grow more diversity. Certain resources, such as effective network bandwidth, costs and patience of the users can be different for similar client devices. The static adaptation policies used by these systems do not handle well this variability in Web content and client resources.

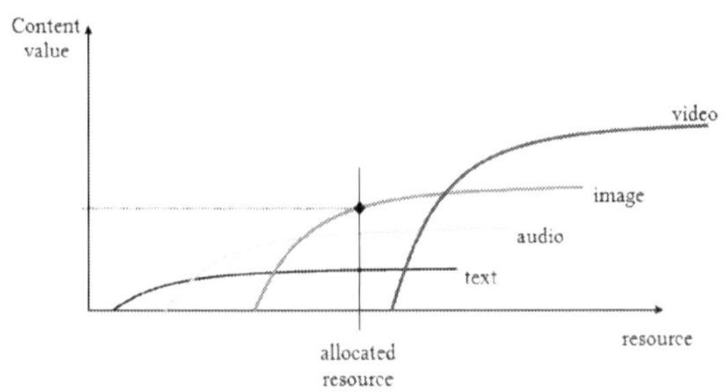

Figure 2. The overlapped content value model of a content item.

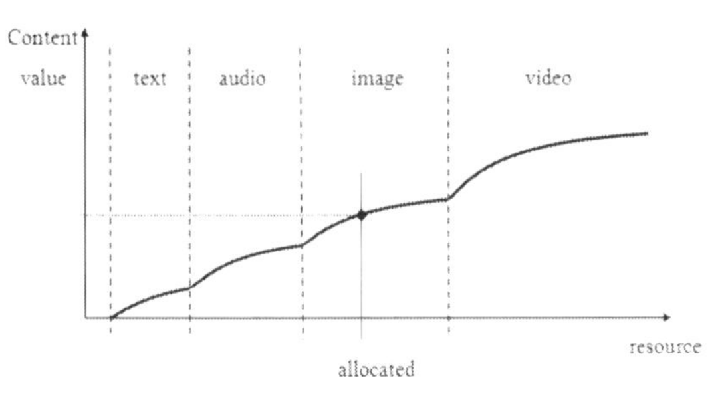

Figure 3. The final content value function of a content item.

Most research results on content adaptation have focused on transcoding of contents within a single format [6] [7] or on a single type of format conversion, e.g., video to images [8]. Media format conversion may be supported in the approach of [9]. However, this approach works with one content item, resulting in little practical use. The approach in [1] is one of few adaptation approaches that can handle multiple formats and multiple contents. However, its resource allocation method is not quite suitable for making decision on media format conversion. Especially, it does not address rapidly changing user/network conditions.

Thang et al. [10] employed the OCV model to represent the content value in different formats according to resource. This model helps finding the conversion boundaries between different formats. The underlying idea is that the conversion boundary between various formats depends on the perceptual qualities of the media formats. Fig. 2 shows the example model of a content that is originally of video format. Here, the content value curve of each format can be assigned manually or automatically. The final content value function of the content is the upper hull of the model, and the intersection points of the curves represent the conversion boundaries between formats. Fig. 3 shows the final content value function and the conversion boundaries of the content. Based on these conversion boundaries, we can quantitatively make the decision on media format conversion so as to maintain an acceptable QoS. The OCV model enables the adaptation engine to determine appropriate media format to be achieved for a given constraint in a quality-aware way. The content value (quality) of a media format can be measured in various utilities. For example, video content value can be computed using both the Peak-Signal-to-Noise-Ratio (PSNR) value and the Mean Opinion Score (MOS) value as follows:

$$Content\_value = z_1 \cdot PSNR\_value + z_2 \cdot MOS\_value \quad (1)$$

where z_1 and z_2 are the appropriate scale factors which are defined by the user, and the sum of them is 1. The criteria for establishing appropriate scaling factors depend on the relative importance between objective quality and subjective quality. If objective quality is comparatively more important than subjective quality, we set z_1 to be greater than z_2. Otherwise, z_1 should be less than or equal to z_2. For more details on computing the OCV model, you are referred to [10]-[12].

III. Proposed Intelligent Media Format Conversion

We propose an intelligent media format conversion technique, which converts the visual information of video content to important image sequence, based on the OCV model in UMA environment. Fig. 4 shows the overall system architecture of the content adaptation employing media format conversion from low quality video to high quality image. Video-to-image format conversion process is as follows: The decision engine takes the original video content and resource constraints as its inputs. Then, the decision engine analyzes the resource constraint and makes optimal decision between format conversion and video transcoding, so that the adapted video has the most value when presented to the user. The media format conversion engine includes the specific operations to adapt the video according to instructions from the decision engine. In Fig. 4, when the given bit-rate is lower than the conversion point, which is generated by the OCV model, video-to-image format conversion is applied. Otherwise, video is scaled by the video transcoder. Under the situation of very limited bit-rate, video transcoder cannot generate satisfactory video quality. For a given resource constraint (specifically, bit-rate as in Fig. 4), the media format that maximizes the utility corresponding to the convent value should be selected for the universal multimedia service.

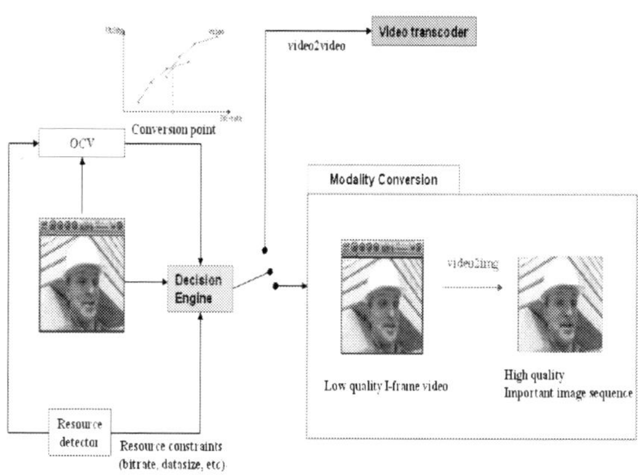

Figure 4. Overall system architecture.

In order to decide the conversion boundary from the video to image, we need to get utility curves: one is video utility curve and the other is image utility curve.

A. Video utility curve

At the given bitrate, PSNR value is estimated according to frame dropping and Quantization Parameter (QP) adjustment. Then, we normalize the PSNR value within utility value 1 in order to map *PSNR* value into OCV model. For generating the scaled video, we use the operation which is combined with frame-dropping and requantization. This process results in the video utility curve shown in Fig. 5. The average *PSNR* values and bitrates of the scaled video are measured to provide the video utility curve. In (2), the content value of video (V) is calculated by multiplying the *PSNR* values with the scale factor of w. This scale factor is used to map the video *PSNR* value into the range [0, 1].

$$V = w \times MV_{PSNR}, \quad where\ w = \frac{1}{MV_{PSNR\_max}}. \qquad (2)$$

The final video utility curve is shown in Fig. 6. From right to left on this curve, each point represents the video streams generated by combining frame-dropping and quantization parameter adjustment. For example, the first point represents the video streams having no frame-dropping with a fixed quantization parameter.

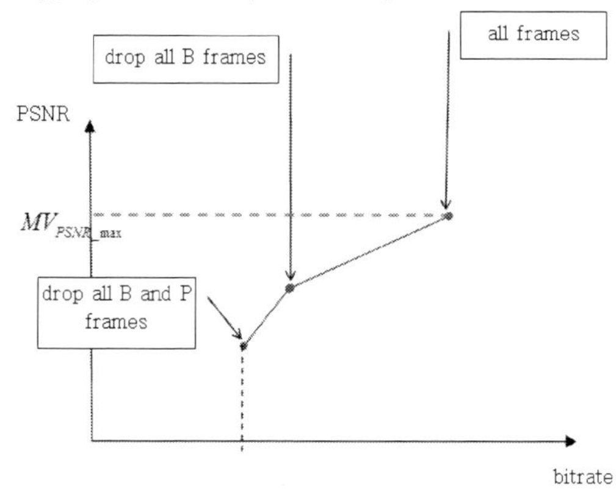

Figure 5. Video utility curve.

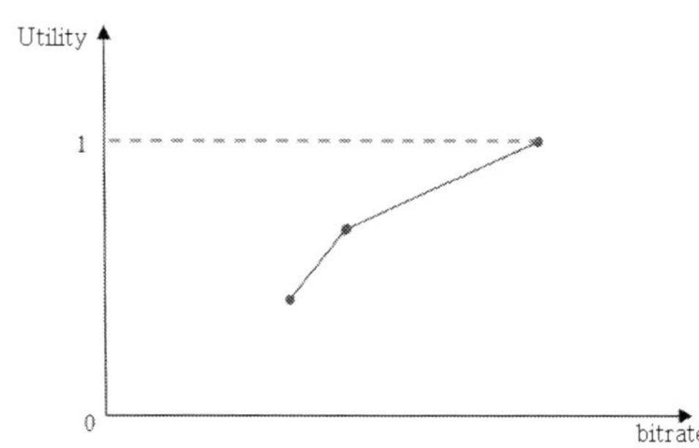

Figure 6. Normalized video utility curve.

B. Image utility curve

For convenience, we suppose the data size of important image sequence is approximately equal to an average value. So, the resource amount of image sequence is linearly proportional to the number of important images. Image sequences are extracted from the full sequence of images (decoded from original video) using various methods described in [13] and [14]. An extracted image sequence is said to represent the best possible summary of the video. Thus the scaling operation for image format is to limit the number of images. Extracted images are encoded in JPEG format such that their qualities are the same as those of the original I-frames. Compared to the full image sequence, any image sequence has an associated semantic distortion D which ranges from 0 to infinity.

We see that, when the image sequence has all the frames, the maximum content value of image format is the same as the original video, which is 1, and then we can set the scale factor of image format to be 1. The distortion D can be changed into content value as follows.

$$V = 1/(1 + A \cdot D), \qquad (3)$$

where A is an unknown constant. It should be noted that (3) is a more generalized case of the formula $V = 1/(1 + D)$ proposed in [1]. The constant A, which actually controls the slope of the image utility curve can be estimated as follows. The video version that contains all original I-frames, called I-frame stream, can also be considered as an image sequence. Then its content value V' can be computed from its semantic distortion D' provided by the extraction method [13] as follows:

$$V' = 1/(1 + A \cdot D'). \qquad (4)$$

Being a video version, the content value of I-frame stream can be evaluated from its *PSNR* value MV':

$$V' = w \cdot MV'_{PSNR}. \qquad (5)$$

From (4) and (5), we have

$$A = \frac{w \cdot MV'_{PSNR} \cdot D'}{1 - w \cdot MV'_{PSNR}}. \qquad (6)$$

C. Mapping of video and image utility curves into OCV model

Fig. 7 shows the video and image utility curves mapped into OCV model [10]. From this utility curve, we can find the conversion point and the resource constraint where the current format is converted.

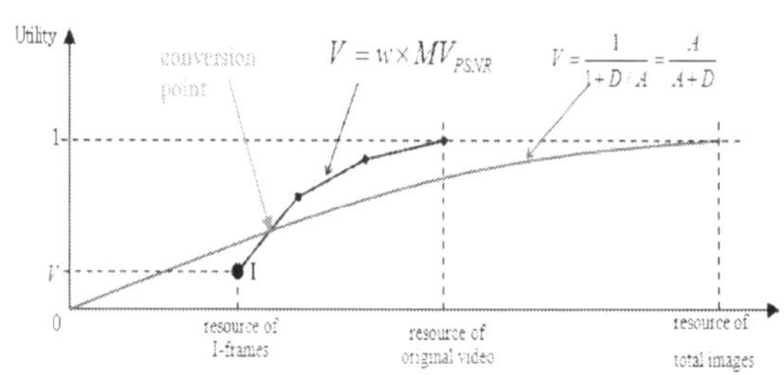

Figure 7. Video and image utility curves mapped into OCV model.

In order to decide the number of extracted images, we propose the decision procedure on the number of extracted images as shown in Fig. 8.

Once we get the decoded JPEG images from input video, we calculate the average of the JPEG image size (Q), which is almost similar to that of an I-frame size. Next, we decide the number of extracted image (N) according to resource constraint (R) and extract the images [13]. Then, we calculate the total data size of the extracted images (T) and the difference value (D) of the total data size of extracted images and the resource constraint (R). In addition, we should check whether the difference value (D) is bigger than zero or not. Then, we need to *update* the number of image to be selected.

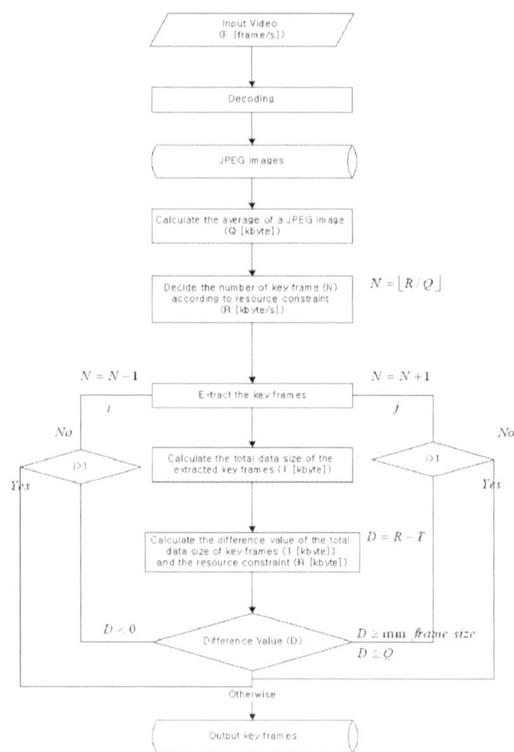

Figure 8. Flow chart for deciding the number of image.

If the difference value (D) is smaller than zero, we decrease the number of image by 1. Otherwise, we increase the number of image by 1. After checking the difference value (D) again, we can find the number of extracted image at last.

IV. Experimental Results

The experiment was performed using a desktop computer system with a Quad-Core 4.0 GHz CPU and 4G Byte memory. For input video, we used a test video sequence with 720p HD (1280x720) resolution, *English.mpg*, for which H.264 compression is applied with the frame rate of 30 fps. Each GOP consists of 15 frames with the structure IBBPBBPBBPBBPBB. The operations of content scaling and media format conversion in the experiment are carried out off-line. That is, a number of content versions of video and image are stored in advance. The content value of the original video is supposed to be 1, and content value of image is mapped into the range [0, 1]. The final video utility curve is shown in Fig. 9.

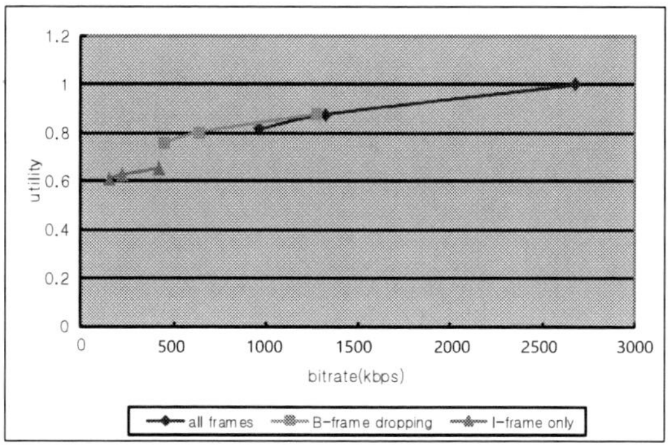

Figure 9. Video utility curve for the test sequence.

When the number of images is 0, the distortion is obviously infinity, and the full image sequence has zero distortion. Also when the image sequence has all frames as the original video, the maximum content value of image format is the same as the original video, which is 1. In order to generate the image utility value, firstly we need to calculate constant A by using (3), (4), and (5). The scale factor w is $1/\max PSNR\ vlue = 1/32.11 = 0.031$ and the distortion of I-frame stream D' is approximately 55.57, which is calculated by the extraction method [13]. Then, its *PSNR* value MV'_{PSNR} is 21.01. Now using (2), we can get constant value *A* as $A = \frac{w \cdot MV'_{PSNR} \cdot D'}{1 - w \cdot MV'_{PSNR}} = 105.18$.

Using the calculated constant A and distortion value, we are able to draw the utility curve shown in Fig. 10. Also, we can map the video utility curve and image utility curve into OCV model shown in Fig. 11. After mapping two utility curves into OCV model, conversion point *B* can be found at 324.2 kbps as shown in Fig. 11. For the perceptual comparison of each content version, we select point *A* (about 147.8 Kbps) as a comparison point. At that point, the video curve indicates I-frame stream with QP=30, and then it corresponds to 5 important images of the image curve.

Fig. 12 shows two kinds of content versions of video and image at 324.2 Kbps. The video version consists of 20 I-frames with QP=20. Meanwhile, the image version consists of only 8 images with original spatial quality.

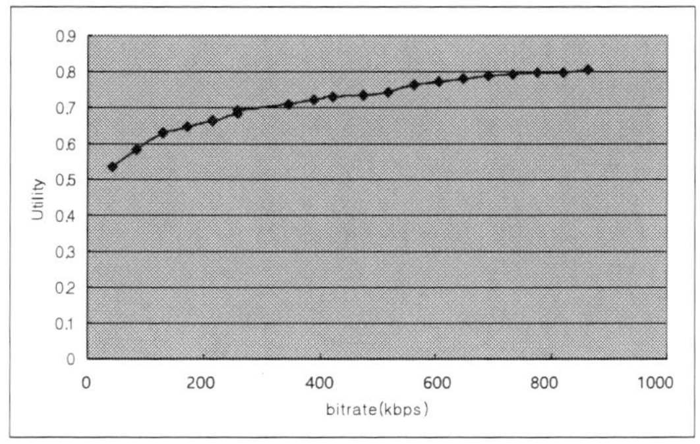

Figure 10. Image utility curve for the test sequence.

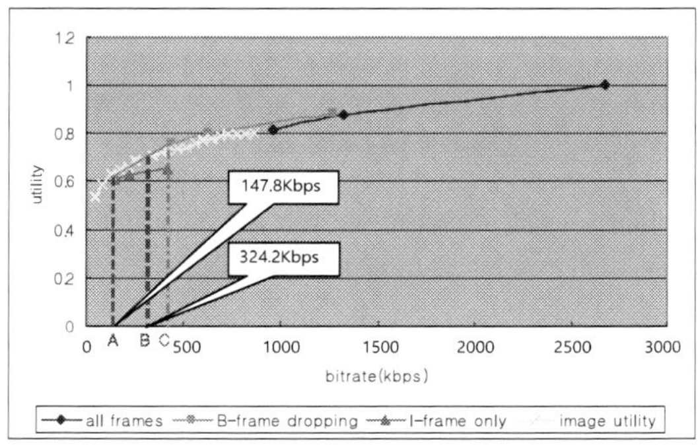

Figure 11. Overlapped Content Value model for the test sequence.

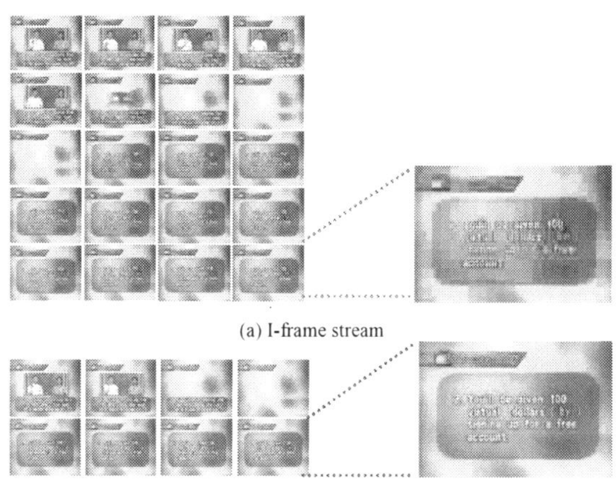

(a) I-frame stream

(b) Image sequence consisting of 8 high quality images

Figure 12. Comparison of the visual content between video and image formats.

In the case of this test video sequence for English education, text is the most important information source. However, we can obtain little information from the degraded I-frame stream as shown in Fig. 12(a). Therefore, although the image version has fewer high quality images due to spatio-temporal trade-off, we can say that the image version has much better human perceptual information than the video version. From the results, we can see that in terms of human perceptual information, the quality of the video version can be destroyed significantly. So, it is reasonable to select the image version to transmit to the end users at this bitrate.

V. Conclusion and Future Work

In this paper, we determined the conversion boundary among different media formats, and present media format conversion technique from video-to-image format. This approach guarantees the acceptable QoS under the obtained conversion boundary. Although conventional content scaling method can sufficiently decrease the bit-rate, it could seriously give rise to the destruction of the important visual information, which the original video originally has. In this case, the proposed media format conversion method can be a good alternative solution to avoid this kind of problem. The experimental results demonstrate: 1) it is better to transmit the important image sequence than to send only I-frame video stream since the important image sequence has most of key frames which I-frame video may missing, 2) the scaled video has little perceptual information at the low bitrate below the conversion point because it almost loses text information, which could be the most important information source, due to serious quality degradation. Meanwhile, the selected important image sequence has much valuable human perceptual information even though it includes a small number of high quality images because of trade-off between spatial and temporal quality.

Acknowledgment

This work was supported by a grant 'Biotechnology & GMP Training Project' from the Korea Institute for Advancement of Technology (KIAT), funded by the Ministry of Trade, Industry and Energy (MOTIE) of the Republic of Korea (N0000961).

References

[1] R. Mohan, J. Smith, and C. Li, "Adapting Multimedia Internet Content for Universal Access," *IEEE Trans. Multimedia*, vol. 11, no. 1, pp. 104-114, Mar. 2009.

[2] MPEG MDS Group, "Study of ISO/IEC 21000-7 FCD - Part 7: Digital Item Adaptation," ISO/IEC JTC1/SC29/WG11 N5933, Brisbane, Australia, Oct. 2003.

[3] A. Fox, S. Gribble, Y. Chawathe, and E. Brewer, "Adapting to network and client variation using active proxies: Lessons and perspectives," *IEEE Personal Commun.*, vol. 55, 2013, pp. 10-19.

[4] J. Smith, R. Mohan, and C. Li, "Transcoding Internet content for heterogeneous client devices," in Proc. *Int. Symp. Circuits and Systems (ISCAS)*, Monterey, CA, 1998, pp. 1-10.

[5] T. Bickmore and B. Schilit, "Digestor: Device-independent access to the World Wide Web," in Proc. *Int. WWW Conf.*, Santa Clara, CA, 2007, pp. 27-35.

[6] N. Bjork and C. Christopoulos, "Video Transcoding for Universal multimedia Access," in Proc. *ACM Multimedia*, pp. 75-79, Nov. 2000.

[7] K. Lee, H. S. Chang, S. S. Chun, H. Choi, and S. Sull, "Perception-based image transcoding for universal multimedia access," *Int. Conf. on Image Processing*, pp. 475-478, 2011.

[8] T. Kaup, S. Treetasanatavorn, U. Rauschenbach, and J. Heuer, "Video analysis for universal multimedia messaging," *IEEE Southwest Symposium on Image Analysis and Interpretation*, pp. 211-215, 2002.

[9] W. Lum and F. Lau, "A QoS-sensitive content adaptation system for mobile computing," *Computer Software and Applications Conference*, pp. 680–685, 2016.

[10] T. Thang, Y. Jung, Y. Ro, J. Nam, M. Kimiaei, and J. Dufourd, "CE report on Modality conversion preference-Part I," ISO/IEC JTC1/SC29/WG11 M9495, Pattaya, Thailand, Mar. 2003

[11] S. Chandra and C. Ellis, "JPEG compression metric as a quality aware image transcoding," in Proc. *USENIX Symp. Internet Technologies and Systems*, Boulder, Colorado, Oct. 2009.

[12] J. Kim, Y. Wang, and S. Chang, "Content-adaptive utility based video adaptation," in Proc. *Int. Conf. on Multimedia & Expo (ICME)*, 2013.

[13] H. Lee and S. Kim, "Iterative Key Frame Selection in the Rate-Constraint Environment," *Image Communication*, Issue 28, pp. 1-15, 2013.

[14] H. Chang, S. Sull, and S. Lee, "Efficient Video Indexing Scheme for Content-Based Retrieval," *IEEE Trans. Circ. Syst. Video Technol.*, vol. 19, pp. 1269-1279, Dec. 2009.

Unsupervised Deep Learning Recommender System for Personal Computer Users

Daniel Shapiro[*] [†], Hamza Qassoud[*], Mathieu Lemay[†] and Miodrag Bolic[*]
[*]School of Electrical Engineering and Computer Science, University of Ottawa, Ottawa, Ontario, Canada
Email: {dshap092, hqass076, mbolic}@eecs.uottawa.ca
[†]Clockrr Inc., and Lemay Solutions Consulting Inc., Ottawa, Ontario, Canada
Email: {daniel, matt}@lemaysolutions.com

***Abstract*—This work presents an unsupervised learning approach for training a virtual assistant recommender system, building upon prior work on deep learning neural networks, image processing, mixed-initiative systems, and recommender systems. Intelligent agents can understand the world in intuitive ways with neural networks, and make action recommendations to computer users. The system discussed in this work interprets a computer screen image in order to learn new keywords from the user's screen and associate them to new contexts in a completely unsupervised way, then produce action recommendations to assist the user. It can assist in automating various tasks such as genetics research, computer programming, engaging with social media, and legal research. The action recommendations are personalized to the user, and are produced without integration of the assistant into each individual application executing on the computer. Recommendations can be accepted with a single mouse click by the computer user.**

Keywords–Recommender systems; Unsupervised learning; Deep learning.

I. Introduction

This work uses a virtual assistant called Automated Virtual Recommendation Agent (AVRA). AVRA follows a Mixed-Initiative (MI) approach to human-computer interaction, where a human and virtual agent work together to achieve common goals. The approach is to offload to AVRA some of the cognitive pressure of understanding onscreen problems and goals visible on the computer screen, and recommending actions to the user as solutions.

AVRA can look into the browser history and screen content history to decipher a simple sequence of events of interest to the user. If the user saw text on the screen in some context and subsequently searched for that text within some small time frame, then AVRA records the event so that it can offer to perform the search when that context and text appear onscreen in the future. In order to decipher which context to train new information into, the AVRA computes with a word embedding model the fit between the new keyword and the keywords already encoded into each context. AVRA also calculates the fit between the screenshot images of the keyword appearing in the user history, and each context already trained into an image processing Convolutional Neural Network (CNN). The image fit is calculated using perceptual hashing [1]. If, for all existing contexts in AVRA, the keyword fit or image fit is too low (as specified by learning hyperparameters), then a new context is created. Training this new context requires obtaining additional training images from the screenshot history, validated using context-specific perceptual hashing. The unsupervised learning algorithm is still in development, and has thus far achieved a 47% accuracy rate in identifying which historical screenshot images are good examples from which to learn the new context.

AVRA learns through the inference of operational knowledge from observations of the computer over time. AVRA monitors the computer screen with regular screen capture images, and analyzes the content of each image to understand what type of visual information is present (the context) and which keywords are on the screen. Each context is associated with a list of keywords, and at any given time there may be multiple onscreen contexts and multiple onscreen keywords. Each keyword in each context is associated with one action. For example, if the Eclipse IDE is present (context=eclipse) and a compiler error is detected in the onscreen text (keyword=NullPointerException), then AVRA can recommend to the user to open a web page containing advice on escaping this error with a try/catch block. In order to offer the most relevant action recommendations, AVRA produces recognition scores for context detection and keyword detection, and combines these scores with a history of user actions to produce an overall score for every possible recommendation.

Several definitions are required in order to discuss unsupervised learning in a compact format. A candidate keyword k is one text snippet within the onscreen text O. The notation $k \in O$ means that the keyword k is in the set O, in this case because it is a substring of O. An action can be referred to as $g \in G$, where g is a particular action and G is the set of all actions known to AVRA. Similarly, a particular context c is one element in a set of contexts learned into AVRA, denoted as $c \in C$. The set of all keywords learned by AVRA is K, and after discovering $k \in O$, AVRA can integrate k to become $k \in K$.

The challenge discussed in this work is to learn new contexts, keywords, and actions without human intervention. How can AVRA autonomously learn new visual contexts into C beyond "eclipse", and new context-specific keywords such as `NullPointerException` into K? Even if learning new contexts and keywords was accomplished, how can AVRA learn which actions G are associated with contexts and keywords? More formally, this unsupervised learning challenge is to:

(TASK 1) Identify keyword k within onscreen text O leading to action g in context c.
(TASK 2) Recognize context c if it appears again.
(TASK 3) Recognize keyword k if it appears again in onscreen text O when context c is recognized.
(TASK 4) Enable AVRA to recommend action g when context c and keyword k are recognized onscreen at the same time.

This work describes a novel approach to unsupervised

learning for a computer assistant. Once AVRA can watch users and draw causal relationships from user actions, it can learn new information unforeseen by its developers. The first step on the path to a working solution was to relax the constraints on the problem and solve easier problems of unsupervised action learning without context learning (Sections III) and supervised context learning (Section IV). The solutions to these simplified problems are then combined and expanded upon in Section V to answer the larger question of how to learn new actions, contexts and keywords. Next, performance experiments are detailed in Section VI. The contribution of this work is to describe how unsupervised learning can be used in a recommender system. Unsupervised action learning without context is discussed in Section III. The methods of unsupervised action learning with supervised context learning are described in Section IV. Section V describes how AVRA can use both unsupervised action learning and unsupervised context learning. Section VI contains a summary of this work and a discussion of future research directions.

II. Prior Art

Deep learning includes three methods for learning: supervised, reinforcement, and unsupervised learning [2]. Supervised Learning (SL) is the best understood and involves training the classifier using many labelled examples. For example, images of cars accompanied by the label "car", alongside images of dogs accompanied by the label "dog" can be used to train a classifier to discriminate between images of cars and dogs. In supervised learning the classifier adjusts weights during each training iteration of processing the dataset in order to minimize the classification error. Unlike supervised learning, reinforcement learning involves training without an immediate reward signal [3][4]. Reinforcement learning is useful in use cases such as autonomous driving cars and strategy games, where the feedback to the learning system only arrives after some end state is reached, or after a significant delay. And finally, Unsupervised Learning (UL) is the process of learning without labelled examples organized into a dataset [5]. This form of learning gets no feedback, and therefore requires that the learner figure out a pattern from raw data and also figure out a metric for evaluating the accuracy of what was learned. In terms of information content, as described in [6], reinforcement learning predicts only a few bits per input sample (e.g., position of steering wheel to control car), supervised learning predicts a few thousand bits (e.g., class labels to add to an image), and finally unsupervised learning predicts anything to do with the input (e.g., given a video, predict images of the next few frames [7]).

Transfer learning is an approach in ML where the training data is augmented by some other already trained model [8, page 243]. The advantage of using transfer learning is that it enables a model to start from some already trained set of learned features and extend this initial set of knowledge by training on additional data, rather than randomly initializing the weights and training from that random starting point. Transfer learning was accomplished in this work using an Inception v3 tensorflow CNN model that was trained on ImageNet images [9]–[11]. The model was extended by training a new last neural network layer on top of the existing fixed network that can recognize new classes of images after training. This final layer of the CNN received a 2048-dimensional input vector for each image, after which a softmax layer is added. As explained in [12], for N labels this CNN learns only N + 2048*N model parameters corresponding to the learned biases and weights. This is a vast decrease in the number of parameters to learn over training all layers of the model.

The training effectiveness of supervised learning can be enhanced by injecting random noise into the inputs to each layer of the neural network during the training process [13] [14], and by randomly dropping out inputs in each layer of the neural network (dropout) [15]. Dropout and random noise injection each help to prevent the model from overfitting the data during training.

Feature engineering is the process of applying domain knowledge and human data analysis to strengthen predictive models such as neural networks [16][17]. The idea of feature engineering is to reorganize existing data into new formats that the learning system can learn more easily. For example, humans perceive the direction "walk straight" more effectively than "walk in the ventral direction orthogonal to the plane formed by the corners of your torso that faces out from your eyes". These two statements contain the same information, but presenting this data in an easy to process format makes all the difference. In feature engineering that can mean re-encoding the data between acquisition and training.

Supervised learning can be thought of as a clustering problem, where a classifier must learn a linear boundary function between two sets of labeled points on a 2 dimensional graph. In reality, this graph could be of higher dimension, the classifier function could be nonlinear, and the graph could contain more than 2 classes, but the idea serves to illustrate the point of what a SL classifier is doing. It learns a classification function based upon labeled data in order to be able to classify novel data. Unsupervised learning can be thought of as a similar clustering problem, with all of the points having no labels. The main difference here is that in the unsupervised learning case, it is not known to the algorithm which points belong on which side of the line. Worse yet, it is not known ahead of time how many clusters the data should break into.

A good example of an unsupervised learning algorithm is Google News story clustering [18]. The system collects similar stories based on their content, and presents them to the user in an organized way. These stories are organized by their content, rather than by an editor. On a related note, this work uses this same dataset, a 300-dimensional set of approximately 3 million vectors extracted/trained from the Google News dataset of approximately 100 billion words [19].

In this work, unsupervised learning is considered in the domain of Recommender Systems (RS). This means learning new recommendations from unlabeled recordings of computer state and user action data. Unlike reinforcement learning and supervised learning, unlabeled data means that there is no error or reward feedback signal available to create a cost function based upon which the quality of new recommendations can be evaluated. The "right" answer is simply not known to the system. The UL algorithm must make its own decisions about creating image classes and text classes (creating keywords and contexts), and deciding the association between them (what keyword belongs in what context).

Deep neural networks and convolutional neural networks do not contain state information. A given input deterministically results in a given output. Other types of neural nets such as Long Short Term Memory (LSTM) or Recurrent Neural Nets (RNN) contain state information and in addition to containing memory units, the output of the neural network can feed back into the input [20]. RNN do not make the Markov assumption, and even so it is difficult for RNN to encapsulate long-term relationships [21]. In this work, LSTM and RNN were not used, as there was a conscious effort to keep the Markovian assumption in an effort to ease the feasibility of developing an unsupervised learning capability.

Unsupervised learning is often applied to facilitate the success of supervised learning [20, page 14]. Often the unsupervised learning is applied to encode raw data into a form that an SL algorithm can succeed with, where the supervised learning algorithm would not succeed on the raw data. For example, pre-training autoencoder weights prior to applying SL with backpropagation [22], and pre-training RNN [23, page 17].

AVRA's unsupervised learning algorithm finds the similarity of keywords to topics, and the similarity of screen images to learned image features. To learn the relationship between keywords unsupervised, a corpus of online text is extracted and analyzed similar to the approaches of [24][25]–[34] and others. To model the semantic relationships between words in the corpus, word embedding is a common approach [24] [30][33]–[36]. Approaches to unsupervised learning applied to semantic word similarity for a corpus obtained from the web include [24] (keyword extraction from spoken documents), [27] (named-entity extraction), [28] (synonym identification), [30] (identifying relationships in a medical corpus), [31] (set expansion), [34] (relation extraction), and [33]. AVRA follows the approach of [33] to iteratively grow topics one keyword at a time based upon the detected context. AVRA also uses the concept of a "Class Vector" introduced in [33] to represent each topic, and the cosine similarity was used in both approaches to measure the distance between vectors. Furthermore, [33] included a crawling mechanism and removed stop words. Named Entity Recognition (NER) was the goal of [33] and the context surrounding the named entity was textual, forming a Bag-of-Context-Words. AVRA instead focuses on keyword recognition (not NER), where the context is visual: what the computer screen looks like when the keyword is detected. Another difference is that [33] focused on different levels of query complexity (Focused, Very Focused, Unfocused) whereas AVRA makes no such distinction between keywords.

III. Unsupervised Action Learning Without Context

Consider a relaxed version of (TASK 1), where there is only one context. The objective is therefore to identify what onscreen text k in the onscreen text O leads to action g. In this relaxed case, (TASK 2) is not necessary, (TASK 3) simplifies to recognizing when text k appears within the onscreen text O, and (TASK 4) simplifies to recommending action g when text k appears onscreen.

Let the input to the unsupervised learning algorithm be the stream of tokenized timestamped Optical Character Recognition (OCR) text $O(t_1)$ produced when processing each computer screen image. Each image is associated with a timestamp t_1. Next, let the actions $g \in G$ be the detected user interest text (e.g., browser search, clipboard history, keystrokes). Each element g in G is an action performed by the user which could conceivably be replayed by AVRA on behalf of the user. Each observed user action is associated with a timestamp t_2, yielding a stream of timestamped actions $G(t_2)$ and corresponding keyword $K(t_2)$. A dictionary F can store the relationship between keywords and actions as $F < k, g >$ allowing AVRA to identify the desired action g when it detects keyword k.

The learning algorithm can iterate through the OCR text $O(t_1)$ and actions $K(t_2)$, and store into F wherever $K(t_2)$ came soon after the OCR text $O(t_1)$ appeared onscreen, and the user interest text $K(t_2)$ was a substring of the onscreen text $O(t_1)$. These constraints are expressed as $[t_2 > t_1]$ and $[K(t_2)$ in $O(t_1)]$ and $[t_2 - t_1 < windowSize]$. Following this approach, the algorithm can learn from scenarios where the user copies onscreen text (a substring of $O(t_1)$) and pastes into a search engine producing the action text $K(t_2)$ for action $G(t_2)$. After learning this pattern in F, AVRA can recommend the relevant action when a keyword appears onscreen, without the user copying and pasting and searching. The algorithm of Figure 1 implements these concepts. It provides a method for determining what onscreen text O leads to action G in this single context problem. The approach is to search for an onscreen $keyword$ that the user searched for in the past (verbatim) after seeing it on the screen.

Input: OCR text of computer screen at time $t1$: $O(t1)$;
Detected user interest text (e.g., browser search, clipboard history, keystrokes) at time $t2$: $G(t2)$
Output: Database of problem / solution pairs
$F < O, G >$

for ***each*** $O(t1)$ *in history* **do**
    for ***each*** $K(t1)$ *in* $O(t1)$ **do**
        for ***each*** $G(t2)$ *in history* **do**
            if $t2 > t1$ *and* $G(t2)$ *in* $K(t1)$ *and* $t2 - t1 < windowSize$ **then**
                $F.store(K(t1),\ G(t2))$
            end
        end
    end
end

Figure 1. Learning Algorithm: What onscreen text O leads to action G

Consider the example where at time $t = 0$, while AVRA is running in the background, the user and AVRA see an image of a dog and the onscreen word dog. Next, at time $t = 1$, some other information is seen on the screen, and finally at time $t = 2$, the user searches for the word "dog" and AVRA stores into F the fact that the recently observed onscreen word "dog" led to the user performing a search action for that word.

IV. Supervised Context Learning

The challenge in training the CNN with supervised learning is acquiring many images that look like a particular context, in order to carry out the supervised context learning. At least 30 images representing the context should be used to train the CNN in order to avoid total failure of the training. However, 300 to 800 training images is a "good" image dataset size for each context. Only when a sufficient number of images have been collected can the images be used to train the new context into the CNN, or reinforce an existing context with new information. Several image collection approaches are possible:

(METHOD 1) Capture an image representative of the context each time AVRA learns a new keyword into F.

(METHOD 2) Collect images from image search engines based upon context-specific keywords.

(METHOD 3) Given one or more images representing a context, collect additional images using reverse image search.

(METHOD 4) Leverage collaborative filtering to collect context-specific images identified by other AVRA users.

For (METHOD 1), collecting the context training images locally with AVRA was accomplished by simply retaining the screen captures stored by AVRA during routine operation. Working backward from the time when K stored a new keyword, the image captured at time t_1 when k appeared onscreen, the image captured at t_1 should be a picture containing the context of interest C_i. The downside of this approach is that it requires many observations to collect sufficient data to train the CNN. This approach was further improved by sampling the images just before and after t_1 and including them in the training data if they were similar to the image taken at t_1. Similarity was established with a perceptual hash comparing the image taken when the keyword was onscreen, and the images taken at nearby timestamps. For example, if the image taken at time t_1 is a picture of the Eclipse IDE showing a stacktrace containing `NullPointerException`, then the next image taken is likely also a picture of the Eclipse IDE. If these images are in fact similar, then the difference in perceptual hash values between the image taken at time t_1 and the image taken at time image t_{1+1} would be small. Similarly the image taken at time t_{1-1} may be a useful training example if the perceptual hash difference from the image taken at t_1 is small. Image similarity can be controlled by tuning an image similarity hyperparameter.

(METHOD 2), scraping representative images from the Internet to form training datasets, was implemented in nodejs. The program cycled through a hand-crafted list of keywords based upon K relating to the desired context (e.g., "eclipse IDE java programming") and submitted these keywords to image search engine APIs. The search engine submissions returned lists of URLs for images and additional information about these images such as image type and size. The image search was narrowed to include only large images with specific image formats. The next step involved manual data validation where non-representative images were deleted by a human operator. A further step of duplicate image deletion was accomplished with an automated tool.

Whereas (METHOD 2) relied on keyword-based search engines, (METHOD 3) involved querying perceptual hash search engines (e.g., TinEye [37] and Yandex [38]). To find novel images related to the already collected image(s), the perceptual hash of the known image can be used to identify similar images. The downside of this approach was that there may be no such images available, or the identified images may be copies of the submitted image with tiny modifications (e.g., added or modified text).

For (METHOD 4), the collaborative filtering of user actions in a distributed framework with many clients, requiring several instances of an action to be observed before learning a pattern is a reasonable expectation. It is the basis of the collaborative filtering concept that data for one user can be applied to another user.

To learn new contexts in an unsupervised fashion, one or more of these approaches must be automated, removing all human intervention. For example, with (METHOD 2) image search keywords are produced manually, and images are validated manually. With (METHOD 1) the user must perform the same action many times, and the image similarity metric must be flexible enough to allow differences between images but strict enough to reject irrelevant images from polluting the training data.

V. Unsupervised Context Learning

Having outlined solutions to unsupervised action learning and supervised context learning, enough of the solution is revealed that one can begin to consider the full scope of the unsupervised learning problem. Consider AVRA's design shown in Figure 2. How can AVRA autonomously identify keywords K within onscreen text O leading to action G in context C?

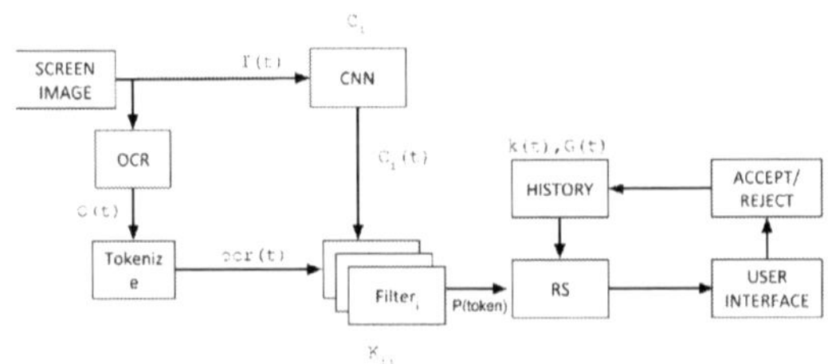

Figure 2. AVRA System Overview.

Consider that AVRA has just detected that a keyword k captured at timestamp t_1 and recognized in image $I(t_1)$ was followed by user action $g(t_2)$. AVRA must decide if this keyword belongs to an existing context or a new one. New challenges emerge when attacking this broader problem definition. First, the fit between a new image $I(t_1)$ and existing trained CNN context C is required to understand how well the new image fits into the set of features that define each context. Second, the relative fit between keyword k and every existing context in C must be quantified in order to decide into which context new information should be stored. Third, AVRA requires an autonomous method for extrapolating novel images from the set of acquired images, as described previously in Section IV.

To obtain the image 'fit', the CNN can tell the unsupervised learning algorithm how much a new image 'looks like' the contexts it was already trained to recognize simply by processing the image in the same way as AVRA interprets screenshots. This capability is exposed by simply processing the image $I(t_1)$ through the CNN and observing the classification confidence score for each context. The output of the CNN indicates how much the image looks like each context.

A trained word embedding model should contain a representation that encodes the semantic understanding of words. The vectors for words can be manipulated to compare ideas, as previously described in the famous $king - man + woman = queen$ example [39]. To find the fit of a new keyword k with an existing context C_i, one or more trained word embedding models are interrogated to find out if k and many keywords of interest K are represented in the model. If so, the cosine similarity between the keywords K already in the context C_i and the new keyword k is computed. More specifically, AVRA's unsupervised learning algorithm relies on the Google News word embedding model to obtain the conceptual distance between words [19]. If a word is not found in the word embedding model, then the distance is set to 0. The average similarity between k and the keywords in context C_i represents the relative fit of keyword k into C_i. If each context contains n keywords, and there are m contexts trained into AVRA, then keyword k must be compared to $m * n$ elements.

At this point the 'fit' between a new keyword and each context is computed as the similarity between a keyword and each keyword in each context. Each of the $m * n$ calculations peers into the Google News word2vec model, requiring several hours to execute. To accelerate the comparison to several seconds, an average vector for all the keywords in each context is computed, and then compared with the candidate keyword. Several approaches are well known for computing a vector to represent a set of words in a word embedding model, including the average vector approach implemented in AVRA [40], and k-means clustering [8, page 5]. One major advantage of this new approach with average vectors is that computing the average vectors is accomplished outside the word2vec model, and so it executes very quickly. Further complicating matters, some keywords AVRA learned during supervised learning are not available (not trained into) in the word2vec model, and so the vector for those keywords in the model does not exist. Therefore, the fit between the candidate keyword and those missing vectors were not taken into account in creating the average vector. To fix this, the fit between the average vector and the vector for the new keyword k is multiplied by a ratio of A (the number of vectors used to make the average vector) and B (the total number of keywords in the context of interest). And so if all the context keywords are in the model, the ratio is 1.0, if none are, then the ratio is 0.0, and if half are in the model, then the ratio is 0.5. The calculation of the mean similarity is computed as the similarity between k and the average vector, multiplied by the ratio.

Another acceleration technique used was memoization. Any intermediate results (e.g., distance('paris','france')) is not re-calculated when the result is needed later on.

As discussed previously, approaches to getting more images representative of a new CNN context requires fully automating one or more of (METHOD 1) (making multiple observations of $k + C_i \rightarrow g$ before learning a new context, and obtaining similar images nearby in time using perceptual hashing), (METHOD 2) (keyword-based image search engines), (METHOD 3) (perceptual-hash reverse image search), and (METHOD 4) (collaborative filtering). (METHOD 1) was already fully automated, and provides a small number of useful images as a starting point for the CNN training dataset. To automate (METHOD 2), images obtained from (METHOD 1) were fed to an image labeling API (Google Vision API [41]) in order to come up with a set of keywords, and these keywords were submitted to image search engines to obtain new image examples. The resulting images were a poor fit for the contexts tested (e.g., console, Eclipse IDE) as a result of the small number of labels that the image annotation API was able to extract from the available images. Obtaining keywords from images was possible, and scraping images based on these keywords was also possible, but the quality of the generated keywords was too low to be useful for an autonomous use case. For example, the labels added to an image of a console window were: Text, Font, Brand, Screenshot, Design, Presentation, Line, and Document. Searching for images using these labels does not return additional images of console windows. (METHOD 2) automation was therefore not successful. Surprisingly, full automation of (METHOD 3) was similarly disappointing. Reverse image search did sometimes return novel examples of the submitted context (e.g., image of a console window returned additional examples of console windows). However, reverse image search tended to return either no results (e.g., a fullscreen image of the Eclipse IDE) identical copies of the submitted image (e.g., an image of a celebrity) or results focusing on the "wrong" features of the submitted image (e.g., for a screenshot of a desktop, the perceptual hash caused the results to be the image shown as the desktop background with the desktop icons removed, focusing on the irrelevant background image at the expense of the real goad of finding images of desktop backgrounds). Full automation of (METHOD 3) was therefore not successful. Collaborative filtering (METHOD 4) was not implemented.

Having described how the text fit and image fit are computed, and how a dataset to train the CNN can be obtained for new contexts, the unsupervised learning process can now be discussed in additional detail. For each new keyword k under consideration, if AVRA has seen enough examples of the keyword (and related images for context training) triggering an action, then AVRA will begin assessing which context the keyword belongs in. This may be a new context or an existing context. This keyword may already exist in one context and now also belongs in another. Let $I_{examples}$ be a list of the images related to one keyword k. AVRA begins by assessing the keyword in relation to the keywords already learned for each context C_i. The average fit between the new keyword k and the existing keywords in C_i is computed using the ratio with average vector comparison approach described above. Next, the average fit between the images $I_{examples}$ and the context is computed by processing them through the CNN and averaging the classification confidence for class C_i. If $I_{examples}$ does indeed contain similar features to the already trained CNN class, then a high average fit is expected. To associate the keyword to an existing class, the average image fit must exceed hyperparameter h_1 and the keyword fit must exceed hyperparameter h_2, and the average image fit multiplied by the keyword fit must exceed any previously encountered "best context fit". In other words, the class with the strongest keyword and image similarity is assigned the keyword unless either the keyword or images are too dissimilar from any existing context. In that case a new context is learned.

If the keyword is learned into an existing context C_i, then the CNN can be retrained with images $I_{examples}$, and the keyword identification system for C_i is also updated to recognize the new keyword. If, however, the keyword is learned into a new context, then AVRA finds additional distinct images according to (METHOD 1), in an attempt to increase the number of images available for training. This larger image set is used to retrain the CNN to identify the new context. The keyword identification system is also updated to recognize the new keyword.

AVRA's unsupervised learning algorithm described in this Section is presented in the algorithm of Figure 3. Similar to

Figure 1, it can learn causal relationships between onscreen keywords and user actions. However, the added advantage in Figure 3 is that it can also learn features from what the screen looks like when the keyword is present (image contexts). On the first line of Figure 3, the observations made by AVRA are processed to identify a set of keywords ($new\_keywords$) that appeared onscreen prior to the user performing a related search. This part of the algorithm work as described in Figure 1. For each keyword k in $new\_keywords$, a list of images $I_{examples}[k]$ is also collected. Next, for each keyword and corresponding action ($[k, g]$), if there were enough causation examples observed, the algorithm checks each context to see which has the highest context fit (lines 6 to 14). If a best context is found, then the keyword k and action g are added to AVRA's database.

This method for unsupervised learning can be viewed as partitioning the space of all images and words into sub-regions by context and keyword. Keyword clustering is one part of the partitioning, and image clustering is the other. The unsupervised learning approach in AVRA incrementally clusters sets of keywords and stereotypes of images. Figure 4 shows the block diagram for AVRA's unsupervised learning approach. A sufficient number of new keyword identifications (TASK 1) causes a decision engine to assesses a keyword $k(t)$ recognized in image $I(t)$. Next, to accomplish context recognition (TASK 2), the fit between the existing CNN contexts and the new image is computed (Context Similarity in Figure 4). Further to (TASK 2), the images provided to characterize the potential new context are extended by testing the images taken just before and after time t with a perceptual hash, and keeping images with a difference less than $h3$ from $I(t)$. The resulting set of images is called $I_{examples}$. The context similarity task returns the list of contexts sufficiently similar to the potentially new context (with a similarity threshold of $h1$). DNN training to recognize a new keyword within a context (TASK 3) is only initiated once a keyword has been assigned a context. To assign a keyword to a context (new or existing), the keyword fit is first computed (Keyword Clustering in Figure 4), and a list of contexts with sufficiently similar keywords is returned. The text similarity threshold is hyperparameter $h2$. If no context has a sufficiently high keyword fit and context fit, n new context is present, and the CNN is retrained to recognize the new context. However, if there are contexts with sufficiently high keyword fit and context fit, the context with the highest combination of context and keyword fit (computed by multiplying them together) is assigned the new $keyword$ k. When the keyword is assigned a context, in addition to the DNN training being initiated, action g is associated to the new keyword k in AVRA's database (TASK 4). To extract user actions from the computer, a browser history program was developed to read out keyword search terms and links from the browser along with visit timestamps and page titles. This information was fed into AVRA's database to form the user action history (G).

The key overlap between AVRA's shallow image processing integration and prior work on fullscreen image processing with a CNN to take decisions (e.g., [4]) is the use of a CNN to process the image of the screen, and then using fully connected layers of a Deep Neural Network (DNN) to make a decision. In the case of AVRA, the DNN output is a recommendation to be ranked based upon supervised or unsupervised learning, whereas in [4] the outputs represent joystick positions learned through reinforcement learning.

Input: Minimum observations of keyword and subsequent action $h0 : 1$; Minimum image fit $h1 : 0.1$; Minimum keyword fit $h2 : 0.1$; Minimum CNN recognition confidence to add new image to training data $h3 : 0.1$; Maximum perceptual hash difference to add new image to training data $h4 : 35$; Detected user search text, URL, and timestamp recorded at time $t2 : G(t2)$; Snippets of onscreen text observed at time $t : ocr(t)$; Maximum time from observation of keyword to action by user $windowSize : 10\ s$; List of CNN contexts $contexts$

Output: Keyword added to new context or existing context, or nothing learned.

```
1  [I_examples, new_keywords] =
     detectNewKeywords(G, ocr, windowSize)
2  for each [k, g] in new_keywords do
3    if length(I_examples[k]) ≥ h0 then
4      best_context_fit = 0
5      best_context = None
6      for each context in contexts do
7        keyword_fit =
           modelTextFit(k, context.keywords())
8        img_fit =
           average(CNN_classify(I_examples[k],
9          context))
10       if img_fit > h1 and keyword_fit >
           h2 and img_fit * keyword_fit >
           best_context_fit then
11         best_context = context
12         best_context_fit =
             img_fit * keyword_fit
13       end
14     end
15     if best_context then
16       train_DNN(best_context, k, g)
17       train_CNN(best_context, I_examples[k])
18     end
19     else
20       c = newContextID()
21       I_examples[k] =
           moreImages(I_examples[k], k,
22         CNN_contexts, h3, h4)
23       train_new_DNN(c, k, g)
24       train_CNN(c, I_examples[k])
25     end
26   end
27 end
```

Figure 3. AVRA's unsupervised learning algorithm.

Having described above the unsupervised learning algorithm in AVRA, consider the example of how an existing context can be extended with a new keyword. First, AVRA sees an image of a dog and the text `dog`. The image at timestamp for $t = 0$ is $0.jpg$. At that time, AVRA has already learned through supervised learning two contexts `Animals` and `Colors`. Each context contains two keywords. The `Animals` context contains keywords `cat` and `mule`, while the `Colors` context contains the keywords `red` and `green`. At timestamp $t = 1$, AVRA detects user action g, where the

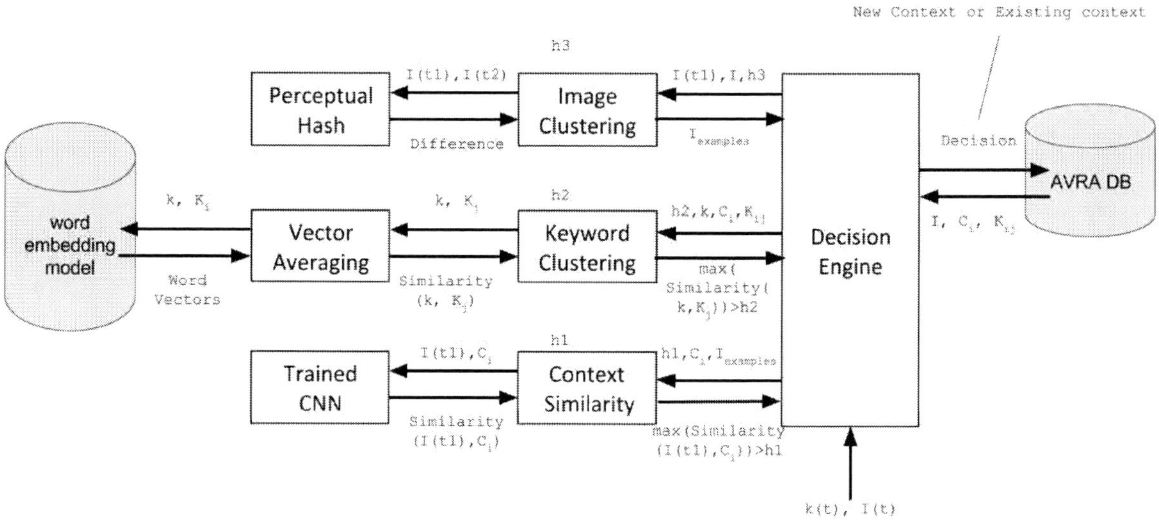

Figure 4. Block diagram for AVRA's unsupervised learning algorithm.

word `dog` is searched for in a browser. The image recorded at timestamp $t = 1$ is $1.jpg$. At time $t = 3$, the unsupervised learning algorithm makes the connection that the text `dog` led to the action `Search(dog)`. The algorithm then loads the hyperparaemters $h1$ and $h2$ as 0.65. Next, the fit of the text `dog` is computed in comparison to the average vector for the context `Animals`, with a result of 0.8. The fit of `dog` with the average vector for the keywords in context `Colors` computes to 0.1. $0.jpg$ is then compared with $1.jpg$ using a perceptual hash to detect if the images are close enough together for $1.jpg$ to be representative of the potential new context. The image difference is too great, and so only $0.jpg$ is used in the next step. The image fit is calculated by passing $0.jpg$ to the CNN for classification. It outputs that $0.jpg$ strongly activates the context `Animals` (0.9 - perhaps detecting the eyes and other body features common to all animals), and also activates the context `Colors` (0.7 - perhaps picking up on the fact that the image of the dog is mostly one solid white color). The ratio for both the `Animals` and `Colors` contexts was 1.0, and so the ratio did not modify the decision at the output in this case. The overall fit of keyword `dog` into context `Animals` was 0.72, exceeding the threshold of 0.65. At 0.07, the overall fit of keyword `dog` into context `Colors` did not exceed the threshold of 0.65, and so it was discarded. With only one context vying to accept the new keyword `dog`, it was added to the context `Animals`.

Consider the second example of AVRA learning a new context. AVRA sees an image of a dog and the text `dog`. The image at timestamp for $t = 0$ is $0.jpg$. At that time AVRA has already learned through supervised learning two contexts `Shapes` and `Colors`. Each context contains two keywords. The `Shapes` context contains keywords `round` and `line`, while the `Colors` context contains the keywords `red` and `green`. At timestamp $t = 1$, AVRA detects user action g, where the word `dog` is searched for in a browser. The image recorded at timestamp $t = 1$ is $1.jpg$. At time $t = 3$ the unsupervised learning algorithm makes the connection that the text `dog` led to the action `Search(dog)`. The algorithm then loads the hyperparaemters $h1$ and $h2$ as 0.65. Next, the fit of the text `dog` is computed in comparison to the average vector for the context `Shapes`, with a result of 0.0. The fit of `dog` with the average vector for the keywords in context `Colors` computes to 0.1. $0.jpg$ is then compared with $1.jpg$ using a perceptual hash to detect if the images are close enough together for $1.jpg$ to be representative of the potential new context. The image difference is too great, and so only $0.jpg$ is used in the next step. The image fit is calculated by passing $0.jpg$ to the CNN for classification. It outputs that $0.jpg$ activates the context `Shapes` (0.6), and also activates the context `Colors` (0.7). The ratio for both the `Shapes` and `Colors` contexts was 1.0 because all of the keywords in each context was used to compose their average vector. The overall fit of keyword `dog` into context `Shapes` was 0.0, below the threshold of 0.65. At 0.07, the overall fit of keyword `dog` into context `Colors` also did not exceed the threshold of 0.65. With no remaining context into which the keyword `dog` can be trained, a new context `newContext` was created and the keyword `dog` was added to it. The arbitrary name `newContext` reflects the fact that AVRA does not know what the overall context is going to store in the future.

A problem surfaced when assessing AVRA's ability to learn new *keywords* into existing contexts created through supervised learning. The word embedding component of the unsupervised learning algorithm was mostly unsuccessful adding to the supervised learning data. It emerged that the problem was the ratio. The ratio is small when many of the keywords from supervised learning (e.g., nullpointerexception) are not contained in the word embedding model generated from the Google News dataset [19], or other general word embedding models. The model in question contains 3 million words, but this was not sufficient. One approach to force the unsupervised learning model to work was to ignore the ratio, setting it to 1.0 instead of calculating the correct value. Setting ratio to 1.0 is of course a sub-optimal solution, but with this approach AVRA was able to learn new *keywords* into existing contexts created through supervised learning.

A better approach to learn new *keywords* into existing contexts created through supervised learning was to re-purpose (METHOD 2) to collect website contents instead of images. The idea was to scrape text from search engine results (web pages), where the search query is built using the keywords AVRA knows about, and the new keyword AVRA wants to classify into a new or existing context. Using the text from these web pages as a corpus, one can train a new word embedding model that can relate a high ratio of the keywords to each other. The drawback of this approach is that scraping the pages and training the word embedding model is very slow. It can take days. Luckily the unsupervised learning process can be trained as an offline server-side process without slowing down the user experience at all. To build the corpus, the first 30 results for each search term were downloaded. Search terms were composed of distinct sets of 3 or 4 keywords (e.g., *horse baseexception chicken*). Stopwords were removed using the NLTK Stopwords corpus by Porter [42] [43, page 47]. Stemming was applied using the `PorterStemmer` module of the `gensim` library [44]. Some web pages from the results were skipped because the server refused the connection, the file on the server was not a web page (e.g., PowerPoint file), or the page contained no text. Each valid link returned by the search engine was processed into a text string, and all of the results were concatenated into a single corpus tokenized by spaces. Next, a word embedding model was trained on the corpus, exposing the similarity between words by computing the cosine similarity in the word embedding model between vectors for words.

At this point in the work, it has been described to the reader how AVRA has the ability to make sense of new words by building its own word embedding models completely unsupervised. Crucially, supervised and unsupervised learning can be combined in AVRA, to accomplish transfer learning. AVRA can learn new things autonomously as long as the related keywords are trained into one of the word embedding models that informs the textual context relationships between them, or the information relating these concepts is obtainable by building a word embedding using documents obtained by searching on the web. Multiple word embedding models could be used by AVRA as a general knowledge reference.

VI. Performance Evaluation for Unsupervised Learning

Learning in AVRA is data driven. In this Section, the operation of AVRA's unsupervised learning algorithm with real data is explored. A high-level view of a word embedding model for several contexts is presented to clarify the ability of AVRA to classify new keywords into existing contexts. Visualization for AVRA's image recognition system similarly reveals that AVRA can successfully discriminate between different sets of images. To collect data quickly, a test automation program was used to model a user using the computer (a 'bot'). This bot was used to carry out use cases such as extending an existing context with new information, and creating a new context in AVRA's model. Examples of extending an existing context and creating a new context are provided as validation of the AVRA prototype's ability to apply unsupervised learning.

1) Unsupervised Learning Extending Existing AVRA Context: Table I presents a real example to show how AVRA extends the Eclipse IDE context created using supervised learning. For this example, 5 existing contexts were included in the computations, to give the reader a sense for the computations AVRA performs without overwhelming the reader with many contexts and keywords. Setting the stage for this example, and with AVRA running in the background, a program generated an error, then opened a browser window to search for keywords related to this error message. When AVRA observed the causal relationship between the onscreen error in the IDE, and the search action in the browser, it stored the data in the AVRA database. When sufficient copies of the action were observed, the unsupervised learning algorithm was triggered to try and learn the new keywords into AVRA's RS.

TABLE I. EXTENDING AN EXISTING CONTEXT AFTER OBSERVING THE USER.

Event	Context Similarity	Word Clustering	AVRA Decision	Correct?
New keyword *thread*	*console* 0.02 **eclipse 0.94** *desktop* 0.01 *facebook* 0.02 *gene* 0.00	**console 0.28** **eclipse 0.15** **desktop 0.30** *facebook* 0.00 **gene 0.25**	Train *thread* into *eclipse*	YES
New keyword *exception*	*console* 0.02 **eclipse 0.94** *desktop* 0.01 *facebook* 0.02 *gene* 0.00	**console 0.16** **eclipse 0.51** *desktop* 0.01 *facebook* 0.00 *gene* 0.01	Train *exception* into *eclipse*	YES
New keyword *throwing*	*console* 0.02 **eclipse 0.94** *desktop* 0.01 *facebook* 0.02 *gene* 0.00	**console 0.14** *eclipse* 0.09 *desktop* 0.01 *facebook* 0.00 *gene* 0.01	Image clustering. Train new context for *throwing*	NO

Examining Table I, AVRA found that images when *thread* was onscreen strongly activated the *eclipse* context (0.95) and that word *thread* was semantically similar to the keywords in *console* (0.28), *eclipse* (0.15), *desktop* (0.30), and *gene* (0.25). Because only one context demonstrated sufficient image and word similarity, the new keyword *thread* was trained into AVRA for the *eclipse* context. Continuing with the second row of Table I, AVRA found that images when *exception* was onscreen strongly activated the eclipse context (0.94) and that word *exception* was semantically similar to the keywords in *console* (0.16), and *eclipse* (0.51). Because, once again, only one context demonstrated sufficient image and word similarity, the new keyword *exception* was trained into AVRA for the *eclipse* context. The unsupervised learning algorithm in AVRA does make mistakes. For example, in the third row of Table I, AVRA recognized the images of the Eclipse IDE but just missed the hyperparameter cutoff of 0.10 to consider the keyword *throwing* semantically similar to the *eclipse* context. Instead of learning *throwing* into *eclipse*, AVRA incorrectly learned the keyword into a new context.

2) Unsupervised Learning Creating New AVRA Context: Table II presents a real example to show how AVRA creates a new context using unsupervised learning. A **bolded** result in the table below indicates a result that exceeded the required threshold. For this example, 5 existing contexts were included in the computations. Prior to the events listed in Table II, the user moved from the a browser window containing a cake recipe to a browser search window and searched for keywords related to the recipe (*chocolate*, *cake*, and *cupcake*). All the while, AVRA was running in the background collecting images and extracting onscreen text. When AVRA observed the causal relationship between the onscreen recipe text, and the search actions in the browser, it stored the data in the AVRA database. When sufficient copies of the action were observed, the unsupervised learning algorithm was triggered to try and learn the new keywords into AVRA's RS.

Starting with the first row of Table II, AVRA found that images of a recipe website taken when the word *cupcake* was onscreen strongly activated the facebook context (0.90) and that word *cupacke* was semantically similar to the keywords in *desktop* (0.18). Because no context demonstrated sufficient

TABLE II. CREATING A NEW CONTEXT AFTER OBSERVING THE USER.

Event	Context Similarity	Word Clustering	AVRA Decision	Correct?
New keyword *cupcake*	*console* 0.02 *eclipse* 0.04 *desktop* 0.03 **facebook 0.90** *gene* 0.01	*console* 0.07 *eclipse* 0.00 **desktop 0.18** *facebook* 0.00 *gene* 0.05	Image clustering. Train *cupcake* into new context *newContext*	YES
New keyword *chocolate*	*console* 0.02 *eclipse* 0.04 *desktop* 0.03 **facebook 0.90** *gene* 0.01 **newContext 0.70**	*console* 0.04 *eclipse* 0.00 **desktop 0.12** *facebook* 0.00 *gene* 0.05 **newContext 0.55**	Train *chocolate* into *newContext*	YES
New keyword *cake*	*console* 0.02 *eclipse* 0.04 *desktop* 0.03 **facebook 0.90** *gene* 0.01 **newContext 0.70**	*console* 0.05 *eclipse* 0.00 **desktop 0.12** *facebook* 0.00 *gene* 0.05 **newContext 0.60**	Train *cake* into *newContext*	YES

image and word similarity, a new context was created in AVRA. Continuing with the second row of Table II, AVRA found that images captured when the word *chocolate* was on-screen strongly activated the *facebook* context (0.90) as well as the new context *newContext* (0.70). The word *chocolate* was semantically similar to the keywords in *desktop* (0.12), and *newContext* (0.55). Because only one context demonstrated sufficient image and word similarity, the new keyword *chocolate* was trained into AVRA for the *newContext* context. For the third row of Table II, AVRA recognized the images of the recipe website, and considered the keyword *cupcake* semantically similar to the context *newContext*. AVRA learned the keyword *cake* into the correct context. This example shows that when the risk of concept drift is highest, for a new context with only a few keywords, AVRA does generally manage to build up the new context. There are cases such as the third row in Table I, where keyword clustering or image clustering fails to group an action into an existing context where it belongs, fracturing the context into two (or more) contexts.

3) Unsupervised Learning Relationships Between Keywords: It is interesting to ask how long it takes to train a new word embedding model for a new *keyword* (e.g., "nullpointerexception") that is not in AVRA's default model, and how well that model works, given the fact that the raw data was built through analyzing web pages returned by a search engine.

To evaluate the ability of the generated model to classify new entities, two small sets of related keywords were created for testing purposes: `Animals` $(horse, dog, cow, pig)$ and `Java` $(baseexception, exception, standarderror, importerror)$, and the similarity (from the cosine distance) to a new keyword `chicken` was measured. An effective model should find that `chicken` has a lower cosine distance to the average vector for `Animals` than it does compared to the average vector for `Java` keywords.

The $23MB$ corpus of text was downloaded and trained in approximately 30 minutes for 9 keywords. $1,744$ of the links produced usable text. In the collected corpus, the frequency of the stemmed keywords was as follows: $hors(8,137)$, $dog(14,412)$, $cow(4,914)$, $pig(9,933)$, $baseexcept(434)$, $except(9,109)$, $standarderror(256)$, $importerror(544)$, $chicken(6,252)$. The average sentence length was 110.9 characters, and $47,566$ distinct keywords were translated into word vectors in the trained model. The model was created under various hyperparameter configurations (random seed value, training iterations between 5 and 50, context window size between 10 and 40) and each configuration was tested 10 times. All of these measurements resulted in assignment of the new keyword `chicken` to the context `Animals`. Generally, there was a negative similarity between the keyword `chicken` and the context `Java`, while there was always a positive similarity between the keyword `chicken` and the context `Animals`. Very surprisingly, the outcome was positive even when the number of dimensions (also called the number of features) used to represent word vectors was varied between 10 and 100. AVRA sometimes misses the context or keyword information, or has higher confidence in unhelpful recommendations than detected helpful recommendations. Two overall challenges in developing AVRA were poor classification of keywords with very short text length (e.g., the terminal command "ls"), and low context detection confidence (e.g., 2% confidence in the correct class). These cases were rare but noticeable. Perhaps the short keyword recognition could be resolved by modifying the DNN input filter hyperparameters. The low confidence context detection cases may be mitigated by collecting additional image data for context training.

VII. CONCLUSION

This work presented AVRA's unsupervised learning approach and explained with examples how AVRA combined supervised and unsupervised learning to accomplish transfer learning. An architecture for a deep learning recommender system for personal computer users was described in this work. Action recommendations produced by this design are personalized to the user and are generated in real-time. The AVRA system mines information from screen capture data, rather than interfacing with individual applications. Recommendations are presented to the user in an intuitive button-based user interface. The architecture described in this work can provide the foundation for further research into recommender system for personal computer users.

Future work planned for AVRA includes user acceptance testing, testing with large sets of contexts and keywords, collaborative filtering and related privacy considerations, the expansion of AVRA's input processing and modeling capabilities, and more on unsupervised learning. Applying content-based image recognition and semantic segmentation of images to achieve face and object classification within a context (and generating related recommendations) is an interesting area to explore.

REFERENCES

[1] J. Buchner, "A Python Perceptual Image Hashing Module," https://github.com/JohannesBuchner/imagehash, 2017, [retrieved: 2017-05].

[2] Y. LeCun, Y. Bengio, and G. Hinton, "Deep learning," Nature, vol. 521, no. 7553, 2015, pp. 436–444.

[3] R. Sutton, "Introduction to reinforcement learning," vol. 135, 1998.

[4] V. Mnih, K. Kavukcuoglu, D. Silver, A. A. Rusu, J. Veness, M. G. Bellemare, A. Graves, M. Riedmiller, A. K. Fidjeland, G. Ostrovski et al., "Human-level control through deep reinforcement learning," Nature, vol. 518, no. 7540, 2015, pp. 529–533.

[5] G. E. Hinton, P. Dayan, B. J. Frey, and R. M. Neal, "The" wake-sleep" algorithm for unsupervised neural networks," Science, vol. 268, no. 5214, 1995, p. 1158.

[6] Y. Lecun, "Ethics of artificial intelligence - general issues," https://youtu.be/tNWqOgNDnCw?t=1h23m21s, [retrieved: 2017-01].

[7] A. Radford, L. Metz, and S. Chintala, "Unsupervised representation learning with deep convolutional generative adversarial networks," arXiv preprint arXiv:1511.06434, 2015.

[8] E. S. Olivas, J. D. M. Guerrero, M. M. Sober, J. R. M. Benedito, and A. J. S. López, "Handbook of research on machine learning applications and trends: Algorithms, methods, and techniques," 2010.

[9] "Imagenet," http://www.image-net.org/, [retrieved: 2017-01].

[10] C. Szegedy, W. Liu, Y. Jia, P. Sermanet, S. Reed, D. Anguelov, D. Erhan, V. Vanhoucke, and A. Rabinovich, "Going deeper with convolutions," in Proceedings of the IEEE Conference on Computer Vision and Pattern Recognition, 2015, pp. 1–9.

[11] M. Abadi, A. Agarwal, P. Barham et al., "TensorFlow: Large-scale machine learning on heterogeneous systems," 2015, software available from tensorflow.org [retrieved: 2017-05]. [Online]. Available: http://tensorflow.org/

[12] P. Warden, "Tensorflow for poets," https://petewarden.com/2016/02/28/tensorflow-for-poets/, [retrieved: 2017-01].

[13] W. M. Brown, T. D. Gedeon, and D. I. Groves, "Use of noise to augment training data: a neural network method of mineral–potential mapping in regions of limited known deposit examples," Natural Resources Research, vol. 12, no. 2, 2003, pp. 141–152.

[14] J. Sietsma and R. J. Dow, "Creating artificial neural networks that generalize," Neural networks, vol. 4, no. 1, 1991, pp. 67–79.

[15] N. Srivastava, G. Hinton, A. Krizhevsky, I. Sutskever, and R. Salakhutdinov, "Dropout: A simple way to prevent neural networks from overfitting," The Journal of Machine Learning Research, vol. 15, no. 1, 2014, pp. 1929–1958.

[16] L. P. Coelho and W. Richert, Building machine learning systems with Python. Packt Publishing Ltd, 2015.

[17] F. Seide, G. Li, X. Chen, and D. Yu, "Feature engineering in context-dependent deep neural networks for conversational speech transcription," in 2011 IEEE Workshop on Automatic Speech Recognition Understanding, Dec 2011, pp. 24–29.

[18] A. S. Das, M. Datar, A. Garg, and S. Rajaram, "Google news personalization: scalable online collaborative filtering," in Proceedings of the 16th international conference on World Wide Web. ACM, 2007, pp. 271–280.

[19] T. Mikolov, I. Sutskever, K. Chen, G. S. Corrado, and J. Dean, "Distributed representations of words and phrases and their compositionality," in Advances in neural information processing systems, 2013, pp. 3111–3119.

[20] J. Schmidhuber, "Deep learning in neural networks: An overview," Neural Networks, vol. 61, 2015, pp. 85–117.

[21] Y. Bengio, P. Simard, and P. Frasconi, "Learning long-term dependencies with gradient descent is difficult," IEEE transactions on neural networks, vol. 5, no. 2, 1994, pp. 157–166.

[22] D. H. Ballard, "Modular learning in neural networks." in AAAI, 1987, pp. 279–284.

[23] J. Schmidhuber, "Learning complex, extended sequences using the principle of history compression," Neural Computation, vol. 4, no. 2, 1992, pp. 234–242.

[24] Y. N. Chen, Y. Huang, H. Y. Lee, and L. S. Lee, "Unsupervised two-stage keyword extraction from spoken documents by topic coherence and support vector machine," in 2012 IEEE International Conference on Acoustics, Speech and Signal Processing (ICASSP), March 2012, pp. 5041–5044.

[25] G. Grefenstette and L. Muchemi, "Determining the characteristic vocabulary for a specialized dictionary using word2vec and a directed crawler," in GLOBALEX 2016: Lexicographic Resources for Human Language Technology, May 2016.

[26] P. Pantel, E. Crestan, A. Borkovsky, A.-M. Popescu, and V. Vyas, "Web-scale distributional similarity and entity set expansion," in Proceedings of the 2009 Conference on Empirical Methods in Natural Language Processing: Volume 2 - Volume 2, ser. EMNLP '09. Stroudsburg, PA, USA: Association for Computational Linguistics, 2009, pp. 938–947. [Online]. Available: http://dl.acm.org/citation.cfm?id=1699571.1699635

[27] O. Etzioni, M. Cafarella, D. Downey, A.-M. Popescu, T. Shaked, S. Soderland, D. S. Weld, and A. Yates, "Unsupervised named-entity extraction from the web: An experimental study," Artificial intelligence, vol. 165, no. 1, 2005, pp. 91–134.

[28] P. D. Turney, "Mining the web for synonyms: Pmi-ir versus lsa on toefl," in European Conference on Machine Learning. Springer, 2001, pp. 491–502.

[29] S. Chakrabarti, M. van den Berg, and B. Dom, "Focused crawling: a new approach to topic-specific web resource discovery," Computer Networks, vol. 31, no. 1116, 1999, pp. 1623 – 1640. [Online]. Available: http://www.sciencedirect.com/science/article/pii/S1389128699000523

[30] J. A. Miñarro-Giménez, O. Marín-Alonso, and M. Samwald, "Applying deep learning techniques on medical corpora from the world wide web: a prototypical system and evaluation," CoRR, vol. abs/1502.03682, 2015, [retrieved: 2017-05]. [Online]. Available: http://arxiv.org/abs/1502.03682

[31] R. C. Wang and W. W. Cohen, "Language-independent set expansion of named entities using the web," in Data Mining, 2007. ICDM 2007. Seventh IEEE International Conference on. IEEE, 2007, pp. 342–350.

[32] R. C. Wang, N. Schlaefer, W. W. Cohen, and E. Nyberg, "Automatic set expansion for list question answering," in Proceedings of the Conference on Empirical Methods in Natural Language Processing. Association for Computational Linguistics, 2008, pp. 947–954.

[33] A. Alasiry, M. Levene, and A. Poulovassilis, "Mining named entities from search engine query logs," in Proceedings of the 18th International Database Engineering & Applications Symposium, ser. IDEAS '14. New York, NY, USA: ACM, 2014, pp. 46–56. [Online]. Available: http://doi.acm.org/10.1145/2628194.2628224

[34] B. Min, S. Shi, R. Grishman, and C.-Y. Lin, "Towards large-scale unsupervised relation extraction from the web," Int. J. Semant. Web Inf. Syst., vol. 8, no. 3, Jul. 2012, pp. 1–23. [Online]. Available: http://dx.doi.org/10.4018/jswis.2012070101

[35] T. Wang, V. Viswanath, and P. Chen, "Extended topic model for word dependency," in Proceedings of the 53rd Annual Meeting of the Association for Computational Linguistics and The 7th International Joint Conference of the Asian Federation of Natural Language Processing, 2015, p. 506. [Online]. Available: http://acl2015.org/

[36] W. Li, X. Xie, J. Hu, Z. Zhang, and Y. Zhang, "Using big data from the web to train chinese traffic word representation model in vector space," in 2016 12th World Congress on Intelligent Control and Automation (WCICA), June 2016, pp. 2304–2307.

[37] TinEye, "TinEye Reverse Image Search," https://www.tineye.com/, [retrieved:2017-02].

[38] Yandex, "Yandex.Images: search for images on the internet, search by image," https://yandex.com/images/, [retrieved:2017-02].

[39] T. Mikolov, W.-t. Yih, and G. Zweig, "Linguistic regularities in continuous space word representations." in HLT-NAACL, vol. 13, 2013, pp. 746–751.

[40] Q. Le and T. Mikolov, "Distributed representations of sentences and documents," in Proceedings of the 31st International Conference on Machine Learning (ICML-14), 2014, pp. 1188–1196.

[41] Google Inc., "Vision API - Image Content Analysis — Google Cloud Platform," https://cloud.google.com/vision/, [retrieved: 2017-01].

[42] M. F. Porter, "An algorithm for suffix stripping," Program, vol. 14, no. 3, 1980, pp. 130–137.

[43] S. Bird, E. Klein, and E. Loper, Natural language processing with Python. O'Reilly Media, Inc., 2009.

[44] R. Řehůřek and P. Sojka, "Software Framework for Topic Modelling with Large Corpora," in Proceedings of the LREC 2010 Workshop on New Challenges for NLP Frameworks. Valletta, Malta: ELRA, May 2010, pp. 45–50, http://is.muni.cz/publication/884893/en.

Modeling of Complex Multiagent Behavior Using Matrix Representation

Sebastian Meszyński, Oleksandr Sokolov
Faculty of Physics, Astronomy, and Informatics
Nicolaus Copernicus University
Toruń, Poland
email: {sebcio, osokolov}@fizyka.umk.pl

Abstract— **Multi-agent systems are systems that solve complex problems by dividing them into smaller problems and imparting each of them to specialized programs called agents. The reliability of such systems strongly depends on the correctness of agents' communication and interaction. Unfortunately, the analysis of the whole system is not an easy task as its component parts, in the form of agents, work in an asynchronous way. An additional problem causing the difficulty in this analysis is the fact that each agent is an autonomous being, therefore, having received information from another agent existing in the same environment, it does not have to change its internal condition. In the following paper, matrix representation and equations, describing dynamics of the multiagent system were implemented by using the basic elements of graph theory and theory of compartment modeling. The analysis of equations and examples presented below, confirm the validity of the thesis that the adopted description is sufficient to describe the interactions between agents in the multiagent system.**

Keywords- multiagent system; agent; linear algebra; matrix.

I. INTRODUCTION

The models used for modeling of any kinds of physical phenomena are the tools utilized to obtain an answer to questions concerning the tested system, without the need for performing the actual experiment. Among the variety of models, i.e., psychological, word or physical models, there are also mathematical models whose relations observed in the system are described by mathematical formulas. The possibility to perform such experiments is called simulation (lat. simulare – simulate). It is a cheap and safe alternative or a complement to experiments with the system.

The quality of simulation's results depends entirely on the quality of the model. Fundamentally, there are two approaches to building a model representing a particular system. The first type of approach is based on the knowledge taken from literature or experience of experts in a given domain and could be used for building more and more precise description of the investigated phenomenon (more complex models are generated). The second one is based on observation of the phenomenon and its behavior on one level of description (using similar agents) and after that building the model and identification of parameters (agent-based approach).

The created model in both approaches needs to be described in a handy form, especially if one wants to analyze it with the use of digital machines. Having the model built, it is necessary to verify the correctness of obtained results. The credibility of the results provided by the model can be acquired using verification or validation.

This paper focuses on the use of a multi-agent system for the modeling of the insulin-glucose system responsible for the blood glucose homeostasis. Even by designing the simplest model based on the multi-agent paradigm, one must rely on a complex analysis of interactions between agents. For this reason, there is not one general formalism of description of these interactions, which would additionally allow for an easy analysis of the functioning of such a multi-agent system. In most cases, the approaches used are chosen depending on the category of problem that is solved by the system. It should be understood that if the multi-agent system was designed to address the issues of game theory, then this formalism would be used to analyze multi-agent system. In case multi-agent system was created for optimization problems, such problems will be used to analyze this system [7][8]. What is presented in this paper is a demonstration of the use of two modeling techniques for the general description of a multi-agent system. On one hand, the theory of compartment models has been used to describe the interaction between the different body regions, called compartments. On the other hand, there is a graph theory, which introduces a general and universal tool for describing the interaction between beings that can represent any mathematical or physical concept. Combining these two techniques allows us to describe the interaction between agents in a multi-agent system (MAS) in two ways. Firstly, it could help to describe the dynamics of the entire multi-agent system, showing the connections between agents, their behavior, and the ability to investigate the whole system. Secondly, it makes possible to include in the same formalism the information associated with each agent. This should be understood as the ability to get information about what behavior is implemented in the body of the agent, which behavior is used to communicate with the environment, and which are only the internal behavior of the agent. One can also get information about which agent is a receiver of the messages and which agents are senders of those messages.

The proposed approach allows describing MAS in two complexity scales - the system as a whole and the agent and its impact on the system. We illustrate now the MAS description and communication on the glucose homeostasis. The selected analytical model (Stolwijk-Hardy model [9]) was converted to a multi-agent system in a lossless fashion. As a result, individual members of this model became the determinants of behavior of individual agents, and in addition, the analysis of such model was maintained by compartmental methods.

The structure of the paper is following. Section II gives a short introduction to multi-agent systems and draws attention on components of agents and their communication standards. In the next section, the matrix representation of multi-agent system is proposed. Section IV illustrates the authors' approach with two simple examples. The conclusion and references summarize the article.

II. MULTI-AGENT SYSTEMS

We present primary ideas concerning multi-agent systems.

A. Concept of multi-agent system and agent

Multi-agent systems are complex systems of agents communicating and cooperating with each other. This construction of the systems enables solving problems of a diffuse or complex calculation. In the studies applying multi-agent systems, the concept of an agent is presented as an autonomous object having the initiative of action based on the observation of the environment, in which it is located. It also has the ability to use the resources of the environment and the motivation to solve the problem it has to face. Such definition of the agent forces him to have inputs called sensors (through which it will be able to receive signals from the environment) and effectors, which can be used to influence the surrounding environment. The most important task of the agent is to decide which of the possible courses of action is best, at the time of acquired knowledge about the problem, in order to achieve the goal.

The issue „agent" is wide and diverse. Nowadays the term is so broadly used that is best described as comprising a heterogeneous body of research and development [1]. Different communities refer to it in various ways. Some scientists will characterize agents as initiatives and reactivity of objects; others emphasize independent learning and communication skills. What can also be invoked is the characteristic that unifies modeling agent the most – it is their decentralization. An extensive discussion of multi-agent systems can be found in positions [2][3]. In contrast to the dynamic system or actions based on models, the multi-agent system does not have a special place of centralization where the dynamics of the system is fixed. What is more, global behavior of the whole system is defined on the basis of the individual behavior of all agents. Each agent has its own inner behavior as a set of rules and behavior for interaction with the environment and other agents. Such description produce a dynamic interaction of agents based on rules.

In many situations, there is a doubt linked to the lack of understanding of the philosophy of using multi-agent systems and returning toward object-oriented programming. What is characteristic of multi-agent systems can be presented in the following subparagraphs:

- Agents possess internal awareness and defined goals to be achieved. The goals can, but do not have to be identical to the objectives of the other agents who are in the same environment. In such case, information obtained from another agent can be taken into account only if it is coincident with its own objective.
- The agent is a dynamic instance which adapts its activity to instantaneous changes in the environment and has certain fixed parameters and characteristics only for him that do not change regardless of the extent of the changes observed in the environment.
- Each agent possesses at least one strand which is responsible for its behaviorism.

The general difference between instance of an agent and the object lies in the fact that the object has variables that change, while the agent variables can be changed only when the agent accepts the request of the sender to change the value of a variable in an immediate way or after the act of negotiation.

B. Communication in multi-agent system

In an environment where there is more than one agent, there must be a mechanism for the exchange of information between the environment and the agent, and between agents. Communication mechanisms are essential for the agents grouped in structures that facilitate co-operation so that they could achieve their goals. Since the multi-agent environments [4][5] are dynamic environments, it is necessary to introduce a mechanism that would allow for informing the agents of the existence of other participants in the system. The literature [6] distinguishes the following approaches:

- Yellow pages, where agent can place information about services it provides
- White pages – the list of all agents in the environment
- Broker – intercessory agent.

In order to create a message and then send it to another agent, so it can receive it and understand it, it is necessary to define common, to all the participants of the act, language of communication and terminology. It should be noted that the language of communication, which is independent of the field, is separated from the language of messages content. Among the communication standards the most popular include:

- KQML (Knowledge Query and Manipulation Language)
- ACL (Agent Communication Language)

Among the examples of the language of message content, the following should be distinguished:

- KIF (eng. Knowledge Interchange Format)
- FIPA standards:
  - SL (Semantic Language)
  - CCL(Content Language)

Having a tool for communication, agents can communicate with each other to achieve a common or an opposing goal. In the first case, we have to deal with the concept of co-operation, in the second case with the concept of competition. As a rule, multi-agent systems are designed to solve complex problems in which agents have control (or can observe), only a certain part of the environment (Figure

1). In order for the multi-agent system to solve the problem, the agent has to have knowledge and control over the entire environment. To do so, agents are organized in the structure where then interact with each other. Interactions between structures and agents are supposed to bring them benefits. Each agent has its preferences for the state in which environment it should be (this is its goal). In order to describe this preference, the concept of utility v, which causes an alignment state of the environment Ω due to the preferences of the agent, is introduced.

$$v : \Omega \rightarrow \Re \quad (1)$$

The environment that corresponds to preferences of the agent will have greater utility value (in other words: the agent will "feel better").

III. MATRIX DESCRIPTION OF MULTI-AGENT SYSTEM

The key consideration in this paper is to propose a modeling paradigm glucose-insulin in the form of a multi-agent system starting with a mathematical description and finishing the implementation of the program. This solution shows how we can implement features of agents for both the macro and micro processes in homeostasis of glycemia. Moreover, at the same time, we can allow operating on two scales: organs and cells scale. This results in a new quality of information. To describe the multi-agent system, the authors used the approach presented in the chapter describing compartment modeling and using the rationality of graph theory (Figure 1). This approach simplifies the interpretation of what is happening in the multi-agent system, therefore, the behaviors of individual agents and their influence on other agents in the considered system can be easily identified.

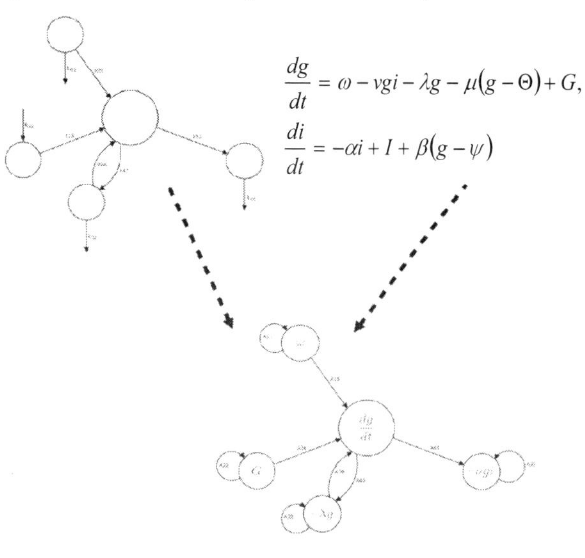

Figure 1. A new concept of describing a multi-agent model.

The analysis of multi-agent system is a difficult task to implement due to the existence of the asynchronous relationships between agents occurring in the system. Additionally, each agent which takes an active part in the multi-agent system has at least two behaviors: the one receiving incoming messages from other agents, and the other one used by it to send the information to the chosen agent. By verification of the model, one can understand two aspects. The first aspect concerns information about acceptable range of internal parameters of model, which guarantees the stability of the model for the incoming information/extortion from outside. The second is the range of input set, which ensures the correct stability and expected representation of the behavior of the modeled system.

We propose to describe multiagent system by using a comparison of network connections between the agents to the connections between vertexes forming a graph. Nomenclature of the vertex is extended by the occurrence of behaviors that identifies the agent's behavior. In this perspective of the problem, the graph which describes the interactions between agents with their associated behaviors is obtained. The assumptions are:

- Behaviors implemented in a given agent create a set of behaviors for the agent, which is a subset of behavior occurring in the multi-agent system:

$$\sum A \in \Phi \quad (2)$$

$$\Phi \subseteq \Omega \quad (3)$$

where:
A - represents some behavior of agent, Φ - represents a set of behaviors of a given agent, Ω - represents a set of behaviors of multi-agent system.

- Agents who pose the same behaviors are not identical with each other. It results from independent activities in terms of time and each agent using the same behavior performs them in various time slots.

- Graph A=(V,E); |V|=n, |E|=m represents multi-agent system basing on the assumption that:
  - n: number of graph vertexes (number of agents),
  - m : number of behaviors appearing in MAS.

- Adjacency matrix $K \in M(n \times n; N)$ is defined in such way that value in i-th line and in j-th column equals:
  - 0: if there is no communication between agents (connection),
  - 1: if there is communication between agents (connection).

  Whereby:
  - k_{ii} represents cyclical route of agent i-th,
  - k_{ij} represents route from agent i-th to agent j-th.
- The sum of the same behavior is the same behavior:

$$\sum_i A_{1i} = A_1 \quad (4)$$

- Behavioral Matrix $A \in M(n \times n; B)$ (where B designates set of behaviors within the scope of the multi-agent system) is defined in a such way that value in i-th line corresponds to behavior responsible for communication between agents i-th and agent j-th , whereby:
  - Behavior A_{ii} represents internal behavior (cyclical) of agent i-th,
  - Behavior A_{ij} represents information exchange from agent i-th to agent j-th.

Taking the above assumptions into consideration, it is possible to describe multi-agent system with the use of matrix equation:

$$A^T K + D = \Phi \tag{5}$$

where:
A^T is the transpose of a matrix of agents' behaviors; K is a matrix of connections between agents; D is a matrix of agents' internal behaviors; Φ is a matrix representing multi-agent system.

Analysis of the above equation will be presented on 3 examples of multi-agent system. Both examples will rely on a different number of behaviors occurring in the multi-agent system.

IV. EXAMPLES

In this paragraph, authors demonstrate examples of the use of matrix to describe the multi-agent system and to select unknown behavior.

A. The example of two-agent description based on the matrix representation

Let us consider the multi-agent system, where two agents A1 and A2 have predefined behaviors and A11 and A22 are internal behaviors and A12 and A21 are external behaviors (Figure 2).

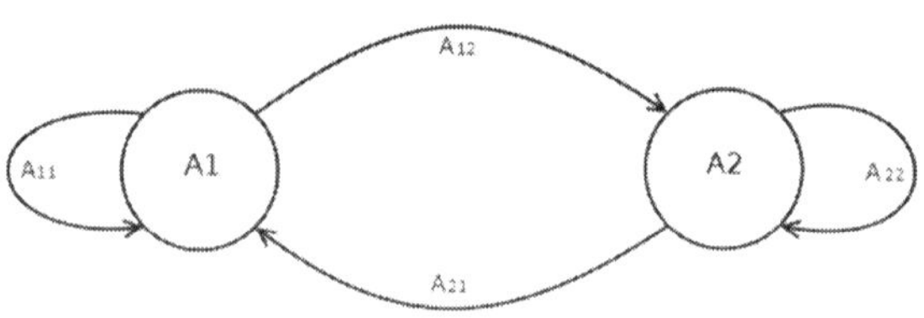

Figure 2. Two-agent system.

For the following example, adequate matrixes will be defined:

$$A = \begin{bmatrix} A_{21} - A_{12} & A_{12} \\ A_{21} & A_{12} - A_{21} \end{bmatrix} \tag{6}$$

$$A^T = \begin{bmatrix} A_{21} - A_{12} & A_{21} \\ A_{12} & A_{12} - A_{21} \end{bmatrix} \tag{7}$$

$$K = \begin{bmatrix} 0 & 1 \\ 1 & 0 \end{bmatrix} \tag{8}$$

$$D = \begin{bmatrix} A_{11} & 0 \\ 0 & A_{22} \end{bmatrix} \tag{9}$$

Substituting to equation (5) we obtain representation of multi-agent system in the form of:

$$[\Phi] = \begin{bmatrix} A_{11} + A_{21} & A_{21} - A_{12} \\ A_{12} - A_{21} & A_{22} + A_{12} \end{bmatrix} \tag{10}$$

Conducting a detailed analysis of the matrix Φ we receive information about:

- First minor (φ_1) of a matrix Φ represents internal and incoming behaviors to agent A_1:

$$\varphi_1 = A_{11} + A_{21} \tag{11}$$

- Second minor (φ_2) of a matrix Φ represents behaviors of data exchange between agents A_1 and A_2:

$$\varphi_2 = A_{21} - A_{12} \tag{12}$$

- Third minor (φ_3) of a matrix Φ represents of data exchange between agents A_1 and A_2:

$$\varphi_3 = A_{12} - A_{21} \tag{13}$$

- Fourth minor (φ_4) of a matrix Φ represents internal and incoming behaviors to agent A_2:

$$\varphi_4 = A_{22} + A_{12} \tag{14}$$

- Trace of a matrix represents behaviors occurring in multi-agent system:

$$Tr[\Phi] = A_{11} + A_{21} + A_{22} + A_{12} \tag{15}$$

The above-mentioned examples were designed to show the application of (5) to describe the multi-agent system and the equivalence with the use of a graph. Description using matrixes is helpful in such a way that, in a compact form, it contains a representation of the dynamics of multi-agent system. It is not relevant what type of behaviors are written using matrix A. That is why the authors consider this record as universal. The results matrix Φ contains much information from which one can restore the functioning of the multi-agent system, basing solely on the content of individual cells of the matrix. Individual cells φ_i make it possible to obtain information on what types of behavior are present in the agent - whether they are its own internal behaviors (e.g., A_{11}) or behaviors associated with taking or receiving information to/from another agent (e.g., A_{21}). Additionally, the sum of the behavior of a given line (e.g., $\varphi_1 + \varphi_2$) is interpreted as the behavior occurring in the agent (e.g., for A_1). The results matrix can also determine whether, in a multi-agent system, there is at least one bidirectional communication between agents. In order to verify whether in the multi-agent system the exchange of information occurs, it is necessary to check whether the following identity is met:

$$Tr[\Phi] = \sum_i \varphi_i \quad (16)$$

In order to verify the above relationship the examples discussed earlier can be used:

$$A_{11} + A_{21} + A_{22} + A_{12} = A_{11} + A_{21} + A_{22} + A_{12} \Leftrightarrow Tr[\Phi] = \sum_i \varphi_i \quad (17)$$

B. The example of matrix representation for identification of desired behavior

The experiment is quite specific. This uniqueness is based on the use of the matrix record, introduced in Section III, to determine unknown behavior in a multi-agent system. The experiment was based on a two-agent representation of the glucose homeostasis system. The first agent represents the entire mechanism of normoglycemia in the case of type 1 diabetic patient. The second agent represents insulin delivery in the form of external administration (Figure 3). The purpose of this experiment is to define the behavior responsible for sending "information" from Agent A1 to Agent A2 so that the dose of insulin delivered contributes to the metabolism of glucose.

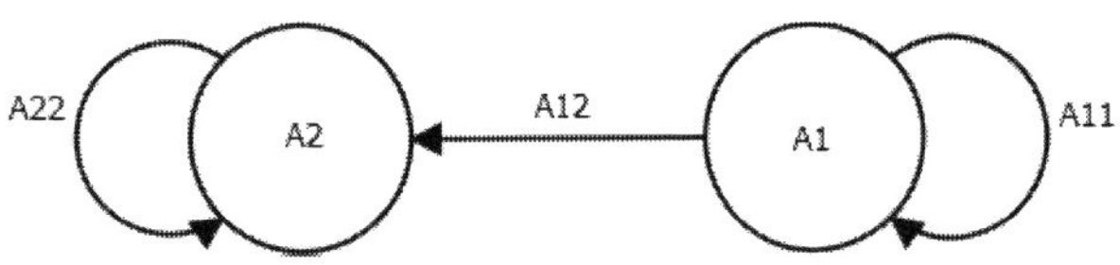

Figure 3. Diagram of multi-agent system for the experiment.

Based on the concepts introduced in the section above, we can define the appropriate arrays, and so the matrix A:

$$A = \begin{bmatrix} -A_{12} & A_{12} \\ 0 & A_{12} \end{bmatrix} \quad (18)$$

matrix K:

$$K = \begin{bmatrix} 0 & 1 \\ 0 & 0 \end{bmatrix} \quad (19)$$

matrix D:

$$D = \begin{bmatrix} A_{11} & 0 \\ 0 & A_{22} \end{bmatrix} \quad (20)$$

The matrix of a multi-agent system is defined by the corresponding relation between the previously mentioned matrices so that the system matrix is:

$$\Phi = \begin{bmatrix} A_{11} & -A_{12} \\ 0 & A_{22} + A_{12} \end{bmatrix} \quad (21)$$

The trace of the matrix:

$$Tr\phi = A_{22} + A_{11} + A_{12} \quad (22)$$

In this particular case, the meaning of the individual behavior is as follows:

- Behavior A_{11} it is responsible for the insulin production that will eventually be introduced into the system. This behavior may also represent a buffer that stores a certain amount of insulin.
- Behavior A_{22} it represents all the phenomena occurring in the glycemic homeostasis system, along with the ways of insulin utilization.
- Behavior A_{12} it is responsible for the exchange of information (from agent A1 to agent A2) - this behavior should be determined.

The purpose here is to define the behavior A12 in such a way as to ensure insulin levels of φ_{A2}=7 [uIU/ml] for Agent A2. Below is a procedure to achieve our goal:

1. Simulation for the conditions specified for a person with type 1 diabetes (without insulin infusion) (Figure 4).

2. Transform the pattern (22) into a form that allows us to calculate the desired behavior. In this case, we get:

$$A_{12} = \varphi_{A2} - A_{22} \quad (23)$$

3. Perform curve fitting procedure (Figure 5) to the points obtained. This procedure was performed in MATLAB environment using the "fctool" command. The fit was done using a linear function. The following form of function is given:

$$f(A_{12}) = -0{,}0914t + 6{,}14 \quad (24)$$

4. The last step was to implement the equation described in Equation (24) into the body of the insulin dispensing agent. The simulation was started and a comparative analysis of data from the insulin-free model and from the model in which the found behavior A_{12}.

Below are the following drawings corresponding to the points mentioned above.

As can be deduced from Figure 6, the concept of using a matrix description to identify unknown behaviors is the most appropriate approach. Using (22), it is possible to select unknown behavior in such a way that the preset value can be maintained throughout the system under consideration. By focusing on the selected part of φ matrix, there is an opportunity to declare such an unknown behavior that will result in a given value from the agent the minor describes. This is the second case presented in this experiment. As a result of matching A_{12}, it has become possible to maintain insulin levels of 7 [uIU/ml] by the agent A2. Of course, the quality of the curve fitting to the measurement points (Figures 4 and 5) directly affects the quality of the results generated by the multi-agent system.

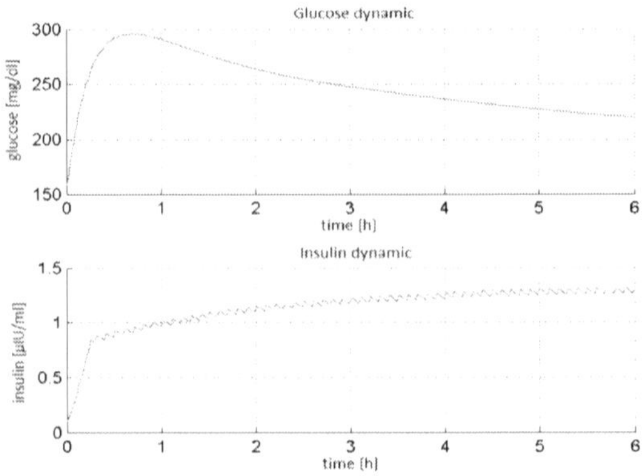

Figure 4. Simulation result for a person with type 1 diabetes - without insulin.

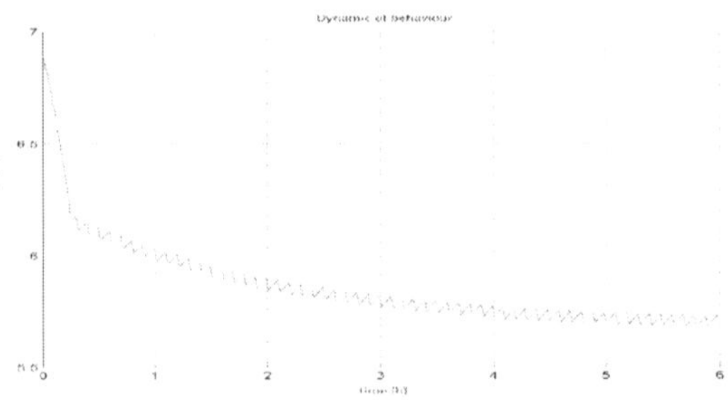

Figure 5. Chart for variability of behavior A_{12}.

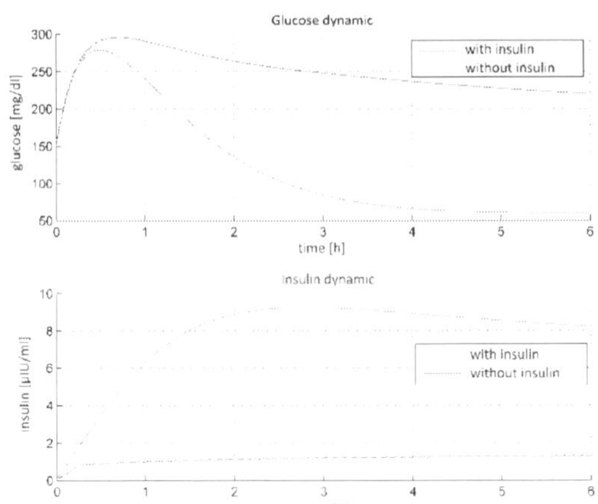

Figure 6. Simulation results for two cases: without insulin (blue curve), including the behavior of insulin dosing into the multiple agent system (red curve).

V. CONCLUSIONS

In this paper, we made the analysis of the multi-agent system with the use of graph theory and matrix calculus. This approach can help us analyze the operation of such system in two ways: quantitative and qualitative ones. The use of matrix record enables performance of analysis of internal multi-agent system involving assignment of behaviors to particular agents. External analysis of the multi-agent system with the use of introduced record allows for description of the relation between agents and for selection of such unknown behavior of agent which will meet the intended purpose or criterion implemented by the multi-agent system. In the second example, it is shown how using matrix equation allows finding the desired behavior of multi-agent system. For the general case in which the agents (and the multi-agent system) process several volumes, each of these factors must be represented by a separate graph of accurate dependency. Generally speaking, each value can represent different graph of connections between agents, and agents can have different numbers and behaviors intended to process these values. The matrix equation (5) proposed by authors, will be the subject of further work towards stability study of multi-agent system.

REFERENCES

1. H. S. Nwana, "Software agents: an overview," *The Knowledge Engineering Review*, 1996, 11(3), pp. 205–244. doi: 10.1017/S026988890000789X.
2. M. Wooldridge, "An introduction to multiagent systems," John Wiley& Sons, 2009.
3. P. Stone and M. Veloso, "Multiagent systems: A survey from a machine learning perspective," Autonomous Robots 8.3: pp. 345-383, 2000.
4. A. Helleboogh, G. Vizzari, A. Uhrmacher and F. Michel, "Modeling dynamic environments in multi-agent simulation," *Autonomous Agents and Multi-Agent Systems* 14.1 : 87-116, 2007.
5. T. Seth and U. Wilensky, "NetLogo: Design and implementation of a multi-agent modeling environment," *Proceedings of agent*, vol. 2004.
6. F. Bellifemine, A. Poggi and G. Rimassa, "Developing multi-agent systems with JADE," *International Workshop on Agent Theories, Architectures, and Languages*, Springer Berlin Heidelberg, 2000.
7. S. Parson and M. Wooldridge, "Game Theory and Decision Theory in Multi-Agent Systems," Kluwer Academic Publisher, 2000.
8. P. J. Wangerman and F. R. Stengel, "Optimization and Coordination of Multiagent Systems Using Principled Negotiation," Journal of guidance, control, and dynamics, vol. 22, No. 1, 1999.
9. S. Soylu, K. Danişman, I.E. Saçu and M. Alçi, "Closed-loop control of blood glucose level in type-1 diabetics: A simulation study." Electrical and Electronics Engineering (ELECO), 2013 8th International Conference on. IEEE, 2013.

Dialog Management for Credit Card Selling via Finite State Machine Using Sentiment Classification in Turkish Language

Gizem Soğancıoğlu, Tolga Çekiç, Bilge Köroğlu, Mert Basmacı and Onur Ağın

R&D and Special Projects Department
Yapı Kredi Technology, Istanbul, Turkey
Email: {gizem.soganciogIu, tolga.cekic, bilge.koroglu, mert.basmaci}@yapikredi.com.tr

***Abstract*—In this paper, we propose a goal-oriented chat bot, which aims to sell a suitable credit card to customers according to their needs. Our proposed chat bot detects customer's needs, uses this information to recommend a credit card, answers specific queries from customers and gathers the required information to start a credit card application process. This goal-oriented dialog management system is designed for Turkish Language and it makes use of a Finite State Machine (FSM) structure to achieve its goals. This design allows the chat bot to facilitate the flow of conversation and prevents giving unrelated answers to customers. The chat bot has unique tasks to perform in each state of FSM. Transitions between states are processed with the events, which are determined by outputs of the sentiment analysis model. Due to Turkish being an agglutinative language we perform morphological analysis of words to perform this task. Besides driving the conversation flow to achieving its goal, the chat bot can detect when customers ask questions and proceeds to the related state where the chat bot retrieves a proper answer. Since sentiment classification model forms the basis for keeping the chat bot in proper states, we experimented with different classification algorithms with different features and compared their successes. K-Nearest Neighbor algorithm using bag-of-words and lexicon features yielded the best results with the 0.822 f-score. Moreover, human evaluations for chat bot showed that using FSM and managing the conversation with the sentiment classification model for Turkish language is a promising solution.**

Keywords–Chat bot; Dialog Management; Sentiment Classification; Finite State Machine; Conversational Bot

I. INTRODUCTION

Intelligent conversation agents, or chat bots, are being considered increasingly for helping people with solving real life problems. In this paper, we present such a system for credit card selling tasks. Our proposed chat bot uses a Finite State Machine(FSM) based dialog flow in conjunction with continuous sentiment analysis of customer utterances to perform its predefined duties such as informing user or detecting what type of product would be more suitable for them, and ultimately successfully completing credit card selling process. We use a finite state machine for our chat bot to always keep track of conversation and also to prevent conversation from going too far away from the subject and the goal that our chat bot is trying to achieve. Additionally, keeping state of the conversation with an FSM provides consistency in responses of our chat bot, which is desired as it is aimed to help customers buy a credit card.

Chat bots have been developed for different purposes. Weizenbaum's ELIZA [1], one of the first dialog systems, and A.L.I.C.E. [2] are examples of general conversational bots. As natural language processing becomes more sophisticated some chat bots have been tailored for specific purposes to help people as virtual assistants. For example, Apple's Siri[3] can assist users in multiple ways or Alaska Airline's chat bot Jenn [4] can help customers in a more domain specific way to find suitable planes to their desired destinations. Our chat bot is similar to the latter example as it can help customers in informing them in credit card domain while it also has the additional goal of selling the product.

Designing our chat bot for Turkish language provides additional challenges and opportunities in natural language processing compared to Indo-European languages such as English. Turkish is an agglutinative language and suffixes to the words are very important and usually replace words. Therefore, many different words seem to appear in a sentence while in fact a few words with different suffixes appear in a text and in some instances some important information crucial to the meaning of the sentence can only be found in suffixes such as negativity of a sentence.For example the word "kitap" (book) becomes "kitabım" (my book) after the suffix "-ım" is appended. When the suffix "-a" is appended to this word it becomes "kitabıma" (to my book) [5]. Also, some consonants change in Turkish language when new suffixes are appended as "kitap" becomes "kitabım", letter "p" is changed into "b". Because of these reasons morphological analysis of words is crucial in Turkish language processing.

This paper is organized in the following way: in Section 2 we describe and give examples of some of the related previous research in this area. In Section 3 we describe our methodology in detail. In Section 4 we explain how we evaluated the success of our system and present experimental results. Lastly, we discuss the possible applications and future research of our work and conclude the paper in Section 5.

II. RELATED WORK

A. Related Work in Dialogue Management

Researchers were interested by chat bots because they can enable trying new natural language processing, machine learning and artificial intelligence methods while providing an interesting platform for people from all walks of life can interact. One of the first examples of using natural language processing techniques to create a chat bot that emulates human conversation is ELIZA [1]. Also a Turkish chat bot inspired by ELIZA was developed by Aytekin et al. [6]

There have also been research on chat bots to emulate daily speech, to give users the feeling that they are talking to a thinking person rather than a machine. A.L.I.C.E. [2] and Mitsuku [7] are such examples of chat bots that try to emulate human conversations.

Some researches have oriented toward making chat bots for more specific purposes rather than just general conversation. For example, IBM's Watson computer is designed to answer questions about world knowledge by processing questions asked in natural language [8]. Apple's Siri is a conversation agent that assists users in various ways, in addition to providing natural language answers to user queries, it can also perform tasks like phone calls or web searches. There are also chat bots that emulate customer service representatives. These chat bots are designed with the purpose of helping customers by answering their questions or solving their problems with the related products. Alaska Airline website's "Ask Jenn" or IKEA's Anna[9] are examples of chat bots acting as customer service representatives. Other chat bots have been developed to help students in educational environments such as EMERGO [10] and CHARLIE [11].

Chakrabarti proposes using finite state machines in chat bots that are designed as support agents [12]. Chakrabarti's FSM tries to keep state by analyzing users' utterances to detect how much user thinks bot is close to solving the problem and uses an external knowledge base to include in its answers. Since our chat bot has a more specific goal, instead of keeping state of where customer is, we track states of how much our chat bot is close to selling the product and use customer sentiments to go to further states.

B. Related Work in Sentiment Analysis

Our chat bot relies heavily on the sentiment analysis of customer utterances. Sentiment analysis is basically detecting or understanding the opinion or the negative or positive sentiment in a sentence or a document. The term sentiment analysis has been coined by Nasukawa et al. [13] Sentiment analysis has especially gained popularity for analyzing social media blogs and mini-blogs, product opinion reviews, wikis [14]. Sentiment analysis have been performed on different lengths of text. Since we expect chat customers to write short messages like a sentence, we focused our research on sentiment analysis on sentences.

Maynard and Funk suggests three types of methods for sentiment analysis: machine learning based, lexicon based and hybrid methods [15]. While machine learning approaches use training for finding common patterns for different sentiments, lexicon based approaches uses language rules for finding the sentiments. Syed et al. uses a lexicon based approach for sentiment analysis in morphologically rich Urdu language [16]. Hybrid methods use aspects from both approaches. As we use both morphological analysis of words and machine learning our sentiment analysis approach is hybrid. Dehkharghani's research provides methods for sentiment analysis in Turkish Language [17].

III. Method

The purpose of our chat bot is to both perform the task of selling a product and answer any questions a customer may have. Therefore, our chat bot keeps track how close it is to complete its task with an FSM and uses sentiment classification methods to change between states. Also, it assists customers in the way of a more traditional chat bot by detecting user questions and returning appropriate replies, while continuing to driving the conversation toward successfully selling a product. For sentiment classification, question detection and answering we use natural language processing techniques adapted to work in Turkish language.

A. Preprocessing

We perform some preprocessing operations on customer utterances before using them for question detection or sentiment analysis. We use preprocessing tasks that is common to natural language processing such as removing punctuations and tokenization. The punctuation marks have been removed are listed below:

- Dot, Comma, Colon, Exclamation Mark, Semicolon, Opening and Closing Parenthesis, Square Brackets, Question Mark, Underscore Character, Dash, Slash Mark, Asterisk.

We also perform a spell checking with the help of Zemberek library[18] so as not to miss the meaning of some mistyped words. Additionally, our chat bot keeps sentences both in their original form and by replacing the Turkish characters with their counterpart English letters. This is done to prevent conflicts that may happen due to usage of non-Turkish keyboards.

B. Dialog Management through FSM

We use an FSM in our credit card selling chat bot to keep track of the state of the conversation, varying needs of the customer and to give information to the customer when needed. Figure 1 shows states and transitions of our FSM design. Since this is a goal-oriented chat bot, the main flow of the FSM includes states for fulfilling the goals of credit card selling tasks. Transitions back and forth between the states are included to address a customer's changing needs or desires. Our chat bot has different sets of available answers for each state and drives the conversation toward other states by asking questions and detecting customer's sentiments for these questions. Our goal oriented system has a main flow of states that controls how close chat bot is achieving its goal and what it needs to do next. On the other hand, "Swearing"' and "Informative State" states are out of the main flow and these states have their special rules for transition.

Our chat bot initiates the conversation by greeting the customer and asking them if they have a predetermined type of card they want to buy. The credit card selling system has five card types it can sell and in 'Start' state whether customer wants a specific card among those or not is detected. This state handles various customer replies by sentiment analysis such as negative replies or discarding some card types, etc. If the customer suggests they have a preferred card type but doesn't indicate which one, "Card Determination" state handles this situation by asking user questions to receive the information of which product they want to buy.

The state "Detect User Needs" is, as the name suggests, where the chat bot asks questions to understand which credit card type might be the most suitable for an indecisive customer. As there are different credit card types tailored for different needs and various customer profiles, the credit card selling bot tries to determine what card is the most suitable for the current customer. While the conversation is on this state, questions are asked to gather information from customer to make this

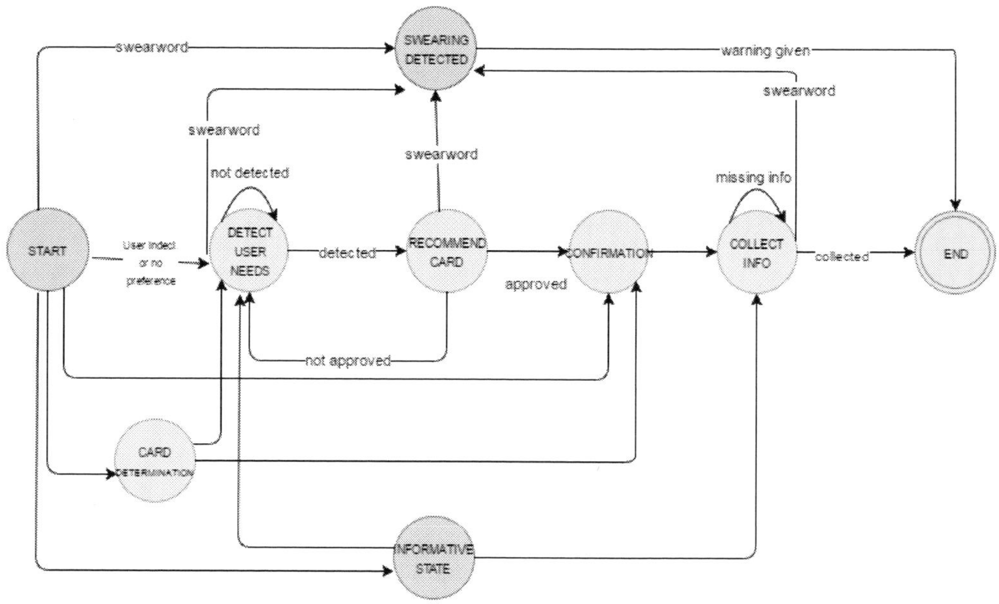

Figure 1. Finite State Machine Diagram of Dialog Flow

decision. Conversation remains on this state until a card is determined to be suitable for the customer.

In the case of a suitable card type for the customer is determined by the chat bot, conversation moves to "Recommendation" state. In this state, detected card is offered to the customer, awaiting for their approval. If the customer does not want to buy that card type, conversation goes back to "Detect User Needs" state, otherwise conversation moves to the "Confirmation" where the chat bot asks the customer for the final confirmation before starting the formal credit card application. Conversation can move to this state from 'Start' as well, if the customer asks to buy a specific card.

Conversation moves to "Collect Information" state once a customer confirms to buy a specific credit card type. During this state of the conversation, chat asks customer questions to learn information required for completing a credit card application. Questions are asked arbitrarily and and customer replies are checked to determine if they are valid. Collecting all the required information, chat bot fulfills its goals by completing a successful credit card application for a customer and a credit card suitable for that customer's needs.

The states "Swearing" and "Informative State" are outside of the main flow and can be reached from all of the other states once customer utters a sentence prompting to either of these states. "Swearing" is basically a control for appropriate speech. If a customer uses a word or a phrase that is deemed taboo in Turkish Language, conversation moves to "Swearing" state and after chat bot issues a warning to the customer the conversation is terminated. Conversation moves to "Informative State" when the customer asks a question anytime during the conversation. Question detection is done morphologically by detecting question words and question suffixes that is usually used in question sentences in Turkish language. In conversation state, chat bot finds an appropriate answer for the question asked by the customer. In order to find an answer to questions, a retrieval-based question answering system is used.

C. Sentiment Classification

As expressed in previous section, sentiment classification algorithm plays an important role for the overall success of the chat bot. Because sentiment of a customer sentence determined by the sentiment classification model is used as a transition event for FSM to change states. It determines the transitions between "Start State - Detect User Needs", "Detect User Needs-Recommendation" and "Recommendation-Confirmation" states. For example, if the system classifies the sentiment of a customer sentence as positive in "Recommendation" state, where the chat bot recommends a proper card type for a customer, it means that customer confirms to buy a recommended card type. In this situation, FSM processes the corresponding event, and passes to "Confirmation" state. This event type moves FSM closer to the END state. Otherwise, when the sentiment of customer utterance is negative, FSM passes to "Detect User Needs" state to help the customer to find the most proper card type for the customer.

Our baseline algorithm and proposed systems are detailed below.

1) Baseline Method: We have implemented two baseline models namely Lexicon-based baseline and Majority-based baseline to measure the real efficiency and success of our sentiment classification system.

Majority-based baseline model classifies any utterance as the most seen label in the training data set. Although this is very common and simple approach, it is a strong baseline.

Lexicon-based baseline system utilizes the lexicons consisting of negative terms and morphological structure of Turkish language. In Turkish, suffix, which makes sentence negative, is added to the end of verb in a sentence. Therefore, first, baseline algorithm checks if a verb in sentence coming from customer contains negative suffix. If it has, system classifies this customer utterance as negative. If it does not, then, algorithm checks if system contains any negative particles defined in lexicon. If it has, algorithm assigns a negative sentiment to sentence, otherwise, assumes it as positive sentence. In summary, baseline system does not use any semantic information, exploits lexical attributes of Turkish Language.

2) Supervised Methods: Since supervised algorithms perform quite successful for sentiment classification problem, we have evaluated different learning algorithms and chose the best performed one. For this task, we needed a labeled data set, which is annotated as positive or negative sentiment. We used a dataset consisting of real web chat conversations between a customer and a customer service representative. This dataset contains more than a million utterances. Although these conversations are based on the solutions of problems, customers face and there were no credit card selling goal they still contain banking domain terminology. We have selected 500 customer utterances among those and 3 different annotators labeled these utterances according to their sentiment. The class (positive/negative) having majority vote for a sentence has been considered as ground truth.

Figure 2 shows the prediction phase (positive/negative) of our sentiment classification module. As shown in Figure 2, firstly, customer message is preprocessed by applying the steps mentioned in Section III-A. Then, this preprocessed message is given to feature extractor module. Features extracted and used in our experiments are listed below:

- Length: is the count of words in a sentence.
- Bag-of-words (BOWs): Text is represented as set of its words in simple vector space.
- countOfPositiveParticles (CPP): is the count of positive terms in a sentence. These positive terms are defined in the lexicon crafted by us.
- countOfNegativeParticles (CNP): is the count of the negative terms in a sentence defined in lexicon crafted by us.
- haveRepeatedLetters (HRL): boolean feature. It considers if a word has repeated letters (nooo!) or not (no!).

Finally, these extracted features are given to trained learning model, which produces a sentiment class of customer message. As learning algorithms, we have used and performed experiments with K-Nearest Neighbor (KNN), Naive Bayes, Random Forest, MultiLayer Perceptron (MLP) and J48 algorithms. For all of these algorithms we used WEKA[19] implementations.

The first algorithm we use for sentiment classification is KNN. Using KNN, we calculate the distances between the utterance which we want to determine its sentiment with labeled utterances from our training set and by looking at sentiments k nearest utterance and choose the classification by a majority vote of these k instances [20]. Euclidean distance is used when calculating distances.

Naive Bayes method based on Bayes Theorem classifies by finding probabilities independently for each feature disregarding any relation that may be present between features [21]. That is why this method is called "naive".

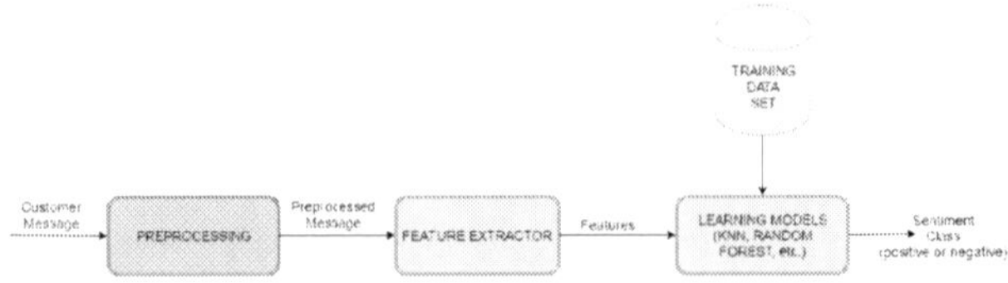

Figure 2. Stages of Sentiment Classification

Random Forest is an ensemble classifier, namely it is a method that uses several classifiers to make a final classification. It uses different decision tress and a final model is generated from the combination of each of these tree classifiers [22].

MLP is a feedforward neural network model. Neural networks are designed after neurons in a human brain, the inputs are processed in by a number of layers with every layer send its feedback to the forward layers [23].

D. Question Answering

As explained above, chat bot drives the conversation by asking questions and analyzing answers, however, when the customer asks a question conversation moves to "Informative State" and the bot answers a question in this state. Question detection is performed by morphological analysis of sentences. In Turkish language, questions are asked by either using question words, which corresponds to wh-questions in English or by adding a question suffix to the appropriate word in question. We use Zemberek for morphological analysis. Zemberek is an NLP tool for Turkish language. We have observed that questions can be detected successfully with morphological analysis.

After detecting a question and moving the conversation to "Informative State" the chat bot tries to find an appropriate answer by retrieving an answer from the knowledge base. The knowledge base contains question-answer pairs for common questions that can be asked about credit cards, and some more specific questions that can be asked about each card type. Chat bot matches the question asked with one of the questions in the knowledge base and returns its answer. Although, knowledge base covers general information about credit cards it is not a very large set and it is not much suitable for models that may require extensive training.

For matching question sentences we preferred q-grams distance calculation. q-grams are substrings of a string with length q. Calculating q-grams distance is based on common q-grams between two sentences. We also experimented with word based similarity calculations such as cosine distance or language modeling but q-grams based similarity performed better for sentence matching task. Since Turkish is an agglutinative language, the amount of different words that appear in a text can be quite high because every suffix essentially produces a new word. Word based similarity measure treats the same words with different suffixes as completely different words. When stemming is used though, information about sentence structure that may be contained in those suffixes cannot be used at all. Hence, a similarity measure that is more focused on characters such as q-grams distance can include both words and their suffixes in distance calculation.

Once the question is answered conversation resumes from the previous state before question was asked. After that, customers can ask more questions if they wish and conversation moves to "Informative State" to answer each question separately.

IV. EVALUATION AND EXPERIMENTAL RESULTS

In this section, we show the experimental results for the overall chat bot and sentiment classification model, which is the part of this study for understanding the customer intent for taking corresponding action. First, we define the evaluation metrics that are used for measure the performance of two systems. Then, we report the corresponding results for each task.

A. Chat bot Evaluations

1) Grice's Maxims: To be able to measure the real efficiency of our system, we needed a consistent evaluation metric. There is not common metric for chat bot evaluation. So, we followed the same way with the study [12], which proposes similar approach with us. They utilize from the Grice's maxims for the evaluation of their proposed chat bot. Grice's maxims was long considered the gold standard for evaluation of human conversations. Maxims for human conversations are defined as follows:

- Quality: speaker tells the truth or provable by adequate evidence.
- Quantity: speaker is as informative as required.
- Relation: response is relevant to topic of discussion.
- Manner: speaker's avoids ambiguity or obscurity, is direct and straightforward.

It was considered that these maxims could be applicable to customer service conversations, between a human customer and a chatter bot agent. And, this maxims are defined as follows[12]:

1) *Quality Maxim:* Agent's responses are factually true.
2) *Quantity Maxim:* Agent provides too little information or too much.
3) *Relation Maxim:* Agent's responses are relevant to the topic of the conversation with respect to the situational context and domain.
4) *Manner Maxim:* Agents responses avoid ambiguity and obscurity.

These four maxims are considered as evaluation metric for this study. To clarify the definitions of this maxims we prepared an example set for the participants of this survey. Annotators gave a score between 1 and 5 for each of the maxim metric where 1 refers the 'strongly disagree', 2 'disagree', 3 'neutral', 4 'agree' and 5 'strongly agree'. Chat bot was evaluated by 20 human participants. Then, definition and example set were given the participants and they are asked for filling the survey by considering the experience they had during the conversation with chat bot.

The average of evaluation results for each maxim has been reported in the Table I. By considering the results, we can say that our chat bot performs quite good to understand the topic of question and answer it relevantly. On the other hand, it seems that even in the situations that it detects the topic of question and answer it in same topic, it does not give the needed answer and the situation causes ambiguity. We can conclude that it is successful to capture the sentiment of customer and process the right transitions. But, when a user ask question, which is processed by informative state, chat bot performs insufficiently.

TABLE I. AVERAGE SCORES FOR MAXIMS

Maxim	*Average Score*
Quality Maxim	3.5
Quantity Maxim	4
Relation Maxim	4
Manner Maxim	3.4

B. Sentiment Classification Results

As it is mentioned in the Section III-C, we manually crafted data set consisting of 500 utterances and this data set was annotated by 3 human annotators. Ground truth of an utterance in data set was considered as the most selected label for that utterance. Evaluations for sentiment classification algorithms have been performed on this data set. 10-fold cross validation method was applied for measuring each algorithm. Since f-score measure is commonly used for evaluation of classification tasks, we reported the results in terms of f-score measure in Table II.

TABLE II. SENTIMENT CLASSIFICATION RESULTS

Learning Model	*Feature*	*F-score*
Lexicon-based Baseline	-	0.650
Majority-based Baseline	-	0.526
KNN (k=1)	BOWs	0.714
	+CNP*,CPP*	**0.822**
	+HRL*	0.806
	+length	0.784
Naive Bayes	BOWs	0.806
	+CNP*,CPP*	0.815
	+HRL*	0.807
	+length	0.773
Random Forest	BOWs	0.790
	+CNP*,CPP*	0.797
	+HRL*	0.790
	+length	0.792
MLP	BOWs	0.724
	+CNP*,CPP*	0.725
	+HRL*	0.719
	+length	0.720

CNP : doesContainNegativeParticle
CPP : doesContainPositiveParticle
HRL : haveRepeatedLetters

To observe the effect of each feature for classification performance, we reported the results as we added a new one. Among baseline systems, Lexicon-based classier, which considers the negative suffix of verb and utilizes the lexicon consisting of negative meaning terms, performed best with the 0.650 in terms of f-score. It can be said that Lexicon-based classifier is an unsupervised and strong baseline. On the other hand, all supervised models performed better than baseline. KNN, which is simple supervised method, performed best among all supervised algorithms. Results show that count of positive and negative terms are distinctive features. On the other hand, length and haveRepeatedLetters features do not contribute the success of any learning model. Therefore, we just used BOWs and CNN, CPP features with the KNN learning algorithm for the sentiment classification part of our chat bot.

V. Discussion and Conclusion

We proposed a chat bot in Turkish Language, which aims to sell customers a proper credit card according to their needs. If the customer already decided the credit card type, it proceeds to the application process. Otherwise, chat bot tries to learn about customers, detect their needs and recommend the most suitable card specifically for that customer. In this study, this process has been provided via FSM. Transitions between predefined states have been performed according to output class of sentiment classification model. FSM has been designed specifically for credit card application. However, it can be easily adapted to any product selling system since it detects customers' needs, suggests a suitable product and and completes the application process of selling that product. All of these steps can be applied to selling most products. Thus, we recommend a general sentiment model based FSM algorithm for product selling. We utilized this method for specifically credit card selling, and experimental results were shown for it.

Since sentiment classification plays an important role in our transitions, we compared different classification algorithms and reported the results in the Section IV. Our experiments show that KNN model using BOWs, doesContainNegativeParticle and doesContainPositiveParticle features obtained the best performance. Moreover, human evaluation results of chat bot according Grice's maxims (Table I) show that the strongest aspect of the chat bot is transition between states accurately. Since the transitions are determined by sentiment classification system, it can be said that users found it working very well. On the other hand, due to low information retrieval performance the question answering in the informative state is the relatively weakest part of the chat bot that needs improving. Since our informative state only considers the lexical similarity between questions, this low performance was expected.

For future work, we aim to improve the performance of informative state by utilizing semantic properties of texts as well. We plan to exploit ontologies and distributional vector representations of texts to capture the semantic relations rather than considering only lexical similarity. Furthermore, a natural language answer generation system that dynamically generates new sentences instead of a choosing from a static list of proper replies would be fine addition. As long as such a system would preserve consistency in grammar and the information presented, it would increase the enthusiasm of customers to try the chat bot. When answers are generated dynamically, customer would feel it more human-like while the FSM still drives the conversation toward fulfilling its goal.

Acknowledgment

The authors would like to thank Şimal Şen, Sinan Kahraman, Deniz Sezen Gezmiş for annotations and feedbacks about chat bot and Nihan Karslıoğlu for her support to improve the system.

References

[1] J. Weizenbaum, "Eliza—a computer program for the study of natural language communication between man and machine," Communications of the ACM, vol. 9, no. 1, 1966, pp. 36–45.

[2] R. S. Wallace, "The anatomy of alice," in Parsing the Turing Test. Springer, 2009, pp. 181–210.

[3] Apple Siri siri. http://www.apple.com/ios/siri/. Accessed: 2017-06-06.

[4] Alaska Air Ask Jenn. https://www.alaskaair.com/. Accessed: 2017-06-06.

[5] E. Emekligil, S. Arslan, and O. Agin, A Bank Information Extraction System Based on Named Entity Recognition with CRFs from Noisy Customer Order Texts in Turkish. Cham: Springer International Publishing, 2016, pp. 93–102.

[6] Ç. Aytekin, A. Say, and E. Akçok, "Eliza speaks turkish: a conversation program for an agglutinative language," in Third Turkish Symp. Artificial Intelligence and Neural Networks, Ankara, 1994, p. 435.

[7] R. Higashinaka et al., "Towards an open-domain conversational system fully based on natural language processing," in COLING, 2014, pp. 928–939.

[8] D. A. Ferrucci, "Introduction to "this is watson"," IBM Journal of Research and Development, vol. 56, no. 3.4, 2012, pp. 1–1.

[9] Ikea Anna. http://www.ikea.com/ms/en_JP/customer_service/splash.html. Accessed: 2017-06-06.

[10] P. Van Rosmalen, J. Eikelboom, E. Bloemers, K. Van Winzum, and P. Spronck, "Towards a game-chatbot: Extending the interaction in serious games," in European Conference on Games Based Learning. Academic Conferences International Limited, 2012, p. 525.

[11] F. A. Mikic, J. C. Burguillo, M. Llamas, D. A. Rodríguez, and E. Rodríguez, "Charlie: An aiml-based chatterbot which works as an interface among ines and humans," in EAEEIE Annual Conference, 2009. IEEE, 2009, pp. 1–6.

[12] C. Chakrabarti, "Artificial conversations for chatter bots using knowledge representation, learning, and pragmatics," Ph.D. dissertation, University of New Mexico. Albuquerque, NM., 2014.

[13] T. Nasukawa and J. Yi, "Sentiment analysis: Capturing favorability using natural language processing," in Proceedings of the 2nd international conference on Knowledge capture. ACM, 2003, pp. 70–77.

[14] D. Alessia, F. Ferri, P. Grifoni, and T. Guzzo, "Approaches, tools and applications for sentiment analysis implementation," International Journal of Computer Applications, vol. 125, no. 3, September 2015, pp. 26–33.

[15] D. Maynard and A. Funk, "Automatic detection of political opinions in tweets," in Extended Semantic Web Conference. Springer, 2011, pp. 88–99.

[16] A. Z. Syed, M. Aslam, and A. M. Martinez-Enriquez, "Associating targets with sentiunits: a step forward in sentiment analysis of urdu text," Artificial Intelligence Review, vol. 41, no. 4, 2014, pp. 535–561.

[17] R. Dehkharghani, B. Yanikoglu, Y. Saygin, and K. Oflazer, "Sentiment analysis in turkish: Towards a complete framework."

[18] Zemberek-NLP. https://github.com/ahmetaa/zemberek-nlp. Accessed: 2017-06-06.

[19] Weka. http://www.cs.waikato.ac.nz/ml/weka/. Accessed: 2017-06-06.

[20] T. Cover and P. Hart, "Nearest neighbor pattern classification," IEEE Trans. Inf. Theor., vol. 13, no. 1, Sep. 2006, pp. 21–27.

[21] P. Langley, W. Iba, and, and K. Thompson, "An analysis of bayesian classifiers," in Proceedings of the Tenth National Conference on Artificial Intelligence, ser. AAAI'92. AAAI Press, 1992, pp. 223–228.

[22] L. Breiman, "Random forests," Mach. Learn., vol. 45, no. 1, Oct. 2001, pp. 5–32.

[23] S. Haykin, Neural Networks: A Comprehensive Foundation, 2nd ed. Upper Saddle River, NJ, USA: Prentice Hall PTR, 1998.

Developing Space Efficient Techniques for Building POMDP Based Intelligent Tutoring Systems

Fangju Wang

School of Computer Science
University of Guelph
Guelph, Ontario, Canada N1G 2W1
Email: fjwang@uoguelph.ca

***Abstract*—In building an intelligent tutoring system (ITS), the partially observable Markov decision process (POMDP) model provides useful tools to deal with uncertainties, which are major challenges in achieving adaptive teaching. However, the POMDP model is very expensive. When a method of policy trees is used in decision making, the number of trees and sizes of individual trees are typically exponential. The great space complexity obstructs application of the POMDP model to ITSs. In our research, we developed space efficient techniques to address the space complexity problem. The techniques minimize the number and sizes of trees, and reduce space consumption of the tree database. Encouraging results have been achieved: the techniques enabled us to build a system with a manageable size, to teach a practical subject.**

Keywords–Intelligent system; intelligent tutoring system; adaptive teaching; partially observable Markov decision process; space efficiency.

I. INTRODUCTION

In recent years, intelligent tutoring systems (ITSs) have been playing increasingly important roles in computer supported education, which is a remarkable development in education and training. ITSs have been built as teaching/learning aids, and has been beneficial to students and teachers in fields including mathematics [13], physics [8], computer science [13], Web based education [2], and military training [13].

A key feature of ITSs is adaptive teaching. In each tutoring step, an ITS should be able to take the optimal teaching action based on information about its student's current knowledge states. An ITS achieves adaptive teaching by tracing student knowledge states, and taking teaching actions based on the states. The core modules in an ITS include a domain model, a student model, and a tutoring model. The *domain model* stores the domain knowledge. The *student model* contains information about student states. The *tutoring model* represents the system's tutoring strategies.

Uncertainties in observing and tracing student states have been major difficulties in building adaptive teaching systems. Quite often, it is difficult to know exactly what the student's states are, and what the most beneficial tutoring actions should be [13]. The partially observable Markov decision process (POMDP) model provides useful tools for dealing with uncertainties. Recently, researchers have been applying POMDP techniques in building ITSs [6] [7].

A POMDP is an extension of a Markov decision process (MDP) for modeling processes in which decisions have to be made when uncertainties exist. In a POMDP, there is a state space, which is not completely observable. The decision agent infers its information about states based its actions and observations, and represents the information as a *belief*. In making a decision, it updates its belief, solves the POMDP for an optimal *policy*, and uses the policy to choose an action.

Great computational costs are primary obstacles to building a POMDP-based ITS. In a POMDP, both space and time complexities are typically exponential. To build a POMDP-based ITS for real world applications, we must address the problems of computational complexities. In earlier stages of our research, we developed techniques to reduce state spaces [9], and to minimize the numbers of policy trees that comprised solution spaces [10]. (The approach of policy trees is for POMDP solving. It will be discussed in details later.)

Although we have achieved progress, problems with space complexity are far from being solved. In an ITS for a practical subject, a policy tree database might become unmanageable in size and a single policy tree might exhaust the available memory space. In this paper, we report our new techniques for further reducing the size of a POMDP solution space in an ITS. The techniques were aimed at minimizing the sizes of individual trees.

In Section II, we review the work related to our research. In Sections III, IV and V, we briefly introduce the technical background of the POMDP model, and an ITS on POMDP, and discuss the space efficiency issues in a POMDP based ITSs. In Section VI, we describe our space efficient techniques, and in Section VII, present and analyze some experimental results.

II. RELATED WORK

The work of applying POMDP to computer supported education started in as early as 1990s [1]. In the early years, POMDP was used to model mental states of individuals, and to find the best ways to teach concepts. More recent work included [3] [4] [6] [7] [11] [12]. The work was commonly characterized by using POMDP to optimize and customize teaching, but varied in the definitions of states, actions, and observations, and in the strategies of POMDP-solving. In the following, we review some representative work in more details.

The technique of faster teaching by POMDP planning is the work reported in [6]. The technique was for computing approximate POMDP policies, with the goal to select actions to minimize the expected time for the learner to understand concepts. The researchers framed the process of choosing optimal actions by using a decision-theoretic approach, and formulated teaching as a POMDP planning problem. In the POMDP, the states represented the learners' knowledge, the transitions modeled how teaching actions stochastically changed the learners' knowledge, and the observations indicated the probability that a learner would give a particular response to a tutorial action.

The researchers developed a method of forward trees for solving the POMDP. Forward trees are variations of policy trees. For the current belief, a forward trees was constructed to estimate the value of each teaching action, and the best action was chosen. The learner's response, plus the action chosen, was used to update the belief. And then a new forward tree was constructed for selecting a new action. The costs for storing and evaluating a forward tree is exponential in the task horizon and the number of possible actions. To reduce the costs, the researchers restricted the trees by sampling only a few actions, and by limiting the horizon to control the sizes of trees.

In [4], a technique of gap elimination was developed to make POMDP solvers feasible for real-world problems. The researchers created a data structure to describe the current mental status of each student. The status was made up of knowledge states and cognitive states. The knowledge states were defined in terms of gaps, which are misconceptions regarding the concepts in the instructional subject. Observations are indicators that particular gaps are present or absent. The intelligent tutor takes actions to discover and remove all gaps.

To deal with time and space efficiency problems, the researchers developed two scalable representations of states and observations: state queue and observation chain. By reordering the gaps to minimize the values in d, a strict total ordering over the knowledge states, or priority, can be created. A state queue only maintained a belief about the presence or absence of one gap, the one with the highest priority. The state queues allowed a POMDP to temporarily ignore less-relevant states. The state space in a POMDP using a state queue was linear, not exponential.

The existing techniques for improving time and space efficiency in POMDPs have made good progress towards building ITSs for practical teaching. However they had limitations. For example, as the authors of [6] concluded, computational challenges still existed in the technique of forward trees, despite sampling only a fraction of possible actions and allowing very short horizons. Also, how to sample the possible actions and how to shorten the horizon are challenging problems. As the authors of [4] indicated, the methods of state queue and observation chain might cause information loss, which might in turn degrade system performance in choosing optimal actions.

III. Partially Observable Markov Decision Process

A POMDP consists of S, A, T, ρ, O, and Z, where S is a set of states, A is a set of actions, T is a set of state transition probabilities, ρ is a reward function, O is a set of observations, and Z is a set of observation probabilities. At a point of time, the decision agent is in state $s \in S$, it takes action $a \in A$, then enters state $s' \in S$, observes $o \in O$, and receives reward $r = \rho(s, a, s')$. The probability of transition from s to s' after a is $P(s'|s, a) \in T$. The probability of observing o in s' after a is $P(o|a, s') \in Z$. Since the states are not completely observable, the agent infers state information from its observations and actions, and makes decisions based on its inferred *beliefs* about the states.

An additional major component in POMDP is the *policy* denoted by π. It is used by the agent to choose an action based on its current belief:

$$a = \pi(b) \tag{1}$$

where b is the belief, which is defined as

$$b = [b(s_1), b(s_2), ..., b(s_Q)] \tag{2}$$

where $s_i \in S$ $(1 \leq i \leq Q)$ is the ith state in S, Q is the number of states in S, $b(s_i)$ is the probability that the agent is in s_i, and $\sum_{i=1}^{Q} b(s_i) = 1$.

Given belief b, the optimal π returns the optimal action. For a POMDP, finding the optimal π is called *solving the POMDP*. For most applications, solving a POMDP is a task of great computational complexity. A practical method for POMDP-solving is using *policy trees*. In a policy tree, nodes are actions and edges are observations. Based on a policy tree, after an action (at a node), the next action is determined by what is observed (at an edge). A path in a policy tree is a sequence of "action, observation, ..., action". Figure 1 illustrates a policy tree, where a_r is the root action, o_1, ..., o_K are possible observations, and a is an action. In a finite horizon POMDP of length H, a policy can be a tree of height H.

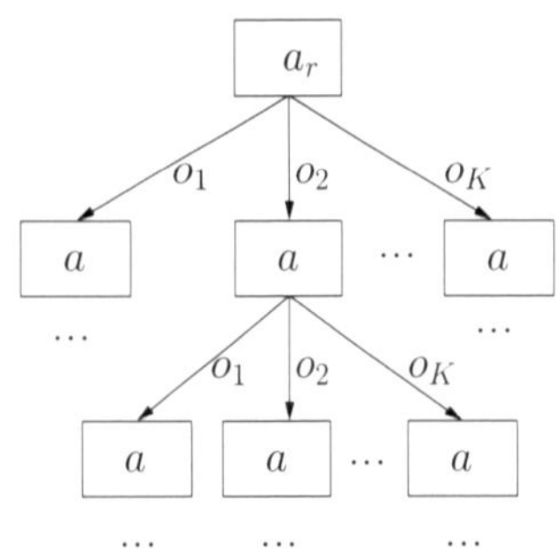

Figure 1. The general structure of a policy tree.

In the method of policy trees, making a decision is to choose the optimal tree and take its root action. Each policy tree is associated with a *value function*. Let τ be a policy tree and s be a state. The value function of s given τ is

$$V^{\tau}(s) = \mathcal{R}(s, a) + \gamma \sum_{s' \in S} P(s'|s, a) \sum_{o \in O} P(o|a, s') V^{\tau(o)}(s') \tag{3}$$

where a is the root action of τ, γ is a discounting factor, o is the observation after the agent takes a, $\tau(o)$ is the subtree in τ which is connected to the node of a by the edge of o, and $\mathcal{R}(s, a)$ is the expected immediate reward after a is taken in s, calculated as

$$\mathcal{R}(s, a) = \sum_{s' \in S} P(s'|s, a) \mathcal{R}(s, a, s') \tag{4}$$

where $\mathcal{R}(s, a, s')$ is the expected immediate reward after the agent takes a in s and enters s'. The second term on the right hand side of (3) is the discounted expected value of future states.

From (2) and (3), we have the value function of belief b given τ:

$$V^{\tau}(b) = \sum_{s \in S} b(s) V^{\tau}(s). \quad (5)$$

Thus we have $\pi(b)$ returning the optimal policy tree $\hat{\tau}$ for b:

$$\pi(b) = \hat{\tau} = \arg\max_{\tau \in \mathcal{T}} V^{\tau}(b), \quad (6)$$

where $\mathcal{T}$ is the set of trees to evaluate in making the decision.

From the above description, we can see that making a decision (by using (3), (4), (5), and (6)) requires computation over the entire state space S and solution space $\mathcal{T}$. The two spaces are typically exponential. They have been a bottleneck in applying POMDP to practical problems.

IV. An Intelligent Tutoring System on POMDP

We developed an experimental system as a test bed for our techniques, including the policy tree technique for intelligent tutoring. In this section, we describe how we cast an ITS onto the POMDP, and how we define states, actions, and observations.

The instructional subject of the ITS is basic knowledge of software. The system is for teaching concepts in the subject. It teaches a student at a time, in a turn-by-turn interactive way. In a tutoring session, the student asks questions about software concepts, and the system chooses the optimal tutoring actions based on its information about the student's current states.

Most concepts in the subject have prerequisites. When the student asks about a concept, the system decides whether it should start with teaching a prerequisite for the student to make up some required knowledge, and, if so, which one to teach. The *optimal* action is to teach the concept that the student needs to make up in order to understand the originally asked concept, and that the student can understand it without making up other concepts.

We cast the ITS *student model* onto the POMDP states, and represent the *tutoring model* as the POMDP policy. At the current stage, the student model contains information about knowledge states. In the architecture, ITS actions are represented by POMDP *actions*, while student actions are treated as POMDP *observations*.

At any point in a tutoring process, the decision agent is in a POMDP state, which represents the agent's information about the student's current state. Since the states are not completely observable, the agent infers the information from its immediate action and observation (the student action), and represents the information by the current belief. Based on the belief, the agent uses the policy to choose the optimal action.

We define states in terms of the concepts in the instructional subject. In software basics, the concepts are *data*, *program*, *algorithm*, and so on. We use a boolean variable to represent each concept: variable $\mathcal{C}_i$ represents concept C_i. $\mathcal{C}_i$ may take two values $\surd C_i$ and $\neg C_i$. $\surd C_i$ indicates that the student understands concept C_i, while $\neg C_i$ indicates that the student does not.

A conjunctive formula of such values may represent information about a student knowledge state. For example, $(\surd C_1 \wedge \surd C_2 \wedge \neg C_3)$ represents that the student understands C_1 and C_2, but not C_3. When there are N concepts in a subject, we can use formulas of N variables to represent student knowledge states. For simplicity, we omit the $\wedge$ operator, and thus have formulas of the form:

$$(\mathcal{C}_1 \mathcal{C}_2 \mathcal{C}_3 ... \mathcal{C}_N) \quad (7)$$

where $\mathcal{C}_i$ may take $\surd C_i$ or $\neg C_i$ $(1 \leq i \leq N)$. We call a formula of (7) a *state formula*. It is a representation of which concepts the student understands and which concepts the students does not.

In an ITS for teaching concepts, student actions are mainly asking questions about concepts. Asking "what is a query language?" is such an action. We assume that a student action concerns only one concept. In this paper, we denote a student action of asking about concept C by $(?C)$, and use (Θ) to denote an *acceptance* action, which indicates that the student is satisfied by a system answer, like "I see", or "I am done". The system actions are mainly teaching concepts, like "A query language is a high-level language for querying." We use $(!C)$ to denote a system action of teaching C, and use (Φ) to denote a system action that does not teach a concept, for example a greeting. As mentioned, ITS actions are represented by POMDP actions, while student actions are treated as POMDP observations.

V. Addressing the Space Problems

A. The Space Problems

When states are defined in terms of concepts in the instructional subject, the number of state formulas is 2^N, where N is the number of concepts in the subject. When the method of policy trees is used for POMDP-solving, in a finite horizon POMDP of length H, the number of nodes in a policy tree is

$$\sum_{t=0}^{H-1} |O|^t = \frac{|O|^H - 1}{|O| - 1} \quad (8)$$

where $|\ |$ is the size operator. At each node, the number of possible actions is $|A|$. Therefore, the total number of all possible H-horizon policy trees is

$$|A|^{\frac{|O|^H - 1}{|O| - 1}}. \quad (9)$$

The complexities result in great difficulties in creating and storing states and policy trees in memory. In the following, we report our techniques for addressing the space problems.

B. Prerequisite Relationships

We develop our techniques based on information about pedagogical orders for learning/teaching contents in instructional subjects. Prerequisite relationships between concepts in a subject are pedagogical orders of the concepts. If, to understand concept C_j the student must first understand concept C_i, C_i is referred to as a prerequisite of C_j. A concept may have zero or more prerequisites, and a concept may be a prerequisite of zero or more other concepts. In this paper, when C_i is a prerequisite of C_j, we call C_j a *successor* of C_i. Prerequisite relationships can be represented in a directed acyclic graph (DAG). Figure 2 illustrates a DAG representing direct prerequisite relationships in a subset of concepts in software basics.

We observed, through examining tutoring processes of human teachers and students, that concepts asked by a student in successive questions usually had prerequisite/successor

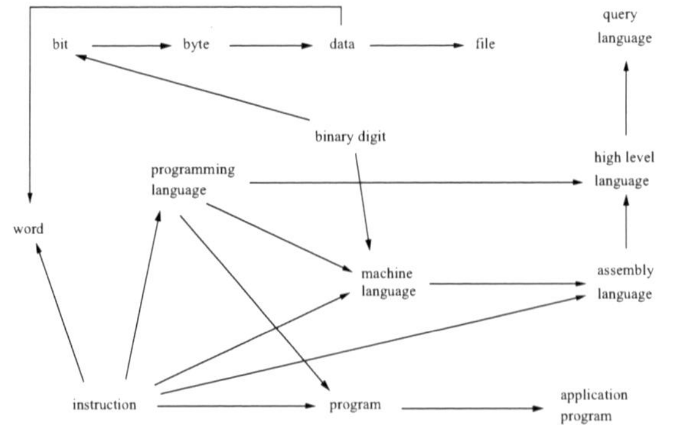

Figure 2. The DAG representing direct prerequisite relationships in a subset of the concepts in software basics. An arrow indicates "is a prerequisite of".

relationships with each other. Sometimes, after the teacher answered a question, the student asked about a prerequisite of the concept in the original question. This happened when the student realized that he/she needed to make up the prerequisite. Sometimes, after a teacher's answer, the student asked about a successor of the concept in the original question. This happened when the student had learned the concept and wanted to learn more along the line.

The observation suggests that we could group concepts in an instructional subject based on their prerequisite relationships, and limit computing within a subset of concepts when an ITS answers a question. We have developed a technique for partitioning a state space into sub-spaces and reducing the sizes of sub-spaces. The technique allows an ITS to localize the computing of a tutoring session within a sub-space. For details of the partitioning technique, please see [9]. In the next session, we describe the space efficient techniques for creating and storing policy trees.

VI. Space Efficient Techniques for Policy Trees

A. Design Consideration

In this section, we present our policy tree techniques for reducing the solution space of a POMDP, including design consideration, structures of solution space and policy trees, and decision making with the trees. We then describe a space saving structure, which enables creating large policy trees in limited memory. Our techniques can be applied to any ITSs, in which instructional subjects can be subdivided into small components to teach, and the components have pedagogical orders with each other.

It can be seen from (6), (8) and (9), when a technique of policy trees is applied, the costs (in time and space) for making a decision depend on the size of $\mathcal{T}$, the horizon H, and the sizes of S and O. The design goal of our techniques is to minimize the H, and the sizes of $\mathcal{T}$, S, and O that are involved in making a decision, with least loss of information.

As mentioned, we observed that successive student questions likely concern concepts that have prerequisite/successor relationships with each other. In our research, we define tutoring sessions to include such questions, and answers to them. A *tutoring session* is a sequence of interleaved student and system actions, starting with a question about a concept, possibly followed by answers and questions concerning the concept and its prerequisites, and ending with a student action accepting the answer to the original question. If, before the acceptance action, the student asks a concept that has no prerequisite relationship with the concept originally asked, we consider that a new tutoring session starts.

For example, a tutoring session may start with a question about *application program* and ends with an acceptance action. In the session, there may be questions and answers about *application program*, and about its prerequisites like *program*, *programming language*, etc. (according to the DAG in Figure 2). If before the session ends, the student asks a question about *file*, another tutoring session starts.

Tutoring sessions play an important role in our techniques. By dividing a tutoring process into such sessions, we can limit computing in a session to a subset of concepts that have prerequisite/successor relationships with each other. We partition the state space into sub-spaces, and localize the computing in a session within a sub-space. In this way, we reduce $|S|$ involved in making a decision [9]. Based on the partitioned state space, we split the solution space.

B. Structure of Solution Space

We classify questions in a session into the *original question* and *current questions*. The original question starts the session, concerning the concept the student originally wants to learn. We denote the original question by $(?C^o)$, where C^o is the concept concerned in the question and superscipt o stands for "original". A current question is the question to be answered by the system at a point in the session, usually for the student to make up some knowledge. We denote a current question by $(?C^c)$, where the superscipt c stands for "current". Concept C^c is in $(\wp_{C^o} \cup C^o)$, where $\wp_{C^o}$ is the set of all the direct and indirect prerequisites of C^o. A current question may be asked by the student, or made by the system. The original question is also the current question, right after it is asked. In the above example of tutoring session, the question concerning *application program* is the original question. if there is a question about *programming language*, it is a current question.

In a session, the tutoring agent chooses an optimal policy tree from a tree set to answer a question (see (6)). Since the agent's ultimate goal is to teach C^o, and current questions in the session concern prerequisites of C^o, we can include only the policy trees for teaching concepts in $(\wp_{C^o} \cup C^o)$ in the tree set that is evaluated in the session started by $(?C^o)$.

The entire tree set $\mathcal{T}$ can thus be split into subsets of $\mathcal{T}_{C^c}^{C^o}$, where C^o is a concept that can be in an original question and C^c is a concept in $(\wp_{C^o} \cup C^o)$, where $\wp_{C^o}$ includes all direct and indirect prerequisites of C^o. The computing for choosing an action to answer a current question evaluates one subset only: when the original question is $(?C^o)$ and current question is $(?C^c)$, the tree set to evaluate is $\mathcal{T}_{C^c}^{C^o}$. In computing (6) for answering the current question, the $\mathcal{T}$ in the equation is substituted with $\mathcal{T}_{C^c}^{C^o}$.

Tree set $\mathcal{T}_{C^c}^{C^o}$ includes trees for concepts in $(\wp_{C^c} \cup C^c)$, i.e., for C^c and its prerequisites. To answer $(?C^c)$, the agent evaluates all of them, to decide to teach C^c or one of its prerequisites. Let C be a concept in $(\wp_{C^c} \cup C^c)$. In $\mathcal{T}_{C^c}^{C^o}$, there is one or more trees for C. To simplify the discussion here, we assume one tree for C. We denote the tree for C in $\mathcal{T}_{C^c}^{C^o}$ by $\mathcal{T}_{C^c}^{C^o}.\tau_C$. Next, we discuss the structure of $\mathcal{T}_{C^c}^{C^o}.\tau_C$.

C. Structure of a Policy Tree

As discussed, in a tutoring session started by $(?C^o)$, the goal of the agent is to teach C^o. In a policy tree for answering a current question, the leaf nodes must be a student action that accepts $(!C^o)$, which is an action to teach the concept in the original question. A path in the tree includes possible questions and answers concerning prerequisites of C^o. Also, since possible student questions in the session concern prerequisites of C^o, we limit the observation set O to include concepts in $\wp_{C^o}$ only. (Student questions are treated as observations.)

The root of $\mathcal{T}_{C^c}^{C^o}.\tau_C$ is $(!C)$, i.e. an action teaching $C \in (\wp_{C^c} \cup C^c)$. When C has M prerequisites C_1, ... C_M, the root has $M+1$ children. The first M children are sub-trees rooted by $(!C_1)$, ... $(!C_M)$ and connected by edges of $(?C_1)$, ... $(?C_M)$. The last child is a sub-tree rooted by $(!C^u)$, where C^u is one of the direct successors of C. This sub-tree is connected by an edge of acceptance action (Θ). For each direct successor of the concept at the root, we construct a tree. The semantics of such root-children structure is that after $(!C)$, if the student asks about a prerequisite of C, teach that prerequisite, if the student accepts $(!C)$, teach one of the direct successors of C.

In a policy tree, each sub-tree is structured in the same way. That is, the root has an edge for each of its prerequisites and an acceptance edge. However, if a prerequisite has been taught in the path from the tree root, the edge is not included. If a root is $(!C^o)$ for answering the original question, its acceptance edge connects to an action terminating the session.

Figure 3 illustrates policy tree $\mathcal{T}_{ML}^{ML}.\tau_{ML}$, where ML stands for *machine language*. The prerequisite relationships are based on Figure 2. ML has three direct and indirect prerequisites IN (*instruction*), BD (*binary digit*), and PL (*programming language*). Therefore the root has three edges for the prerequisites and an acceptance edge. Since the root is for answering the original question, the acceptance edge connects to a terminating action (represented by a horizontal bar). Figure 4 shows policy trees $\mathcal{T}_{ML}^{ML}.\tau_{PL}$, $\mathcal{T}_{ML}^{ML}.\tau_{IN}$, and $\mathcal{T}_{ML}^{ML}.\tau_{BD}$. Figure 5 shows policy trees $\mathcal{T}_{PL}^{PL}.\tau_{PL}$ and $\mathcal{T}_{PL}^{PL}.\tau_{IN}$.

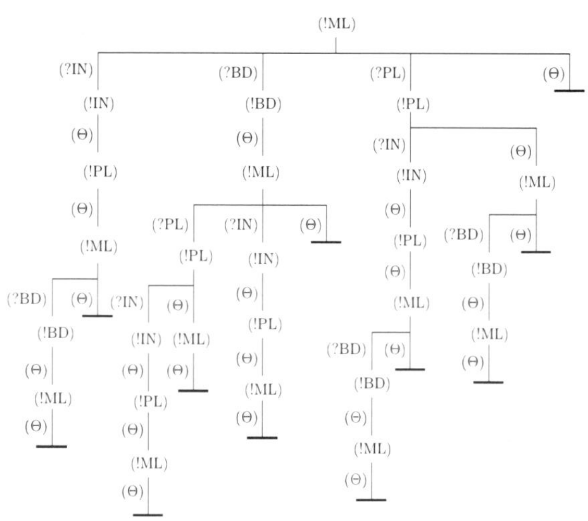

Figure 3. Policy tree $\mathcal{T}_{ML}^{ML}.\tau_{ML}$.

The policy tree structure helps improve efficiency in both space and time. Firstly, it minimizes the number of trees to

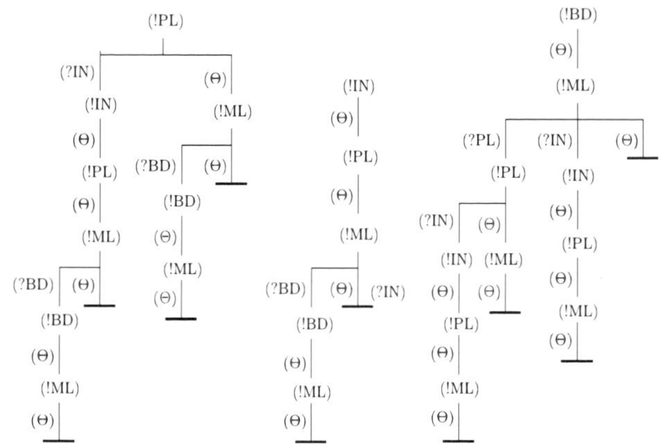

Figure 4. Policy trees $\mathcal{T}_{ML}^{ML}.\tau_{PL}$ (left), $\mathcal{T}_{ML}^{ML}.\tau_{IN}$ (middle), and $\mathcal{T}_{ML}^{ML}.\tau_{BD}$ (right).

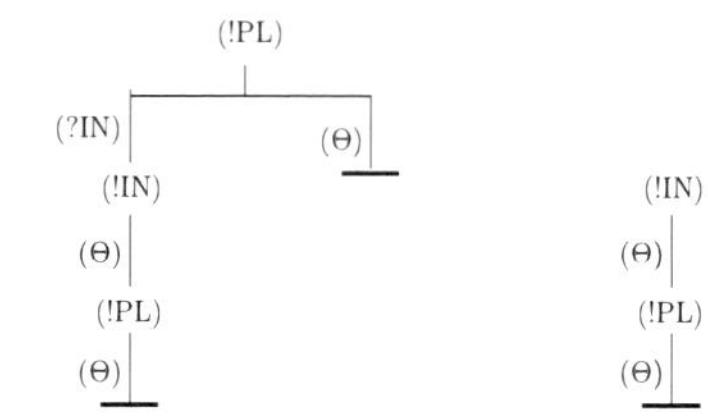

Figure 5. Policy trees $\mathcal{T}_{PL}^{PL}.\tau_{PL}$ (left) and $\mathcal{T}_{PL}^{PL}.\tau_{IN}$ (right).

evaluate. To answer $(?C^c)$ in a session started by $(?C^o)$, the agent evaluates the trees in $\mathcal{T}_{C^c}^{C^o}$ only, instead of all the possible trees. Secondly, it minimizes the costs for evaluating individual trees. A tree deals with only the concepts in $(\wp_{C^o} \cup C^o)$. We can thus minimize the set of observations O. We can also minimize the tree height: a path concerns related concepts only, and unnecessary actions are excluded at the earliest possible point. As discussed before, H and $|O|$ determine the costs for evaluating a tree. Minimizing H and $|O|$ helps minimize tree sizes and thus the space and time costs. In addition, this structure causes no information loss. In a tree, all the possible student actions (observations) have been taken into account.

For better time efficiency, we construct ready-to-use policy trees and store them in a tree database. When the agent needs to make a decision with certain original question and current question, it searches the database for a tree set, and evaluates trees in the set only.

D. Decision-Making with Policy Trees

In a tutoring session started by $(?C^o)$, to answer current question $(?C^c)$, the agent evaluates trees in $\mathcal{T}_{C^c}^{C^o}$ by using (6), and choose the optimal one. In using (6), it substitutes $\mathcal{T}$ with $\mathcal{T}_{C^c}^{C^o}$. For example, when the original and current questions are both (?ML), the agent evaluates the four trees in $\mathcal{T}_{ML}^{ML}$ showed in Figures 3 and 4. It finds the tree of the highest value (optimal tree) based on its current belief.

A policy tree is not a tutoring plan that the agent must follow in the future. It is the choice for the current step. After the optimal tree is selected, the agent takes the root action. After taking the action, it terminates the session or has a new current question, depending on the student action (observation):

1) If the student action is (Θ), and the (Θ) edge connects to a terminating action, the agent terminates the current tutoring session;
2) If the student action is (Θ), and the (Θ) connects to a ($!C$), the agent considers ($?C$) as the current question in the next step.
3) If the student action is ($?C$), the agent considers ($?C$) as the current question in the next step.

In the next step, to answer the current question which is determined by using rules 2) and 3), the agent chooses an action in the same way, i.e. by evaluating a set of policy trees, and so on. Continue the above example with (?ML) being both the original and current questions. If the policy tree for ML is the optimal, the agent takes action (!ML). After (!ML), if the student action is (Θ), the agent follows the edge of (Θ) in the tree, and takes the terminating action to finish the session. Whereas, if after (!ML) the student action is (?PL), the agent considers that (?PL) is the current question in the next step. It evaluates the trees in $\mathcal{T}_{PL}^{ML}$, and continues until it takes a terminating action.

E. Structure for Dealing with Limited Memory

In constructing a tree database, the system creates each policy tree in memory before storing it. To evaluate a policy tree, the system first loads it into memory. Although our technique can minimize the numbers of nodes and edges in individual trees, and we use efficient data structures for tree nodes and edges to reduce memory usage, some trees are still very large. Those are trees for concepts having large numbers of prerequisites. A single tree can be bigger than the memory space available to run the ITS. Dealing with limited memory is a challenging issue in applying a method of policy trees.

The structure we developed for policy trees offers flexibilities in creating and loading policy trees in memory. Let ($?C^o$) and ($?C^c$) be original and current questions ($C^c \in (\wp_{C^o} \cup C^o)$). As described, we create tree set $\mathcal{T}_{C^c}^{C^o}$, which includes policy trees for C^c and all its prerequisites. Let C', C'', ... be prerequisites of C^c. The trees are $\mathcal{T}_{C^c}^{C^o}.\tau_{C^c}$, $\mathcal{T}_{C^c}^{C^o}.\tau_{C'}$, $\mathcal{T}_{C^c}^{C^o}.\tau_{C''}$, ... According to our rules for structuring policy trees, $\mathcal{T}_{C^c}^{C^o}.\tau_{C'}$, $\mathcal{T}_{C^c}^{C^o}.\tau_{C''}$, ... are subtrees of $\mathcal{T}_{C^c}^{C^o}.\tau_{C^c}$. They are connected to the root by edges of ($?C'$), ($?C''$) ... This structure allows us to physically create $\mathcal{T}_{C^c}^{C^o}.\tau_{C'}$, $\mathcal{T}_{C^c}^{C^o}.\tau_{C''}$, ... only, and create $\mathcal{T}_{C^c}^{C^o}.\tau_{C^c}$ as a root and pointers to the trees. This approach can solve the problem that $\mathcal{T}_{C^c}^{C^o}.\tau_{C^c}$ exhausts the available memory.

For example, when the original and current questions are both (?ML), and ML has prerequisites PL, IN and BD, tree set $\mathcal{T}_{ML}^{ML}$ includes four trees: $\mathcal{T}_{ML}^{ML}.\tau_{ML}$, $\mathcal{T}_{ML}^{ML}.\tau_{PL}$, $\mathcal{T}_{ML}^{ML}.\tau_{IN}$, and $\mathcal{T}_{ML}^{ML}.\tau_{BD}$. The four trees are illustrated in Figures 3 and 4. We can see that $\mathcal{T}_{ML}^{ML}.\tau_{PL}$, $\mathcal{T}_{ML}^{ML}.\tau_{IN}$, and $\mathcal{T}_{ML}^{ML}.\tau_{BD}$. are the first three subtrees of $\mathcal{T}_{ML}^{ML}.\tau_{ML}$. We can physically create $\mathcal{T}_{ML}^{ML}.\tau_{PL}$, $\mathcal{T}_{ML}^{ML}.\tau_{IN}$, and $\mathcal{T}_{ML}^{ML}.\tau_{BD}$. For $\mathcal{T}_{ML}^{ML}.\tau_{ML}$, we include root (!ML) and edges (?IN), (?BD), and (?PL) only.

Another structural feature of the policy trees can be used to save storage space. When C^{o_1} is a prerequisite of C^{o_2}, The trees in $\mathcal{T}_C^{C^{o_2}}$ can be used in $\mathcal{T}_C^{C^{o_1}}$ with minor changes. Take $\mathcal{T}_{ML}^{ML}.\tau_{PL}$ and $\mathcal{T}_{PL}^{PL}.\tau_{PL}$ (illustrated in Figures 4 and 5) as an example. The two trees are both for PL but in different tree sets ($\mathcal{T}_{ML}^{ML}$ and $\mathcal{T}_{PL}^{PL}$). PL is a prerequisite of ML. By substituting (!ML) in $\mathcal{T}_{ML}^{ML}.\tau_{PL}$ with a terminating action (represented as a horizontal bar), the tree can be used as $\mathcal{T}_{PL}^{PL}.\tau_{PL}$. This allows us to create and store a tree in a tree set and use it in multiple sets with minor changes. This structure may help save storage space for the tree database.

VII. EXPERIMENTS

We experimented our system using a data set of software basics. This data set contains 90 concepts. A concept has zero to five prerequisites. In the following, we first present the results concerning system performance in adaptive tutoring, and then the results concerning space usage.

30 students participated in the experiments, randomly divided into two groups of the same size. Each student studied with the ITS for about 45 minutes. The students were adults who knew how to use desktop or laptop computers, or smart phones, and application programs, including Web browsers, email systems, text processors, and phone apps. None of the students took a course on computer software before the experiments. The ITS taught students in the first group with the POMDP turned off. When a student asked about a concept, the system either taught the concept directly, or randomly selected a prerequisite to teach. The ITS taught students in the second group with the POMDP turned on. The system chose the optimal action when answering a question.

The performance perimeter was *rejection rate*. Roughly, if right after the system taught concept C, the student asked a question about a prerequisite of C, or said "I already know C", we considered the student rejected the system action. For a student, the rejection rate is calculated as the ratio of the number of system actions rejected by the student to the total number of system actions for teaching the student. The rejection rate of a student could be used to measure how the student was satisfied with the teaching, and thus measure the system's abilities to choose optimal actions.

TABLE I. NUMBER OF STUDENTS, MEAN AND ESTIMATED VARIANCE OF EACH GROUP.

	Group 1	Group 2
Number of students	$n_1 = 15$	$n_2 = 15$
Sample mean	$\bar{X}_1 = 0.5966$	$\bar{X}_2 = 0.2284$
Estimated variance	$s_1^2 = 0.0158$	$s_1^2 = 0.0113$

We applied a two-sample t-test method to evaluate the effects of the optimized teaching strategy to the teaching performance of an ITS. For the two groups, we calculated means $\bar{X}_1$ and $\bar{X}_2$. Sample mean $\bar{X}_1$ was used to represent population mean μ_1, and $\bar{X}_2$ represent μ_2. The alternative and null hypotheses were:

$$H_a : \mu_1 - \mu_2 \neq 0, \qquad H_0 : \mu_1 - \mu_2 = 0$$

The means and variances calculated for the two groups are listed in Table I. The mean rejection rate in Group 1 was 0.5966 and the mean rejection rate in Group 2 was 0.2284. The statistical analysis suggested we could reject H_0 and accept H_a. That is, the difference between the two means was significant.

In the following, we discuss the results related to space usage. As described, we partitioned the state space, so that we

TABLE II. NUMBERS OF CONCEPTS, TREE SETS, TREES, AND TREE HEIGHTS IN SUB-SPACES.

Sub-space	# of concepts	# of tree sets	# of trees	Max set size	Max inheight
1	21	98	285	18	30
2	23	134	456	25	22
3	20	111	388	22	26
4	27	188	753	29	37
5	25	173	684	26	32
6	26	169	682	31	35

could localize computing in a tutoring session within a sub-space. For each sub-space, we created tree sets, each of which contained policy trees to be evaluated for certain questions. For the data set of software basics, our algorithms partitioned the state space into six sub-spaces.

Table II lists the numbers of concepts, tree sets, and trees in each sub-space. It also lists the maximum size of tree sets and maximum tree height in each sub-space. It can be seen that the largest tree set contained 31 trees, and the maximum tree height was 37. That is, in the worst case, to answer a question the system evaluated a set of 31 trees of maximum height 37. Such tree sets and heights did not create major efficiency problems for a modern computer. When the experimental ITS run on a desktop computer with an Intel Core i5 3.2 GHz 64 bit processor and 16GB RAM, the response time for answering a question is less than 300 milliseconds. This includes the time for calculating a new belief, choosing a policy tree, and accessing the database of domain model. For a tutoring system, such response time could be considered acceptable.

TABLE III. MEMORY CONSUMPTION OF ITS COMPONENTS.

ITS Component	Storage usage (MB)
States	3
$P(s'\|s,a)$	5,319
$P(o\|a,s')$	44
$R(s,a)$	13
Tree database	3,671
Policy tree values	37

Table III includes the information about storage usage. The ITS components consuming memory/disk space are states, state transition probabilities $P(s'|s,a)$, observation probabilities $P(o|a,s')$, expected rewards $R(s,a)$, and policy trees. We also saved tree values (computed by using (3)) for possible re-use, for better response time. The tree values were re-computed when the probabilities were updated. The tree database consumed 3,671 MB. Our techniques for structuring policy trees helped reduce the tree database to a manageable size. Before the space-saving structures were used, the tree database consumed about three times the space, and some policy trees could not be created because the available memory was exhausted.

We also experimented the techniques with a data set of statistics. This data set included all the 231 concepts taught in a textbook on introductory statistics [5]. The state space was partitioned into 28 subspaces. The techniques were effective in dealing with space efficiency issues with this subject. In this paper, we will not present the experimental results because of the limited page space.

VIII. CONCLUSION

The issue of space efficiency has been a major obstacle in building a POMDP-based intelligent tutoring system. Policy trees may consume very large space, even exhaust the available memory to crash a system. We developed a set of techniques to address the space problems caused by policy trees. With the techniques, we could minimize the number of trees, and minimize the sizes of individual trees. We could further reduce the space consumption by allowing trees to share the same tree components. Encouraging results have been achieved in experiments.

ACKNOWLEDGMENT

This research is supported by the Natural Sciences and Engineering Research Council of Canada (NSERC). Patrick Hartman implemented part of the system and conducted some of the experiments.

REFERENCES

[1] A. Cassandra, "A survey of pomdp applications", *Working Notes of AAAI 1998 Fall Symposium on Planning with Partially Observable Markov Decision Process*, Oct 23-25, 1998, Orlando, FL, USA. AAAI Press, Palo Alto, CA, USA, July, 1998, pp. 17-24.

[2] B. Cheung, L. Hui, J. Zhang, and S. M. Yiu, "SmartTutor: an intelligent tutoring system in web-based adult education", *The journal of Systems and software*, Elsevier, Cambridge, MA, USA, vol. 68, pp. 11-25, 2003, ISSN: 0164-1212.

[3] H. R. Chinaei, B. Chaib-draa, and L. Lamontagne, "Learning Observation Models for Dialogue POMDPs", in *Canadian AI'12 Proceedings of the 25th Canadian conference on Advances in Artificial Intelligence*, May 28-30, 2012, Toronto, ON, Canada, Springer-Verlag, Berlin, Heidelberg, 2012, pp. 280-286, ISBN: 978-3-642-30353-1.

[4] J. T. Folsom-Kovarik, G. Sukthankar, and S. Schatz, "Tractable POMDP Representations for Intelligent Tutoring Systems", *ACM Transactions on Intelligent Systems and Technology*, New York, NY, USA vol. 4, pp. 29:1-29:22, 2013, ISSN: 2157-6904.

[5] G. W. Heiman, *Basic Statistics for the Behavioral Sciences, Sixth Edition*, WadSworth, Cengage Learning, Belmont, CA, 2011, ISBN-13: 978-0-8400-3143-3.

[6] A. N. Rafferty, E. Brunskill, L. Thomas, T. J. Griffiths, and P. Shafto, "Faster Teaching by POMDP Planning", in *Proceedings of Artificial Intelligence in Education (AIED) 2011*, June 28 - July 2, 2011, Auckland, New Zealand. Springer, New York, NY, USA, July, 2011, pp. 280-287, ISBN: 078-3-642-21869-9.

[7] G. Theocharous, R. Beckwith, N. Butko, and M. Philipose, "Tractable POMDP Planning Algorithms for Optimal Teaching in SPAIS", in *IJCAI PAIR Workshop (2009)*, July 11-17, 2009, Pasadena, CA, USA. AAAI Press, Palo Alto, CA, USA, July, 2009, ISBN: 978-1-57735-426-0.

[8] K. VanLehn, B. van de Sande, R. Shelby, and S. Gershman, "The Andes Physics Tutoring System: an Experiment in Freedom", in Nkambou et-al eds. *Advances in Intelligent Tutoring Systems*, Berlin Heidelberg: Springer-Verlag, 2010, pp. 421-443, ISBN: 3642143628.

[9] F. Wang, "Handling Exponential State Space in a POMDP-Based Intelligent Tutoring System", in *Proceedings of 6th International Conference on E-Service and Knowledge Management (IIAI ESKM 2015)*, Okayama, Japan, July, 2015, pp. 67-72, ISBN: 978-1-4799-9957-6.

[10] F. Wang, "A new technique of policy trees for building a POMDP based intelligent tutoring system", in *Proceedings of The 8th International Conference on Computer Supported Education (CSEDU 2016)*, Rome, Italy, April, 2016, pp. 85-93, ISBN: 978-989-758-179-3.

[11] J. D. Williams, P. Poupart, and S. Young, "Factored Partially Observable Markov Decision Processes for Dialogue Management", in *Proceedings of Knowledge and Reasoning in Practical Dialogue Systems*, 2005.

[12] J. D. Williams, and S. Young, "Partially observable Markov decision processes for spoken dialog systems", *Computer Speech and Language*, Elsevier, Cambridge, MA, USA, vol. 21, pp. 393-422. 2007, ISSN: 0885-2308.

[13] B. P. Woolf, *Building Intelligent Interactive Tutors*, Burlington, MA, USA: Morgan Kaufmann Publishers, 2009, ISBN 978-0-12-373594-2.

Distributed Sensor Network for Noise Monitoring in Industrial Environment with Raspberry Pi

Natalia Blasco, María de Diego, Román Belda, Ismael de Fez, Pau Arce, Francisco José Martínez-Zaldívar, Alberto González, Juan Carlos Guerri
Institute of Telecommunications and Multimedia Applications
Universitat Politècnica de València
Valencia, Spain
e-mail: nablasu@iteam.upv.es, mdediego@dcom.upv.es, robelor@iteam.upv.es, isdefez@iteam.upv.es, paarvi@iteam.upv.es, fjmartin@dcom.upv.es, agonzal@dcom.upv.es, jcguerri@dcom.upv.es

Abstract— **Monitoring the noise in working places is essential to protect the health of workers. There are two main factors that must be taken into account, and thus controlled, when considering noise exposition during the working hours: the level of perceived noise and the time exposed to that level of noise. In industrial environments, these two factors represent a high priority due to the quantity of equipment inside the factory. In this paper, we present a low cost system to measure and monitor noise conditions in an industrial environment. The proposed solution is based on ad hoc wireless probes and a server in the cloud, which acts as a centralized data sink. Specifically, the probes are based on Raspberry Pi 3, while the server may be placed anywhere on the Internet. The proposed system helps to detect critical levels of noise for workers, sending warning messages to predefined contacts by means of a text message or email when hazardous situations occur.**

Keywords- Wireless Acoustic Sensor Network (WASN); Raspberry Pi 3; Industrial environment; Monitoring; Ad hoc networks.

I. INTRODUCTION

According to the findings of the World Health Organization (WHO), noise is the second largest environmental cause of health problems, just after the impact of air quality (particulate matter) [1].

Different regulations about noise monitoring in working environments have appeared along the years. Among them, apart from the aforementioned [1], from the World Health Organization / Europe, we highlight [2], which was published by the International Labour Organization (ILO) in 1977.

Particularly, noise exposure is higher in industrial working environments due to ambient noise produced by machines. Possible side effects resulting from high noise exposure are due to both the amount of sound energy received and the duration of exposure.

In this scenario, the levels and durations of the supported noise are difficult to predict because of the inherent characteristics of audio waves. Therefore, monitoring the real exposure to noise is very helpful to prevent negative health effects and to improve working conditions.

In this sense, usually sound level meters are used to analyze workplaces exposure to noise. However, the measures collected by these devices are not in real time, but they are taken at certain intervals of time instead. In this paper, we propose the use of a low-cost Wireless Sensor Network (WSN) in order to continually monitor workplaces and, therefore, obtain a better picture of the noise exposure of workers.

In the literature we can find several proposals about WSN. For instance, [3] presents a WSN for industrial environments and proposes different strategies to improve the link quality. Unlike [3], our solution is based on Raspberry Pi. In this sense, [4] presents an industrial application using Raspberry Pi in order to carry out the maintenance of a machine. Another use case for acoustic WSN with Raspberry Pi, apart from industrial environments, is the monitoring of noise in smart cities, as proposed in [5].

The rest of the paper is structured as follows. Section 2 presents the system architecture, which is composed of three main blocks: sensor network, cloud and user interface. Section 3 explains the experimental results obtained. Finally, Section 4 presents the conclusions and the future work.

II. SYSTEM ARCHITECTURE

An example of the proposed system can be observed in Figure 1. As the figure depicts, there are three main elements in the architecture: the WSN system installed in the factory; the cloud; and the user interface, used to monitor the state of the network.

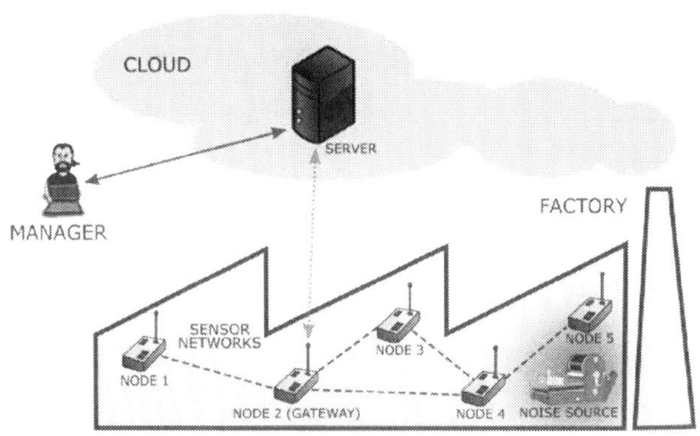

Figure 1. Example of the proposed system architecture.

The figure shows a distributed sensor network composed of five nodes creating an ad hoc Wi-Fi network. As the figure depicts, there is a main node (in the example, the node

2), which acts as a gateway. That is, the main node is in charge of communicating with the rest of nodes and with the server located in the cloud. To that extent, the main node has Internet connection (for instance, direct connection with the local area network of the building or by means of a 3G/4G connection). In an ad hoc network, each node is part of the routing by forwarding data to other nodes until finding the main node (the gateway), which will upload the data to the server. In this way, each node performs functions of router and host.

On the other hand, the manager of the system will access the server located in the cloud to get the information provided by the sensor network. The manager will consult this information by means of a web user interface and will be able to change the audio recording configuration of the nodes.

The following sections present the main details of each one of the three blocks that compose the system proposed.

A. *Overview of the sensor network*

The sensor network is in charge of continuously monitoring the noise levels and generating alerts when the measured noise levels exceed a certain limit. In the example shown in Figure 1, the noise source generates a critical noise that is detected by node 5. This node sends the information of the sound pressure level, which is routed by the ad hoc network until the main node (node 2). The gateway sends this information to the server. In addition, the server can generate an alert by means of a text message or email.

As previously explained, the sensor system is an ad hoc network, which uses Optimized Link State Routing (OLSR) as a routing protocol. OLSR, defined in RFC 3626 [6] and updated in RFC 7181 [7], is a proactive link-state protocol. OLSR uses an optimized system to broadcast routing control and TC (Topology Control) messages by means of special nodes called MPRs (Multipoint Relays). The MPRs selection is carried out through metrics of willingness, connectivity and symmetry of the links with the neighbor nodes.

The main advantages of this kind of deployment are the scalability and the fact that nodes can move freely maintaining the connectivity and updating routing information. As a drawback, we highlight the autonomy of the nodes, which makes them dependent on batteries or power supply. In the study case, nodes can be located in those places with potential risk noise situations. In this way, nodes are connected to the power line, thus avoiding the need to use batteries, although they can work with them, allowing location independence.

Figure 2 shows the appearance of a node, in which the main components can be seen. The base component of each node is a Raspberry Pi 3 model B. This board has a built-in Wi-Fi 802.11n card to create the ad hoc network without needing an external antenna.

As the Raspberry Pi models do not have an integrated microphone input, it has been necessary to use an external USB microphone, which provides its own sound card. Also, in order to provide geolocation, the GPS can be connected through the USB interface. Note that, in order to show the possibilities of the system, the GPS module has been added to the solution presented. The use of this module can be optional in static indoor installations if nodes are in fixed positions.

In this way, a solution based on the use of low-cost components leads to a very cost efficient system. Sensors run Raspbian OS. It is important to note that the service executed on the boards, called agent, has been the focus of the main development carried out. Specifically, the agent has been developed using Python 3 language for the main tasks of the service (such as the application lifecycle, multithreading, recording and reporting the measurements). In addition, in order to process the recorded audio data, Octave through Oct2py interface has been used.

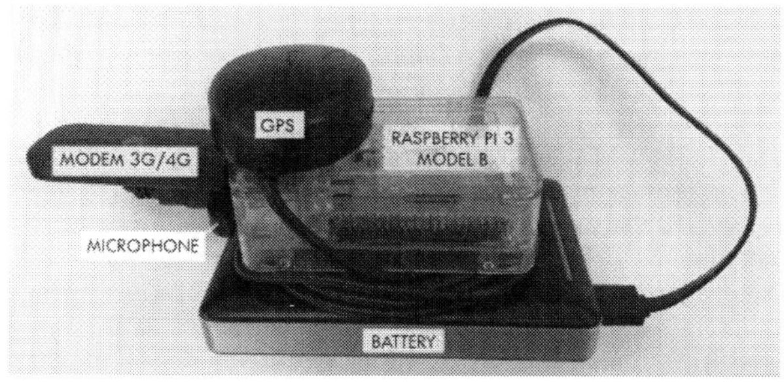

Figure 2. Picture of the node.

Moreover, a piston phone is used to calibrate the microphone in the sensors. First, the difference between the measurement taken by the piston phone and the one obtained with the chosen microphone is calculated. Then, this difference is used in all audio samples to show the correct value of the sound pressure level in the application.

The proposed system captures audio and processes the samples, calculating the sound pressure level in fragments of time. It is worth highlighting that this process is carried out by the Raspberry Pi 3, thus minimizing the data transmitted (and saving bandwidth) because only the processed data values are sent.

B. *Cloud*

Another block of the proposed system architecture (as shown in Figure 1) is the cloud. Data values of the audio recordings are stored on a server in the cloud.

The server receives the sound pressure level from the raspberries in the ad hoc network and saves the data of each node in a database. Apart from the sound pressure level and the node identifier, the database also stores the timestamp of the beginning and the end of the recording.

The database is composed of different tables that allow to organize the collected data in an appropriate way. Sensors can be classified into groups, which can be rather useful to interpret the information. For example, in the industrial environment each node can be assigned to different groups, such as the floor where the node is, the department, the type of machine, etc. Thus, each node can belong to more than one group and it is possible to add as many nodes and groups as required to the network.

C. *User interface*

The last block of the proposed system is related to the management of the architecture. A manager will be able to monitor the network, the audio configuration of the nodes and the database.

To that extent, a web user interface was developed, which is used to consult and manage the data. The web page is structured in two different parts: the monitoring section, and the administration part. The former shows a page with a list of groups and, when selecting a specific group, a table with the properties of the sensors belonging to that group is shown. An example is depicted in Figure 3. Also, the web site shows a map with the geolocation of the nodes. As we can see in the figure, each marker referred to the position of each node has a certain color, depending on the noise level detected in that particular moment: green, for sound pressure levels among 0 and 65 dB_{SPL}; yellow, for sound pressure levels higher than 65 dB_{SPL} and lower than 100 dB_{SPL}; and red, for sound pressure levels higher than 100 dB_{SPL}.

If a certain node collects a measure higher than a specified limit of the sound pressure level, a warning will be shown in the web page. In addition, it is possible to send an alert by means of a text message.

On the other hand, the administration section is only for registered users. Apart from the functionalities of the monitoring section, registered users are able to interact with the database and modify the existing nodes or groups. Moreover, the section allows to load a specific configuration for a node, modifying the configuration table of the nodes. This table contains different parameters related to audio recording (such as the record time or period) and for calculating the audio sound pressure level (such as the integration time or the weighting mode).

III. Experimental Results

The evaluation of the nodes for testing the Wireless Acoustic Sensor Network (WASN) with Raspberry Pi 3 have been carried out inside the Universitat Politècnica de València (Figure 4). The network is composed of three nodes located in a small area without obstacles and with direct view. As the figure depicts, there is a source of noise, specifically, noise coming from construction works. This noise source is found nearby of node 1, and further away from the two other nodes.

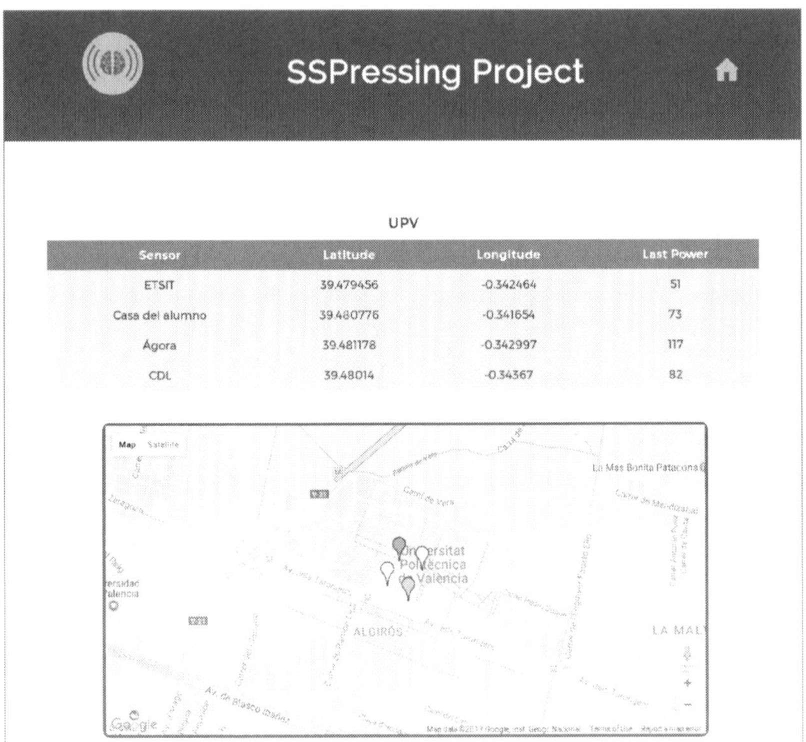

Figure 3. User interface of the monitoring section.

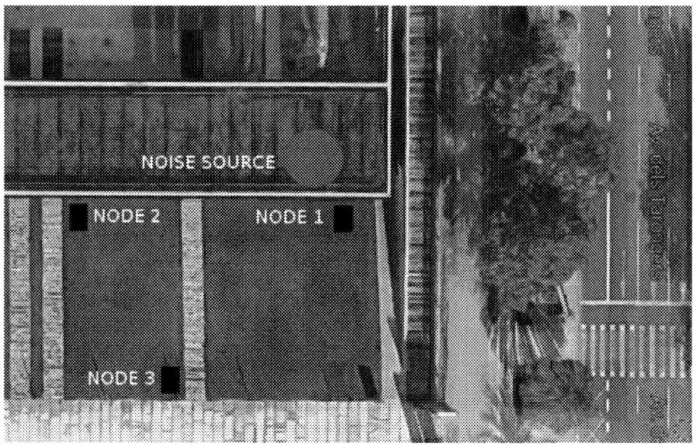

Figure 4. Detail of the network deployment at the Universitat Politècnica de València.

In the evaluation carried out, each node has recorded each second the sound level pressure measured during more than 1 hour (specifically, 74 minutes). The sampling frequency has been 44.1 kHz. The noise level of the three nodes over time is shown in Figure 5. In the x axis, it is shown the hour in which the measure has been taken (from 16:18 until 17:32 in intervals of 1 second). In the y axis, the sound pressure level in dB is displayed. This pressure level is also reflected in the figure by different colors: green tonalities indicate areas with acceptable sound pressure levels, whereas orange and red ones indicate dangerous areas in terms of noise level.

As expected, the node 1 is the node that measures the highest noise level, since it is the nearest node to the source of noise. Specifically, the average sound pressure level measured by node 1 is 83.35 dB, which represents a rather high noise level. In this sense, node 2 and node 3 present a similar evolution over time, although with sound pressure levels much lower (an average noise level of 69.32 dB and 62.46 dB, respectively). These results are in consonance with the distance from each node to the noise source.

In the figure, we can see three alerts corresponding to instants of time when the noise level exceeds 100 dB (specifically, instants of time 16:18, 16:20 and 17:30). Although these noise peaks are detected by the three nodes, only node 1 considers these peaks as alarms, since the measured value exceeds the defined threshold, as the Figure 5 depicts. As previously mentioned, these high sound pressure levels for a long time exposure can be harmful to the health of workers. In this way, the proposed system can help manage the noise level suffered by the employees during their working hours.

IV. Conclusion and Future Work

This paper has presented a system for monitoring the noise exposure in industrial environments. The proposed system is based on an ad hoc network and the use of Raspberries Pi 3. The solution hereby presented represents a low-cost system for audio monitoring which can be considered as a general model that allows to be extended (by adding new functionalities) and used in other environments related to Internet of Things.

As presented, one of the main advantages of the proposed system is the capacity to expand the WASN with more nodes in order to create a network tailored to users' needs. In addition, the network deployment is autonomous and rather portable, because of node size. Finally, remote monitoring allows to manage the information in real time, such as configuring the nodes or checking the warnings.

As a future work, in order to improve the benefits of the prototype proposed, further work to exploit data processing possibilities (such as machine learning for automatic noise classification) will be carried out. Among other improvements, we highlight the use of algorithms for classifying the audio in order to identify the source of the noise, thus better detecting certain alarming situations.

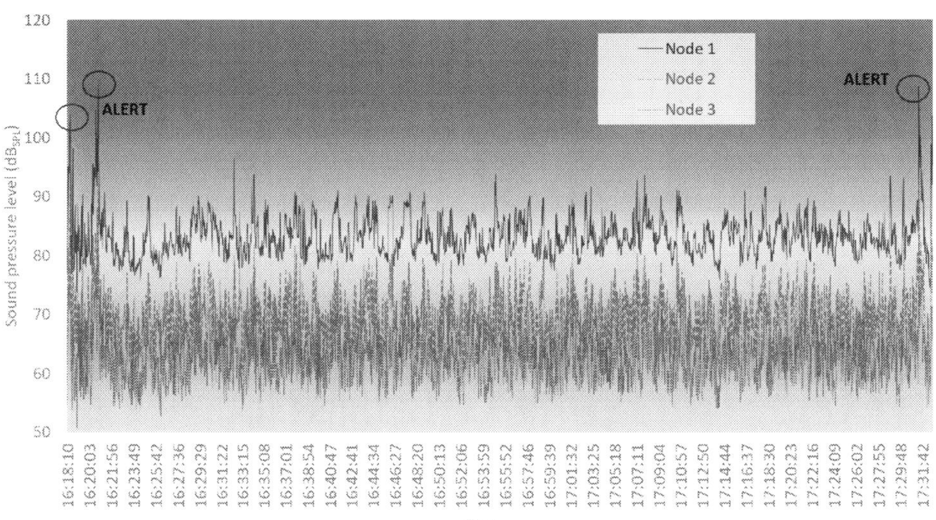

Figure 5. Evaluation of the sound pressure level, inside the UPV, measured outdoors.

ACKNOWLEDGMENT

This work is supported by the "Programa Estatal de I+D+i orientada a los Retos de la Sociedad" from the Government of Spain under the project "Smart Sound Processing for Digital Living (SSPressing)" (TEC2015-67387-C4-4-R).

REFERENCES

[1] World Health Organization Europe, "Night noise guidelines for Europe," 2009, available online at: http://www.euro.who.int/__data/assets/pdf_file/0017/43316/E92845.pdf?ua=1, accessed: Jun. 2017.

[2] International Labour Office, "Protection of workers against noise and vibration," ILO Codes of Practice, 1977, avaible online at: http://www.ilo.org/wcmsp5/groups/public/---ed_protect/---protrav/---safework/documents/normativeinstrument/wcms_107878.pdf, accessed: Jun. 2017.

[3] K. S. Low, W. N. N. Win, and M. J. Er, "Wireless Sensor Networks for Industrial Environments," Int. Conf. on Computational Intelligence for Modelling, Control and Automation and Int. Conf. on Intelligent Agents, Web Technologies and Internet Commerce (CIMCA-IAWTIC), Vienna, Austria, Nov. 2005, pp. 271-276, ISBN: 0-7695-2504-0.

[4] T. A. Onkar and P. T. Karule, "Web based Maintenance for Industrial Application using Raspberry-pi," Online Int. Conference on Green Engineering and TEchnologies (IC-GET), Coimbatore, India, Nov. 2016, pp. 1-4, ISBN: 978-1-5090-4556-3.

[5] J. Segura-Garcia, S. Felici-Castell, J. J. Pérez-Solano, M. Cobos, and J. M. Navarro, "Low-cost Alternatives for Urban Noise Nuisance Monitoring using Wireless Sensor Networks," *IEEE Sensors Journal*, vol. 15, no. 2, pp. 836-844, 2015.

[6] T. Clausen and P. Jacquet, "Optimized Link State Routing Protocol (OLSR)," IETF RFC, vol. 3626, Oct. 2003.

[7] T. Clausen, C. Dearlove, P. Jacquet, and U. Herberg, "The Optimized Link State Routing Protocol (OLSR) version 2," IETF RFC, vol. 7181, Apr. 2014.

Intelligent Tools for Electrical Energy Domain in Smart City

Ary Mauricio Burbano, Antonio Martín
Higher Polytechnic School
Seville University
Seville, Spain
e-mail: aryburcen1@alum.us.es, toni@us.es

Carlos León
Technical High School of Computer Science
University of Seville
Seville, Spain
e-mail: cleon@us.es

***Abstract*— More technological tools that can improve energy efficiency are being used. The generation, transmission, and energy distribution undoubtedly needs management equipment. This article is an effort to expose information acquisition technologies, local service, communications, and service platform. In addition, it explains how artificial intelligence, the Internet of Things and ontology, help to master energy to improve its supervision and thus increase energy efficiency in cities. Developers and engineers in the electricity sector need to know what the new tools can be used in electrical networks and homes. It is important for smart cities that people involved in the generation and distribution of electric power, know and apply these technologies. The main goal of this paper is to present intelligent tools and their characteristics for the people involved in the energy sector that could use these in energy projects or efficiency energy projects.**

Keywords- Electric; energy; intelligent tools; artificial intelligence; communications; ontology.

I. INTRODUCTION

Many technologies have been developed to improve the lifestyle in cities. Technological advance in electronics generate better tools to increase energy efficiency in cities each year. All these electronic devices are connected to the Internet or intranet, where computers store information and organize thousands of data of energy consumption. However, technology has taken another step with artificial intelligence (AI), where computers process information and make decisions. Commonly, when people think in AI, they imagine robots that can speak with humans, make cars, and more recently, help people in physical. But the true development this moment is software, not hardware. Programs are now competent enough that to do jobs that are annoying for humans; for example, in the energy management of electric lines or energy consumption at home, the sensors can communicate in real time and make decisions to solve problems in a few seconds. If the problem is in the electric line and the solution is not possible, the machine sends a signal to the operator to check the fault. That is possible thanks to the communication and the electronic tools that communicate energy data to the computers to build the solutions in real time.

For the energy domain, there are many technical developments to improve management of this sector. One of these is ontology. Ontologies are constructed using appropriate formal languages called ontology languages, based on the logic of first order predicates, frameworks or descriptive logic. According to the literature [1], an ontology language must describe what it clearly means clearly for the machine. Therefore, an ontology language needs to include the ability to specify vocabulary and the means to formally the way it will work to automate reasoning. Especially today, with the fast evolution of the Web and the recent emergence of the Semantic Web, the emphasis is placed on ontology languages suitable for the Internet, which is based on established Web standards. Web ontology languages allow defining different vocabularies, and they are specifically designed to facilitate Web sharing.

Authors in this paper present intelligent tools that help energy users improve energy efficiency. In the first section, the authors talk about the tools in energy domain; in the second section, they speak about the internet of things. The third section is about Artificial Intelligence, the fifth section presents an example of ontology in the energy domain and finally, in the sixth section the conclusions are presented.

II. ICT IN THE ENERGY DOMAIN

Information and Communication Technology (ICT) is one of the key tools for the development of a smart city. The level of the advancement of ICT affects the strategy of planning for the development of smart cities. With ICT, it is possible to have whole digital platforms interconnected that support applications and private and public services. Cities tend toward models that allow reducing the personal and global energy consumption, that support the big imbalance between energy generation capacity and municipal energy consumption [2].

There are many tools that have played a great role in building and developing smart homes and cities. Among these are the internet, wireless networks, and systems such as Wi-Fi, Bluetooth, and Zigbee; Smart Phones including LTE, 3G, 4G, and 5G cell systems; body area sensor networks, smart grids and renewable energy, optical fiber systems and high-speed networks, Internet of Things (IoT), wireless sensor networks (WSN), Vehicle Ad Hoc Networks (VANET), global positioning systems (GPS), geographic information systems (GIS), wireless navigation systems, world wide web (WWW), social networks, smart TV, radio frequency ID (RFID), sensor-enabled smart objects, actuators and sensors, cloud computing systems, intelligent transportation systems (ITS), biometric systems, e-based systems including e-commerce, e-government, e-business and e-service systems, network infrastructures, data management systems, analytics. Wireless power transfer (WPT) is used to transfer power over short distances using magnetic fields [3].

Figure 1. Technologies for Smart Cities

Every day, more ICT´s are implicit in our life; smart city devices (SCDs) have increased the influence of technology in our work, friends, and family. As a generic approach, SCDs types are divided into two main groups: reactive and active devices. Reactive devices are dumber devices that only receive some information and acts.

The generic objective of the reactive devices (R-SCDs) is increasing their energy efficiency without sacrificing performance [4]. One difference between reactive devices and active (A-SCDs) is that smarter devices can pursue a complete communication amongst other SCDs and operators.

Nowadays, people need energy for almost all activities in their daily life. SCDs have various elements that can be used in our lives, such as listening to music, talking, playing, shopping, health, financing etc. The apps now are very common, with infinite possibilities to achieve more energy efficiency. There are apps about house energy, car energy that indicate energy consumption and how many calories one's body has burned. This information could be analyzed and processed to improve our energy consumption. SCD´s are possible to use in all energy cycles; when energy reaches a home, many sensors, capacitors, Data logger and other devices are working to obtain the most efficiency possible. The Smart city must use elements, information management and interconnect various platforms that operate locally and autonomously. The layers of smart city models, from the technology point of view, are the following:

A. *Adquisition of information*

The layer of information acquisition uses sensors that receive information from the environment where they are integrated. The local service layer stores and registers the information of sensors with date and hour to transmit to the services platform. In all cases, this layer does not exist because the sensors and actuators are intelligent and are controlled directly by the services platform.

The sensors are elements, which collect information from different types and are transformed into an electric signal that could be sent and proceed. The digital signal only has two possible values or states, all or nothing, for example, 0 V o 24 V. The analog signal has a continuous range of possible values, for example of 0 to 10, equivalent a measurement range of a physic variable, temperature 0 to 100 ºC [2]. Besides, the data readers as detectors that perceive a determinate value. The simple sensors collect one or more measurements must be considered. Complex sensors collect information from a huge number of aspects. Identification sensors allow the identification of an object incorporating information from it. At Industrial level, we can see the example of ENDESA that leading smart meter installation in Spain with over 8 million smart meters, accounting for 72 % of the current fleet of 11.6 million meters [5].

The capture devices of complex data are elements that captured data through cameras or lectors. The actuators are elements that transform a digital or analog signal through data bus in one action there. Exists all or nothing actuators of the digital signal, as relays or contactors, that allow, for example, the turning on or turning off a group of lamps. The regulation actuators of the analog signal generate one analog outlet, which allows moderating the light level. Many of these sensors and actuators can be consulted and active through the Internet, each grid used their own standards, protocols, and formats of data representation. This is a problem when it wants to homogenize a solution, that is why it is important to try to open standards or have one platform that help to manage and interconnect these heterogeneous devices.

B. *Local Service*

There exists equipment that collects the signals of the sensors or detectors and sends the orders to actuators located in the installation. It also reports the information recollected from the sensors to the services' platform and receives orders from this. The number of sensors that are controlled by the equipment comes from digital inputs for the detectors and analogue inputs for the analog sensors. In Figure 2, we can see the basic structure of interconnection of these control elements.

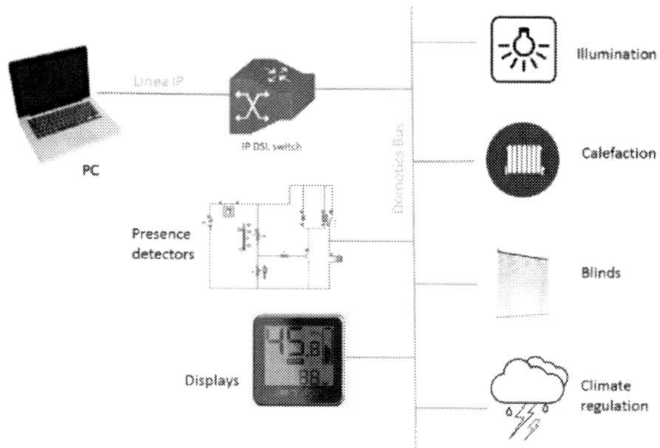

Figure 2. Control Elements

The principal equipment in the local service is the Data logger, which is a device that stores information for the sensors and detectors, with the date and the hour when it has been produced. The Data logger does not receive orders neither signals for realizing functions of actuation, but only gives information to the service platform. However, there exists programmable automata that functions with specific programming. This type of equipment gives to the smart city the advantage of the flexibility, being able to adapt the individual form to the needs of each installation.

C. *Communications*

The transmission information layer is the infrastructure of communications that sends and receives necessary data for the application of global service. With the communication networks, the interconnection of the energy domain is possible and facility the collection of data through sensors for its later treatment and makes decisions. The networks implicated are very heterogeneous, the interoperability and transparency are very important. To support information collection, distribution, automated control and optimization of the power system, the smart grid communication system will rely on two major subsystems: a communication infrastructure and a middleware platform. The communication infrastructure consists of a set of communication technologies, networks, and protocols that support communication connectivity among devices or grid sub-systems and enables the distribution of information and commands within the power system. Basic requirements for such communication infrastructure are scalability, reliability, timeliness, and security. The middleware platform consists of a software layer, which is situated between the applications and the underlying communication infrastructure, providing the services needed to build efficient distributed functions and systems. A middleware runs on the devices that are part of the smart grid communication infrastructure. It supports data management services for example data sharing, storage, and processing, standard communication and programming interfaces for distributed applications and computational intelligence and autonomic management capabilities [6].

The storage and analysis of the information layer is where all data are stored and also where it takes place the process for the analytic system to improve the management platform of the different services. The storage, in some cases of long duration, as the capacity of the process, allows the huge volumes of information generated for the grids of sensors and control equipment. As Guelzim says "Smart homes and cities will rely on the Internet of Things (IoT) devices, sensors, RFID chips, and smart electric meters, among others, to provide added value services to citizens and homeowners. However, these devices generate a large amount of data, big data, data sets, which are so big that traditional data processing techniques are not adequate to manage them" [7].

The technique known as Big Data allows adding the information flows that come to the huge sensor network of the city, convert it to useful and apply knowledge to make decisions of management of the smart city services. Big Data is a term, which design growth the availability and the exponential uses of structured and disorganized information. A definition of Big Data could be "Big Data is not about size, but it's about granularity". The ability of software systems to identify individuals and personalized data is the ironic implication of "Big". It is the ability to focus on the minutiae of the individual, in real time [1]. Data are fundamental in all service in the framework of the smart city. The data management is a complex job because normally they are consumed in real time, are diverse and present different formats. A tentative estimation of the amount of digital information produced by mankind is 280 EB of data [8].

D. *Service Platform*

Finally, the services' platform is the principal platform in the smart city domain, which is formed by various modules and management platforms and have interfaces with the final user. This platform offers a set of common modules to the multiple service and allows the operators to have a better and efficient service. The platform receives the processed information and interprets them, then it performs the actions according to the service of their destination. In the whole process, ICT increase the efficiency of the application of the generation, distribution, and energy consumption. Also, the control center could process the information and give to humans the possible failures solutions. With this technology, now the computers not only send and store information, also process the information. This implies guarantee of the interoperability at different levels; in hardware, the sensors, capacitors and data logger will be connected inwardly, and in software, the communication protocols, data structure and semantic will connect.

When talking about energy efficiency in smart cities it is important to talk about the ICT tools standardization, that allow increasing the security and clarity of energy sector, through of the contribution and information in real time between installations and the users. On the other hand, it encourages the multidirectional communication amongst different persons that influence in the energy consumption of the installation and the buildings. The main challenges of the future applications of SCD networks in smart cities can be listed as follows: lack of central control that has a complete information about the topology, integration and application simplicity, excessive amounts of system need, compatibility between SCDs and networks. To overcome these challenges, software-centered control structures need to be developed [9].

III. Internet Of Things

As utilities seek to modernize their grid infrastructure and day-to-day operations and services, enabled technologies are gaining increasing importance in enabling digitization and delivery of new energy models. The IoT is one of the major technologies that will shape the future of the digital world including Smart World, and Smart Cities and Homes. It is a mesh network of physical objects that either exchange data in P2P mode or communicate and relay information with the service provider [10].

There are many connected objects today such as electronic appliances, laptops, cameras, meeting, news as can see in Figure 3 that rely on RFID technology. IoT objects can be sensed and controlled across local area network or wide area networks.

Figure 3. Internet of Things

This allows the creation of many products and opportunities to better integrate the physical infrastructure with the digital systems. Many experts expect >10 billion IoT objects by year 2020 [7]. Big industry players such as Microsoft, IBM, Cisco, Siemens, and Google already play an important role in helping draft and put in place such technologies by offering cloud-based IoT services and devices.

IV. Artificial Intelligence

A step forward is using artificial intelligence (AI) to improve saving and efficiency energy. With AI, citizen can delegate the decision to improve efficiency to the computer. At the home level, computers can take the decision about the information of the Smart energy management system (SEMS). When SEMS detect a high consumption at night at home, the system could turn off a home appliance that is guilty of the excess. The computer could also turn on the home appliances when the cost of energy is low, for example, the washing machine could be turned on at night.

As the authors said, the energy domain needs the optimization of the resources, this achieves with the measurement, monitoring of the grids and the used energy analysis at buildings. Besides, with the concept of the green city, a city without greenhouses gases, with green transport, green buildings, include more variables to consider. This creates serious limitations when it comes to analyzing the data, especially if the analysis requires data from different fields, for example: technical, political, social, economic, environmental [11]. On the other hand, the difficulties of accessing multiple data sources and integrating them into a unified data model increases in the case of large volumes of data stored in data sources that support the models. Data describing the characteristics of similar articles using different standardization systems, different units of measurement applied [12]. As Keirstead said, it requires a systemic approach to understand "The combined process of acquisition and use of energy to meet the demands of a given urban area" by means of an urban energy system model, i.e., "a formal system that represents the combined processes of energy acquisition and used to meet the demand for energy services" [13].

Because of these difficulties, many researchers are using ontology to facilitate the interoperability between data model, which have been constructed by different experts from several domains using multiple techniques [14]. The Ontology is a taxonomy of concepts with attributes and relationships that provide a consensual vocabulary to defining semantic networks of units of information. Specifically, it is formed by a taxonomy that relates concepts and by a set of axioms or rules of inference, through which new knowledge can be inferred [15]. In the field of urban energetic systems, a shared ontology could facilitate the interoperability between data models building for different experts of various domains that use multiple techniques. There are various examples where are ontologies used. In the SEMANCO project for example, the semantics technologies have used standard tables to create models of urban energy systems, capable to evaluate the energy efficiency of urban zone. A semantic energy information framework brings together data sources at different scales and from different domains [16]. Another developed ontology with a similar objective is DogOnt [17], which aims to represent the different forms of energy production, depending on the construction, the number of occupants living in it, the devices, etc. DogOnt offers the ability to describe the location and capabilities of a home automation device and its possible configurations, device/network support, description of houses independently, including architectural elements. Another example is SynCity (short for "Synthetic City"), a platform for modeling urban energy systems [13]. The SynCity Urban Energy Systems (UES) ontology serves primarily as a library of domain-specific components, consisting of a series of object classes that describe the main elements of an urban energy system and specific cases of these classes.

V. THE ENERGY ONTOLOGY

The Energy Ontology (EO), shown in Figure 4, provides a flexible and extensible structure for modeling information about energy consumption, generation and storage, able to combine easy usage with the possibility to provide detailed descriptions. The ontology introduces a basic set of properties and classes to encode the most common energetic information used for system energy management that can be easily further extended using more specialized subclasses. The capability of OWL language can be also exploited to link EO with other ontology as ELM/OWL.

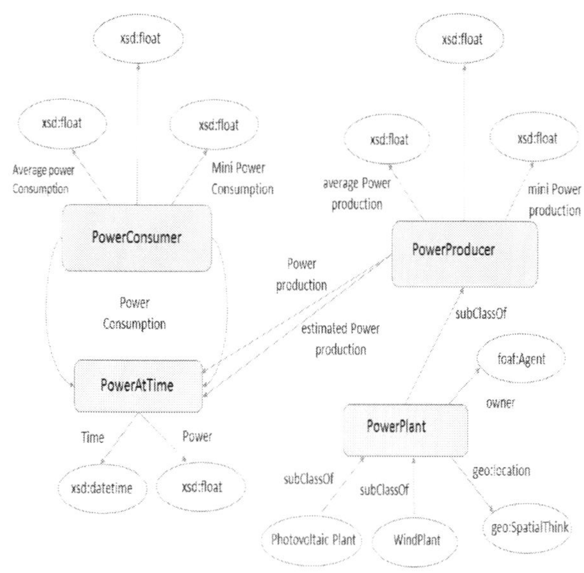

Figure 4. A graphical representation of same classes and properties of the Energy Ontology

EO introduces two basic classes representative of the two main categories that classify the energetic behavior of devices and plants: Power Consumer and Power Producer. These classes expose basic properties to encode information about power production and consumption features like the minimum, maximum and average amount of power consumed/produced. Dealing with energy management it is important to store information of power consumption/ production combined with time information. In this way, for example, historical power consumption can be created and maintained to be use for estimating future consumptions or for defining the user consumption profiles. With such purpose, EO provides the Power at Time class that allows describing the amount of power at a certain time [17].

An intelligent energy management for a complex home environment requires encoding and processing a wide number of information about actual and expected energy consumption and production. Dealing with solar and wind energy generation, the power output changes remarkably according to season, daytime and weather conditions. Particularly, the power output of a photovoltaic installation varies considerably on season scale, due to the different solar irradiation and weather conditions. Even more dramatically on a daily scale, due to solar irradiation ranging from the zero during the night to a maximum during the central hours of the day. Therefore, commonly, the system draws energy from the grid when the production is not sufficient to cover the energy needs, while releases energy to the grid when the produced energy exceeds the needs. Maximizing the amount of produced energy that is consumed locally in the house, is convenient both in terms of efficiency, avoiding energy loss in grid transportation, and profit, because the price at which energy is bought from the grid is higher than the price at which energy is sold to the grid, since power companies add delivery charges to energy price. In addition, reducing the request of energy from the public grid, which mostly relies on fossil sources especially in the rush hours, means to reduce pollution [18].

A dynamic and intelligent task scheduling it is then necessary to exploit at best the produced energy for performing more tasks as possible when there is a surplus of produced energy and to limit later energy draw from the grid when energy production is scarce or null. This requires the management of a wide number of information, relying on them to implement intelligent control logic. It's necessary not only to have a real-time measure of the consumed/produced energy but also to esteem how much energy will be produced in the next hours or days and how much energy the users will consume. Solar irradiation forecast curves, based on an average esteem of the solar irradiation measured on a region in the previous years, and weather forecast services can be used to get a row esteem of energy production. Forecast energy consumption can be evaluated using user's energy consumption profiles, derived from the statistical analyzing of system logs of energy consumption, and considering the energy requested from already scheduled task. It's necessary also to rely on services descriptions to infer if and how much a service can be deferred or performed in advance and consider the time required for task completion. Moreover, it is necessary to evaluate the amount of energy required to perform each service to assign a priority for task execution and to manage eventual conflicts.

VI. CONCLUSIONS

The digitization of city infrastructure is already a fact and is opening a world of opportunities in which all the stakeholders are called to be positioned and create value from that. For example, the development of the Smart Grids should adapt the regulatory framework and do big investment in the grids, such as monitoring, equipment of consumption and smart meters in the consumer installations.

A smart city of the future should have more participation of renewable energy than hydro and fossil fuels. In this city the transport and energy distribution will be through superconductors, all the energy system will be supervised by a master center that analyzes the information that arrives from the sensors and remote terminal units (RTU). This expert system solves the problems and failures, informs the operators if it is necessary to fix a point of the line. The Master learns the new cases and stores the cases for futures problems. So, when the energy arrives at homes, it comes with a few losses thanks to master center and then it is up to the user to be efficient.

In the cities, every day there are installed various energy efficiency technologies, whereby electric utilities and companies in the sector must make known the operation of these tools. For this reason, the decision makers in the electricity sector should create programs to disseminate this technology, and with the help of users, achieve significant reduction that minimizes the bill cost.

REFERENCES

[1] Pulido, J.R.G. Ruiz, M.A.G. Herrera, R. Cabello, E. Legrand, S, and Elliman, D, Ontology languages for the semantic web: a never completely updated review. Knowl. Based Syst, 2006, pp. 489-497,.

[2] Colado, Sergio. *SMART CITY; hacia la gestión inteligente.* Barcelona: Marcombo, pp. 91-101, 2014.

[3] Tseng, R. Von, Novak B. Shevde, S, and Grajski KA, Introduction to the alliance for wireless power loosely-coupled wireless power transfer system specification version 1.0. In: Proceedings of the 2013 IEEE wireless power transfer conference, WPT'1, pp. 79, 83, 2013.

[4] Akgul, OU, and Canberk B, Self-organized things (sot): an energy efficient next generation network management. Comput Common, pp. 74:52–62, 2016.

[5] Vollkwyn, C. (in press). Smart in the Spanish power sector. Metering and smart energy international (MSEI), Issue 4, pp. 32-40, 2016.

[6] Ancillotti, Emilio. Raffaele, Bruno, and Marco Conti. The role of communication systems in smart grids: Architectures, technical solutions and research challenges, Computer communications. The International Journal for the Computer and Telecommunications Industry, pp. 1-22, 2013.

[7] T, Guelzim. M.S, Obaidat, and B Sadoum. Introduction and overview of key enabling technologies for smart cities and homes. Smart Cities and Homes. Elsevier, pp. 11, 2016.

[8] Hilbert, M, and Lopez, P., The world's technological capacity to store, communicates, and compute information. Science, pp. 60–5, 2011.

[9] Akgul, OU, and Canberk B. Software defined thinks: A green network management for future smart city architectures. Smart cities and Homes, Key Enabling Technologies. Cambridge: Morgan Kaufmann. Elsevier, pp. 41-44, 2016.

[10] Atzori, L. Iera, A, and Morabito, G. The Internet of things: a survey. Comput Networks. The International Journal of Computer and Telecommunications Networking, pp. 787–805, 2010.

[11] Heiple, S, and Sailor, D. J. Using building energy simulation and geospatial modeling techniques to determine high-resolution building sector energy consumption profiles. Energy and Buildings. An international journal devoted to investigations of energy use and efficiency in buildings, pp. 1426–1436, 2008.

[12] Nemirovskij, G. Nolle, A. Sicilia, A. Ballarini, I, and Corrado, V. Data integration driven ontology design, case study smart city.In: proceedings of the 3rd international conference on web intelligence, mining and semantics (WIMS' 13), pp.34-46, 2013.

[13] Keirstead, J. Samsatli, N, and Shah, N. SynCity: an integrated tool kit for urban energy systems modeling. In: 5th Urban Research Symposium. University of Marseille, pp. 52, 2009.

[14] Van Dam, K., and Keirstead, J. Re-use of an ontology for modeling urban energy systems. In 3rd international conference on next generation infrastructure systems for eco-cities. Shenzhen: Harbin Institute of Technology, pp. 11-13, 2010.

[15] León, Fernández. Desarrollo de una ontología para la seguridad en caso de incendio en la edificación, Unpublished doctoral dissertation, Universidad de Sevilla,pp 36-50, 2008.

[16] Corrado, V, and Ballarini, I. Guidelines for Structuring Energy Data, Report of SEMANCO Project. Retrieved January 10, 2017, from http://semanco-project.eu/index/files/SEMANCOD3.2_20130121.pdf, 2013.

[17] Bonino, B,and Corno, F. DogOnt e ontology modeling for intelligent domotics environments. In: The Semantic Web e ISWC. Springer Berlin Heidelberg, pp. 790-803, 2008.

[18] Grassi, M. Nucci, M, and Piazza F. Towards an ontology framework for intelligent smart home management and energy saving. Proceedings of the 20 II IEEE International Conference on Networking, Sensing and Control Delft, pp. 56-59, 2011.

Bagged Fuzzy k-nearest Neighbors for Identifying Anomalous Propagation in Radar Images

Hansoo Lee, Jonggeun Kim, Suryo Adhi Wibowo and Sungshin Kim
Department of Electrical and Computer Engineering
Pusan National University
Busan, 46241, Republic of Korea
Email: {hansoo, wisekim, suryo, sskim}@pusan.ac.kr

***Abstract*—Several advanced observation devices, such as radiosondes, satellites, and radars, are utilized in practical weather prediction. The weather radar is an essential device because of its broad coverage with excellent resolution. However, the radar inevitably observes meteorologically irrelevant signals. An anomalous propagation echo is a nonprecipitating echo generated by significantly refracted radar beam towards ground or sea surface. In the case, the radar misrecognizes the surface as a meteorological phenomenon. The false observation results may decrease the accuracy of weather prediction result. Therefore, we propose a novel classification method for identifying anomalous propagation echoes in the radar data by combining fuzzy k-nearest neighbors and Hamamoto's bootstrapping algorithm. By using actual occurrence cases of anomalous propagation, we confirm that the proposed method provides good classification results.**

Keywords–Fuzzy k-nearest neighbors; bootstrap aggregating; anomalous propagation; weather prediction.

I. INTRODUCTION

There are several advanced devices to observe meteorologically related events in the atmosphere, such as satellite, ground-based weather radar, radiosonde, and so on. The ground-based weather radar is one of the essential devices because of its wide array of advantages, such as high resolution and a wide range of observation [1]. The primary purposes of utilizing the weather radar are locating precipitation echoes and calculating quantitative precipitation estimation.

The radar transmitter should emit intense electromagnetic waves, and the radar receiver should be designed to obtain weak signals due to the following reasons: the intervals and sizes of the expected reflecting objects such as raindrops and snowflakes; exceedingly small amounts of the waves can return to the radar receiver. As a result, the observed outcomes inevitably contain unwanted signals. Furthermore, the ground-based weather radar is frequently affected by return signals that do not originate from the precipitation echoes, such as stationary or moving objects in the atmosphere. Even refracted radar beams towards the ground make significant false signals in the radar image.

In actual weather prediction, hence, there is a quality control process [2] to remove the nonprecipitating echoes. The quality control process highly relied on the expert's knowledge at the beginning. However, currently applied quality control process utilizes data mining courtesy of advances in techniques. For example, an anomalous propagation, which appears by abnormally refracted radar beam towards ground or sea surface, is one of the representative nonprecipitating echoes. There are many successful research results using data mining method for identifying the anomalous propagation: artificial neural network [3][4][5], fuzzy inference system [6][7], Bayesian classifier [8][9] and case study [10].

In this paper, we propose a novel approach of k-nearest neighbor algorithm by combining Hamamoto's bootstrapping method and fuzzy set theory for identifying the anomalous propagation echo. The k-nearest neighbor is one of the most popular data mining techniques because of its simple operation principle and good performance. Also, Hamamoto's bootstrapping method, which is a variant of the bootstrap aggregating method, has already proved its ability to improve classification accuracy by comparative studies.

The rest of the paper organized as follows. In Section 2, we describe the characteristics of anomalous propagation echo. In Section 3, we explain not only the proposed algorithm but its components in detail. After experimental results and analysis in Section 4, we elucidate conclusions and future works.

II. ANOMALOUS PROPAGATION ECHO

The weather radar observes floating objects in the atmosphere by transmitting and receiving intense electromagnetic waves as other kinds of remote sensing devices do. Therefore, pathways of the waves highly depend on the atmospheric conditions, such as temperature, humidity, and so on. The conditions refract the paths to abnormal directions. As shown in Figure 1, the pathways can be classified into four different types: sub-refraction, normal refraction, super-refraction and ducting.

The sub-refraction indicates a radar beam path refracted the opposite direction of the surface more than the normal refraction. And the super-refraction means a radar beam path bent the direction of the surface more. Further, a radar beam can be stuck in a certain atmospheric layer if it refracted more severe than a critical gradient. Considering that the weather radar assumes the altitude of the objects based on the normal refraction, the other types of refracted radar beams can cause a severe error in radar data.

As shown in Figure 1, there is a chance to miss the precipitation echo when the sub-refraction occurs. Even if the refracted radar beam can detect the precipitation echo, the miscalculated altitude of the echo causes erroneous observation results. Also, when the super-refraction or ducting occur, the

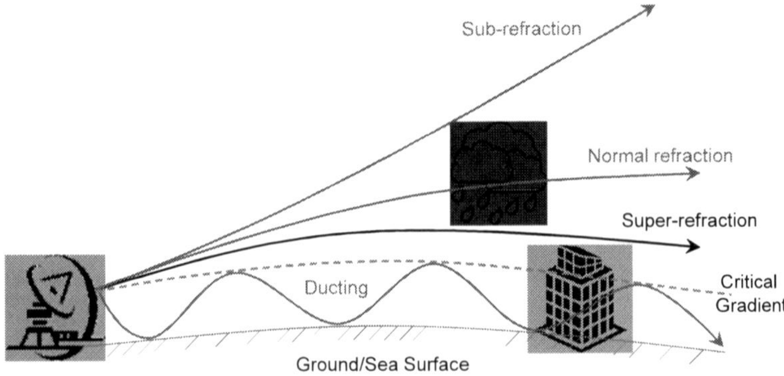

Figure 1. Anomalous propagation echo

radar beam faces on the surface as shown in Figure 1. Then the weather radar will get return signals that do not originate from the precipitation echoes, such as geographic features or meteorologically unrelated floating objects in the atmosphere. Usually, the refracted radar beams towards the surface make severe false observation results in the radar data. For example, the wrong rainfall estimation like an overestimation of rainfall quantity. Furthermore, it also can miss the precipitation echo.

In weather prediction process, meteorologists utilize several complex rules to identify the anomalous propagation echo in radar images. The representative rules are listed as follows.

1) The echo has near-zero Doppler velocity.
   a) On ground surface $= 0$ m/s.
   b) On sea surface ≈ 0 m/s.
2) The echo has discontinuous reflectivity distribution in vertical and horizontal directions.
3) The echo usually locates at low altitude which makes difficult to separate precipitation echoes at the similar region.

According to the list, it is reasonable to consider Doppler velocity, reflectivity, and altitude as classification attributes. In this paper, we chose six classification inputs based on the features: minimum and average Doppler velocity; minimum, maximum and average reflectivity; centroid altitude.

III. Bagged Fuzzy k-Nearest Neighbors

The nearest neighbor algorithm, first introduced in [11], is a nonparametric method for pattern classification based on instances. It has become an active research area in machine learning since proposed. Its popular variant, called the k-nearest neighbor algorithm, is selected as one of the top ten algorithms in data mining [12]. The primary advantages of the k-nearest neighbor algorithm are its simplicity to use and also its often good performance. However, it has also some drawbacks: the necessity of storage, low efficiency of the computation of the decision rule, low tolerance to noise, and high dependency on the given instances [13]. Therefore, lots of researches have been conducted to solve the problems.

The fundamental improvements over k-nearest neighbors are as follows. The first is applying weights in k-nearest neighbors, called as wk-nearest neighbors [14]. The second is generating an artificial training set by using a bootstrapping method. The classic bootstrapping, which changes the training set slightly, has a weak influence to the k-NN because the algorithm is stable. However, bootstrapping method by [15] have a positive effect on improving performances of the k-nearest neighbors classifier. The third is using fuzzy set theory in k-nearest neighbors, called as fuzzy k-nearest neighbors [16].

We select the second and third approaches to improve a performance of k-nearest neighbors algorithm in this paper. The rest of this section organizes as follow. First, we describe the Hamamoto's bootstrapping method and the fuzzy k-nearest neighbor algorithm in sequence. After that, we elucidate our proposed method.

A. Hamamoto's Bootstrapping Method

Bootstrap aggregating, called as bagging, is one of ensemble methods, which uses random sampling methods to improve the performance of the classifier by allowing the classifier to utilize newly created training samples [17]. The classical bagging uses random sampling with replacement to generate samples.

An attempt of combining the bagging with k-nearest neighbors already conducted, but the outcomes were not satisfactory because the k-nearest neighbors is a stable algorithm [17]. In other words, small changes in the training samples do not lead to improving the performance of the classifier significantly. However, Hamamoto's bootstrapping methods [15], one of variant bagging methods, showed remarkable classification results with k-nearest neighbors. We selected the Hamamoto's bootstrapping II method among four different suggestions to creating training samples. The main reason why we chose the way among them is that all the original training samples participate in generating bootstrap samples by the locally weighted sum.

Figure 2 describes the Hamamoto's bootstrapping II method when $k = 3$ in a binary class problem. Let us assume that there are given samples as shown in Figure 2(a). As a first step of the bootstrapping method, it separates the given samples according to its class which is expressed as white

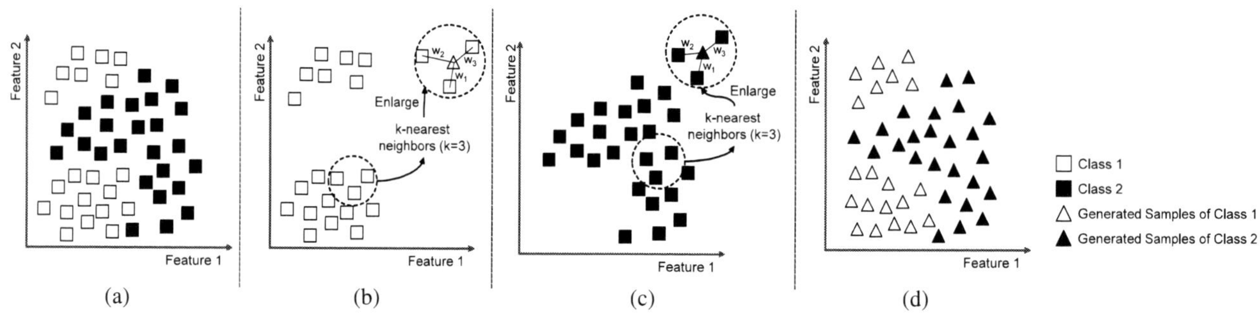

Figure 2. Hamamoto's bootstrap II method: (a) original samples, (b) class 1 data, (c) class 2 data, (d) generated samples

squares in Figure 2(b) and black squares in Figure 2(c). After separation process, it derives nearest neighbor samples of each training sample by utilizing k-nearest neighbor including the selected one. Then, the bootstrapping sample is created using the selected samples and locally weighted sum as shown in (1).

$$\mathbf{x}_i^b = \sum_{j=0}^{r} \omega_j \mathbf{x}_{i,j} = \omega_0 \mathbf{x}_{i,0} + \omega_1 \mathbf{x}_{i,1} + \cdots + \omega_r \mathbf{x}_{i,r} \tag{1}$$

where $\mathbf{x_i^b}$ means the i-th bootstrap sample, and $\mathbf{x_{i,j}}$ indicates the j-th nearest neighbor sample of the i-th original sample. The ω_j means weight derived by (2).

$$\omega_j = \frac{\Delta_j}{\sum_{c=0}^{r} \Delta_c}, \qquad 0 \le j \le r \tag{2}$$

where Δ_j is chosen from a uniform distribution. As shown in Figure 2(b) and Figure 2(c), the bagging samples are represented as triangular-shape, and their color indicates class information. Finally, it is possible to obtain bagging samples, as shown in Figure 2(d), by repeating the mentioned process until all of the original data is selected.

B. Fuzzy k-Nearest Neighbors

The fundamental principle of the fuzzy k-nearest neighbors is to assign membership as a function of the selected sample's distance from its nearest neighbors and memberships of the neighbors in the possible classes [16]. The scheme is similar to the k-nearest neighbors in the sense that there is a search process for the training sample set. However, the class assign process differs significantly from the search process. The membership of the sample x is computed by (3).

$$u_i(x) = \frac{\sum_{j=1}^{k} u_{ij} \left(\frac{1}{\|x - x_j\|^{\frac{2}{(m-1)}}} \right)}{\sum_{j=1}^{k} \left(\frac{1}{\|x - x_j\|^{\frac{2}{(m-1)}}} \right)} \tag{3}$$

where k is the number of nearest neighbors, i indicates class, j is an index of the nearest neighbors, and m is a parameter to determine a type of distance. The most frequently used distance is the Euclidean distance ($m = 2$) when the attributes of the samples are normalized.

Also, it is necessary to define $u_{i,j}$ because the parameter determines class membership as shown in (4).

$$u_{i,j} = \begin{cases} 0.51 + (n_j/k) * 0.49, & \text{if } j = i \\ (n_j/k) * 0.49, & \text{if } j \neq i \end{cases} \tag{4}$$

where n_j is the number of the neighbors which belong to the jth class. This method makes the samples fuzzified by considering the labels of the samples and its neighbors. By utilizing (3), (4), and inverses of the distances from the nearest neighbors, the class of given sample with unknown label can be derived.

C. Proposed Approach

In this paper, we propose a novel nearest neighbor method named bagged fuzzy k-nearest neighbors classifier to improve classification performance by combining two techniques, fuzzy k-nearest neighbors and Hamamoto's bootstrapping II method. Figure 3 shows an overview of the proposed system.

At first, a hierarchical clustering categorizes a given radar data for deriving input attributes. Theoretically, there are a lot of data points to consider in the radar data due to its wide range of observation: for example, over 9 million points should be considered if a radar has 240km observation radius along 10km altitude. Therefore, for deriving attributes efficiently, we applied a hierarchical clustering. After the clustering process, it is possible to use the clusters as training data. From the clusters, we derived six attributes for classification: centroid altitude of the cluster; mean and maximum reflectivity; minimum, maximum and mean Doppler velocity. The reason why we selected these attributes is to reflect expert's knowledge mentioned the previous section.

The training data is used to generate the N number of the artificial training dataset. Simultaneously, the parameter k is derived by k-fold cross validation method using the original training dataset. Including the initial and artificial training datasets, it is possible to implement the bagged fuzzy k-nearest neighbors by utilizing the $(N + 1)$ datasets.

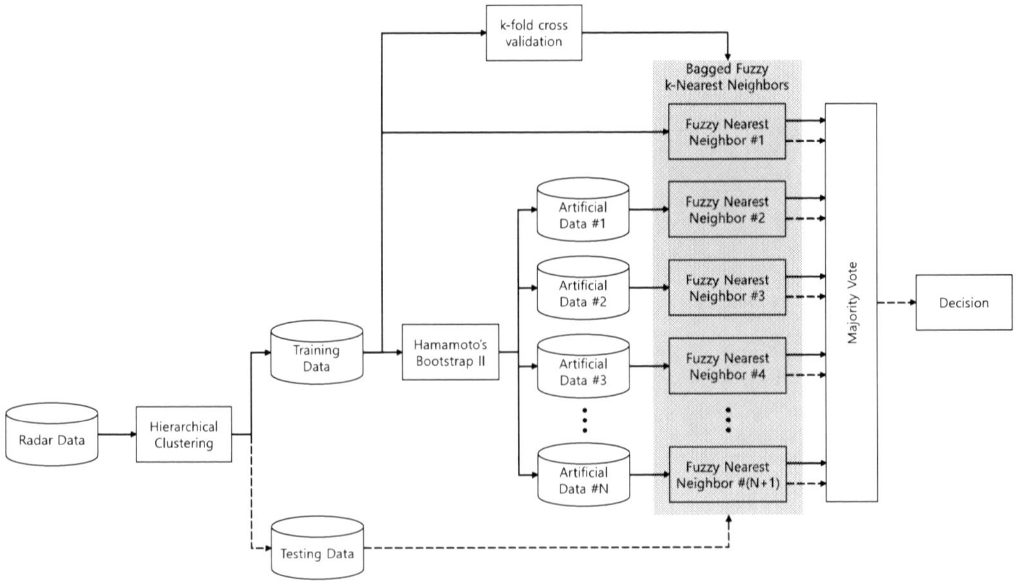

Figure 3. Overview of proposed method

Finally, a sample with an unknown class from the testing dataset can obtain its class by the majority vote process of the proposed classifier as shown in (5).

$$\text{Decision}(X) = \arg\max \sum_{j=1}^{N+1} I\left(\text{FNN}_j(X) = i\right) \quad (5)$$

where X is an attribute vector from learning data, which consists of six elements mentioned above. And $I(\cdot)$ is an indicator function and FNN_j is a j-th fuzzy k-nearest neighbors classifier. Note that the N should be even to avoid a tie result of the majority voting process.

IV. Experimental Results

For evaluating and verifying the proposed method, we used actual anomalous propagation echo occurrence cases. As mentioned earlier, we derived six attributes as inputs for classification according to experts' knowledge: centroid altitude of the cluster; mean and maximum reflectivity; minimum, maximum and mean Doppler velocity.

Figure 4 shows a complicated example of anomalous propagation echo appearance. A significant precipitation echo exists on the left-upper side of Figure 4(a). And the central region shows the anomalous propagation echo. By using the proposed method, we could obtain the successful classification results as shown in Figure 4(b) and (c).

Figure 5 shows another example of the anomalous propagation echo case. Almost all of the observation area is distorted by significant anomalous propagation echo as shown in Figure 5. By using the proposed method, we also could obtain the successful classification results as shown in Figure 5(b) and (c), respectively.

For comparing the performance with other nearest neighbors classifier, we conducted evaluations using accuracy as shown in (6).

$$\text{Accuracy} = \frac{TP + TN}{TP + TN + FP + FN} \quad (6)$$

where TP is true positive, TN is true negative, FP is false positive, and FN is false negative. Also, in this paper, the true indicates the anomalous propagation echo, and the false indicates the non-anomalous propagation echo, respectively.

We compared the proposed method with four kinds of nearest neighbors classifiers: 1-NN, k-NN, fuzzy k-NN, bagged k-NN. 1-NN showed the worst classification accuracy: 84.96%. k-NN showed 87.61%, and bagged k-NN showed 89.52% accuracy. Fuzzy k-NN showed better accuracy than k-NN: 89.05%. And the proposed method derived the best accuracy: 92.38%. From the experimental results, we can conclude that the proposed method can classify the anomalous propagation echo successfully.

V. Conclusion

An anomalous propagation echo is a nonprecipitating echo generated by significantly refracted radar beam towards the surface. The false observation results may decrease the accuracy of weather prediction. Therefore, we proposed a novel approach of k-nearest neighbor algorithm by combining Hamamoto's bootstrapping II method and fuzzy k-nearest neighbors. The fuzzy k-nearest neighbor proves its remarkable performance with simple operation. Also, Hamamoto's bootstrapping II method has demonstrated its ability to improve classification accuracy by comparative studies. By experiments with actual anomalous propagation echo cases, we proved that the proposed method could classify the echo from radar data successfully.

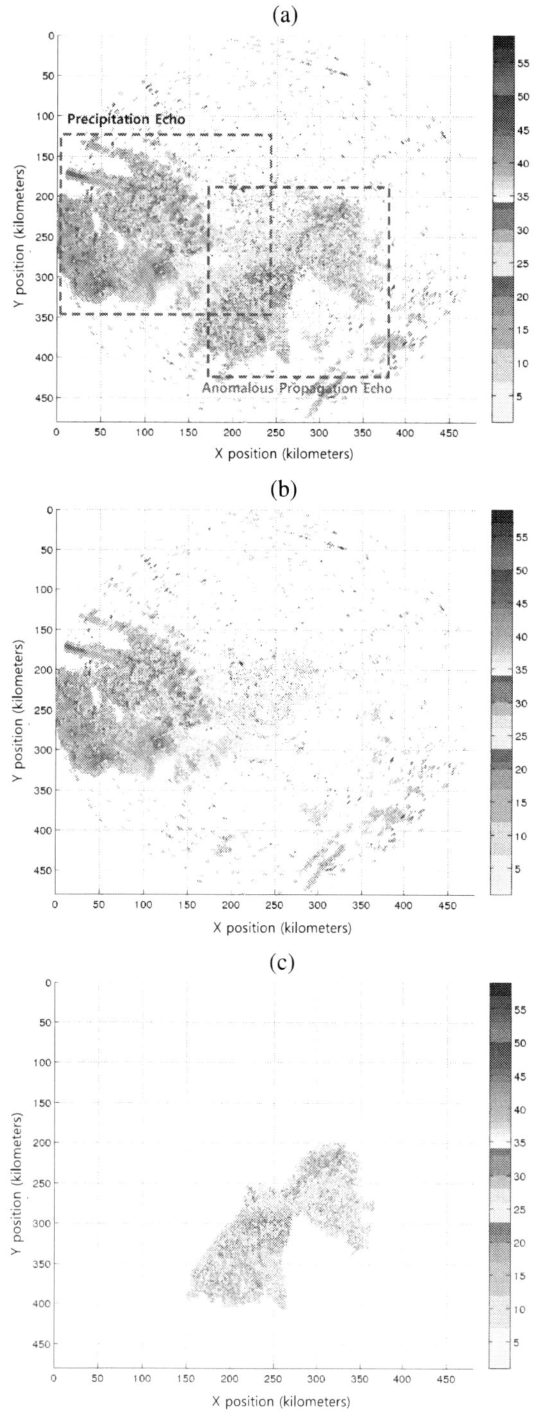

Figure 4. Experimental result, case 1: (a) original radar image, (b) image without classified anomalous propagation echo, (c) classified anomalous propagation echo

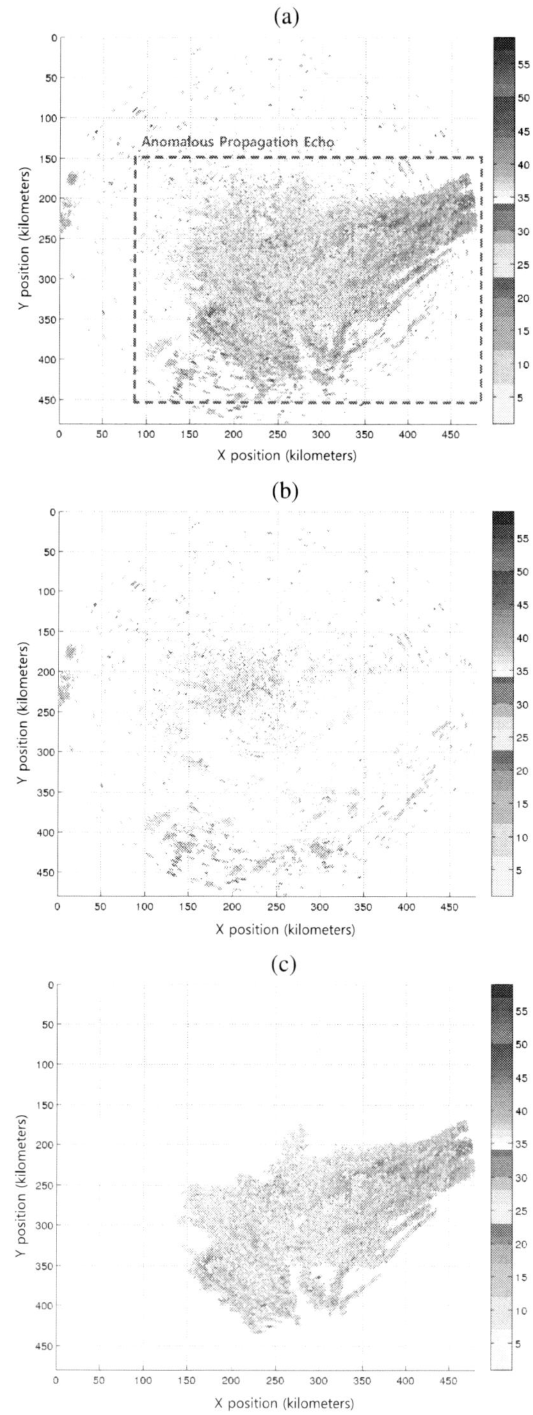

Figure 5. Experimental result, case 2: (a) original radar image, (b) image without classified anomalous propagation echo, (c) classified anomalous propagation echo

In future works, we will try to improve the accuracy of the proposed method. We consider replacing the fuzzification algorithm such as interval type-2 fuzzy logic. Also, we think it is possible to obtain better classification results by combining clustering methods. Further, we will apply the proposed method to the recognition of other echoes, such as chaff echo, interference patterns, and so on.

ACKNOWLEDGMENT

This research was supported by the MOTIE (Ministry of Trade, Industry & Energy), Korea, under the Industry Convergence Liaison Robotics Creative Graduates Education Program supervised by the KIAT (N0001126).

REFERENCES

[1] I. S. Merrill, "Introduction to radar systems," Mc Grow-Hill, 2001.

[2] V. Lakshmanan, A. Fritz, T. Smith, K. Hondl, and G. Stumpf, "An automated technique to quality control radar reflectivity data," Journal of applied meteorology and climatology, vol. 46, no. 3, 2007, pp. 288–305.

[3] R. B. da Silveira and A. R. Holt, "An automatic identification of clutter and anomalous propagation in polarization-diversity weather radar data using neural networks," IEEE transactions on geoscience and remote sensing, vol. 39, no. 8, 2001, pp. 1777–1788.

[4] M. Grecu and W. F. Krajewski, "An efficient methodology for detection of anomalous propagation echoes in radar reflectivity data using neural networks," Journal of Atmospheric and Oceanic Technology, vol. 17, no. 2, 2000, pp. 121–129.

[5] ——, "Detection of anomalous propagation echoes in weather radar data using neural networks," IEEE transactions on geoscience and remote sensing, vol. 37, no. 1, 1999, pp. 287–296.

[6] M. Berenguer, D. Sempere-Torres, C. Corral, and R. Sánchez-Diezma, "A fuzzy logic technique for identifying nonprecipitating echoes in radar scans," Journal of Atmospheric and Oceanic Technology, vol. 23, no. 9, 2006, pp. 1157–1180.

[7] Y.-H. Cho, G. W. Lee, K.-E. Kim, and I. Zawadzki, "Identification and removal of ground echoes and anomalous propagation using the characteristics of radar echoes," Journal of Atmospheric and Oceanic Technology, vol. 23, no. 9, 2006, pp. 1206–1222.

[8] J. Pamment and B. Conway, "Objective identification of echoes due to anomalous propagation in weather radar data," Journal of Atmospheric and Oceanic Technology, vol. 15, no. 1, 1998, pp. 98–113.

[9] J. R. Peter, A. Seed, and P. J. Steinle, "Application of a bayesian classifier of anomalous propagation to single-polarization radar reflectivity data," Journal of Atmospheric and Oceanic Technology, vol. 30, no. 9, 2013, pp. 1985–2005.

[10] W. F. Krajewski and B. Vignal, "Evaluation of anomalous propagation echo detection in wsr-88d data: A large sample case study," Journal of Atmospheric and Oceanic Technology, vol. 18, no. 5, 2001, pp. 807–814.

[11] E. Fix and J. L. Hodges Jr, "Discriminatory analysis-nonparametric discrimination: consistency properties," DTIC Document, Tech. Rep., 1951.

[12] X. Wu, V. Kumar, J. R. Quinlan, J. Ghosh, Q. Yang, H. Motoda, G. J. McLachlan, A. Ng, B. Liu, and S. Y. Philip, "Top 10 algorithms in data mining," Knowledge and information systems, vol. 14, no. 1, 2008, pp. 1–37.

[13] J. Derrac, S. García, and F. Herrera, "Fuzzy nearest neighbor algorithms: Taxonomy, experimental analysis and prospects," Information Sciences, vol. 260, 2014, pp. 98–119.

[14] S. A. Dudani, "The distance-weighted k-nearest-neighbor rule," IEEE Transactions on Systems, Man, and Cybernetics, no. 4, 1976, pp. 325–327.

[15] Y. Hamamoto, S. Uchimura, and S. Tomita, "A bootstrap technique for nearest neighbor classifier design," IEEE Transactions on Pattern Analysis and Machine Intelligence, vol. 19, no. 1, 1997, pp. 73–79.

[16] J. M. Keller, M. R. Gray, and J. A. Givens, "A fuzzy k-nearest neighbor algorithm," IEEE transactions on systems, man, and cybernetics, no. 4, 1985, pp. 580–585.

[17] L. Breiman, "Bagging predictors," Machine learning, vol. 24, no. 2, 1996, pp. 123–140.

Evaluation of Reference Model for Thermal Energy System Based on Machine Learning Algorithm

Minsung Kim
School of Energy Systems Engineering
Chung-Ang University
Seoul, Republic of Korea
email: minsungk@cau.ac.kr

Young-Soo Lee
Thermal Energy System Laboratory
Korea Institute of Energy Research
Daejeon, Republic of Korea
email: yslee@kier.re.kr

***Abstract*—Since thermal energy systems are comprised in a number of heat exchangers and fluid machinery, it is complicated and time consuming to analyze the systems mathematically. For heat pumps, a number of mathematical studies have been carried out to identify their operating status; however, accurate models are very difficult to develop due to numerous cases of different installation and operating conditions. As an alternative way to estimate the performance, a methodology using machine learning algorithm is introduced to develop a reference model. A steady-state detector with a simple low pass filter is applied to filter signals. Once steady state of the system is identified, the real-time measurements are collected to train the system model. From the study, the semi-expert based learning algorithm is effective to develop reference models of heat pump systems.**

Keywords-Thermal energy systems; Steady state; Machine learning; Fault detection and diagnosis.

I. INTRODUCTION

An increasing emphasis on energy saving and environmental conservation requires air conditioners and heat pumps to be highly efficient. In the first place, a variety of research and development on a cycle as well as its basic components have been performed to increase overall efficiency of heat pump systems. A survey of over 55,000 residential and commercial units found the refrigerant charge to be incorrect in more than 60 % of the systems [1]. Another independent survey of 1500 rooftop units showed that the average efficiency was only 80 % of the expected value, primarily due to improper refrigerant charge [2]. To this end, various technologies were reported to analyze the performance of heat pump systems including the function of fault detection and diagnosis [3]-[5].

The development of Fault Detection and Diagnosis (FDD) method includes a laboratory phase during which fault-free and faulty operations are mapped, and an analytical phase during which FDD algorithms are formulated. These techniques typically produce the reference data under the combinations of test conditions which were modulated in laboratory. However, it is very difficult to produce a set of reference data in field systems since the configurations of heat pumps are different. Even in the cases of previous studies performed in laboratories, great efforts are taken to build up reference experiment. From this end, a machine learning algorithm is introduced in this study to produce the reference model out of field operating data of a heat pump system. The reference model was generated at steady states. To generate machine learning procedure, two environmental chambers were programmed randomly reflecting field environment. From the study, a reference model of the heat pump system was obtained very handful and convenient way with an acceptable accuracy.

In this paper, a reference model was described for a heat pump system in section II and the model was statistically evaluated in section III. From the analysis, methodological approach was introduced for a machine learning in section IV.

II. STEADY STATE MODELING OF HEAT PUMPS

In this study, the FDD process was envisioned to be performed every time the system is in steady state. The concept of the steady-state detector originates from noise filter theory. When a system is not steady, thermodynamic system parameters are highly unstable. The variance, or standard deviation, of important parameters is typically utilized to indicate the statistical spread within the data distribution and can be used to characterize random variation of the measured signals.

A. Determination of characteristic variables

Typical temperature-entropy (*T-s*) diagram presenting a vapor compression cycle is plotted in Figure 1. Since temperature measurements are most suitable and costly effective, the 7 parameters were selected as characteristic variables. The selected seven features are: Evaporator exit refrigerant saturation temperature (T_E), evaporator exit refrigerant superheat (T_{sh}), condenser inlet refrigerant saturation temperature (T_C), compressor discharge refrigerant temperature (T_D), condenser exit liquid line refrigerant subcooled temperature (T_{sc}), evaporator air temperature change (ΔT_{EA}), and condenser air temperature change (ΔT_{CA}).

As inputs of the characteristic variables, three parameters were chosen; outdoor dry-bulb temperature (T_{OD}), indoor dry-bulb temperature (T_{ID}), and indoor dew point temperature (T_{IDP}). The reference model was developed with the 3 independent variables and the 7 dependent variables.

The temperature sensors are T-type thermocouples with 0.5°C of uncertainties. Although the above features are limited only by 7 points and the temperature sensors are with

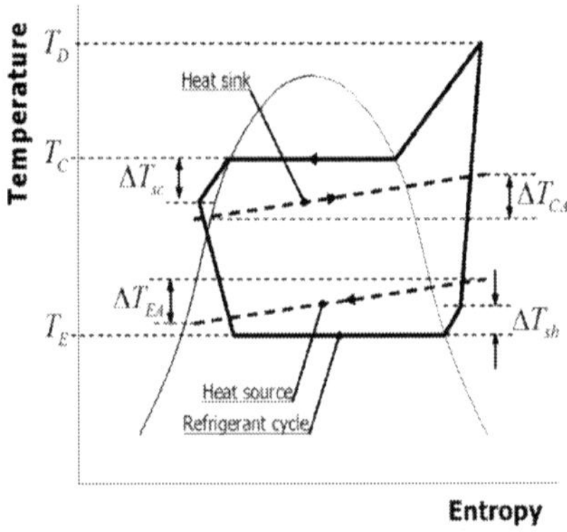

Figure 1. *T-s* diagram of a vapor compression heat pump system

relatively large uncertainties, limited measurements are maintained to reflect field measurements.

The variables were regressed upon the generated from the experimental database. Equations were in the form of the 1st, 2nd, and 3rd order Multivariate Polynomial Regression (MPR) models. After the residuals of the characteristic parameters can be obtained from the system, FDD process identifies defects of the system by analyzing the residuals with thresholds value which determine the system status.

B. Determination of characteristic variables

According to the features defined above, the variables were regressed upon the database generated from the experiments. Equations below show a general form of the regressed equations for the ith feature (or i^{th} dependent variable) as the 2nd and 3rd order MPR models.

$$\phi_i^{(2)} = a_0 + a_1 T_{OD} + a_2 T_{ID} + a_3 T_{IDP} + a_4 T_{OD}{}^2 + a_5 T_{ID}{}^2 + a_6 T_{IDP}{}^2 + a_7 T_{OD} T_{ID} + a_8 T_{ID} T_{IDP} + a_9 T_{IDP} T_{OD} \quad (1)$$

$$\phi_i^{(3)} = \phi_i^{(2)} + a_{10} T_{OD}{}^3 + a_{11} T_{ID}{}^3 + a_{12} T_{IDP}{}^3 + a_{13} T_{OD} T_{ID} T_{IDP} + a_{14} T_{OD}{}^2 T_{ID} + a_{15} T_{OD}{}^2 T_{IDP} + a_{16} T_{ID}{}^2 T_{OD} + a_{17} T_{ID}{}^2 T_{IDP} + a_{18} T_{IDP}{}^2 T_{OD} + a_{19} T_{IDP}{}^2 T_{ID} \quad (2)$$

From the above equations, residuals of the characteristic parameters can be obtained. After the residuals are measured from the system, FDD process identifies defects of the system by analyzing the residuals with thresholds value which determine the system status.

C. Machine learning process

Once the steady-state is identified, key performance parameters were evaluated from the references. We validated measured Coefficient of Performance (COP) – an efficiency parameter – and heating/cooling capacity by comparing the manufacturer's data. If there is no manufacturer's data, the system with no fault incorporated was pre-operated to evaluate the reference operation of the system. Once the key parameters are evaluated as no fault operation, the measured features are used to train the reference module. When the COP or heating capacity is out of range from the reference value, the system is assigned to be at a faulty status and FDD procedure is carried out.

III. Validation of the Machine Learning Based Reference Model

To determine a realistic value of the threshold, validation of the measurements is mandatory. We counted three uncertainties of steady state, repeatability, and model itself. Naturally, the system measurements have uncertainties due to sensors – mostly thermocouples – and due to lack of measurement repeatability. Once the uncertainties by sensors will be evaluated, model uncertainty will be evaluated by the sensor uncertainties. In this section, the uncertainties are evaluated in statistical values.

A. Uncertainties due to steady-state variation and lack of measurement repeatability

The uncertainty of a thermocouple may come from measurement noise and drift. Considering that the measurement noise behaves like zero-mean white noise, its natural variation can be characterized closely by the steady-state standard deviation, $\sigma_{i,SS}$. Thermocouple drift is the measurement bias that varies over longer time periods than noise. However, the thermocouple drift can be regarded as negligible in this research since the same built-in sensors are used for model development and application to the tested system for FDD, thus their bias has been considered in the reference model measurements for this investigation. To observe the repeatability of the system measurements, we analyzed 38 repetitive tests of Kim et al. (2006) [6]. The feature standard deviations from repeatability tests, $\sigma_{i,Repeat}$, are listed in Table 1. In the table, the measurement uncertainties were provided due to by due to steady-state variation, $\sigma_{i,SS}$, and due to by the variation from test-to-test (measurement repeatability), $\sigma_{i,Repeat}$, for similar test conditions. These two values will be used to calculate the total residual threshold uncertainty for each feature.

TABLE I. STANDARD DEVIATION OF THE SELECTED FEATURES

Units of °C	T_{sh}	T_{sc}	T_E	T_D	T_C	ΔT_{CA}	ΔT_{EA}
Steady-state standard deviation ($\sigma_{i,SS}$)	0.124	0.052	0.024	0.058	0.035	0.063	0.058
Standard deviation from repeatability tests ($\sigma_{i,Repeat}$)	0.101	0.156	0.084	0.280	0.166	0.088	0.111

B. Uncertainties due to the reference models

Since measurements are used with the reference model predictions to determine residuals, the square-root of the sum of residuals presents a non-Gaussian root-mean-square (RMS) error. Thus we analyze the no-fault measurements distribution in detail to provide the methodology for determining a proper value of the threshold ε_i. In most cases, it is hard to obtain a reference model covering all operating conditions. To train a reference model after installation, a real-time decision of fault-free or faulty status is mandatory. In contrast to the steady-state and repetition uncertainty, the model uncertainty comes from the imperfections associated with any mathematical model. We define average bias of the model estimation as the averaged residual between the model and current measurement in no zero-mean noise.

$$\sigma^2_{i,\mathrm{NF}} = \sigma^2_{i,\mathrm{SS}} + \sigma^2_{i,\mathrm{Model}} \quad (3)$$

TABLE II. NET MODEL UNCERTAINTIES OF THE FEATURES USING THE 1ST, 2ND, AND 3RD ORDER MPR MODELS

Model uncertainties, $\sigma_{i,\mathrm{Model}}$ (°C)	T_{sh}	T_{sc}	T_E	T_D	T_C	ΔT_{CA}	ΔT_{EA}
1st order MPR model	0.557	0.244	0.549	0.799	0.179	0.150	0.581
2nd order MPR model	0.328	0.197	0.147	0.319	0.047	0.040	0.131
3rd order MPR model	0.197	0.133	0.123	0.250	0.029	0.019	0.071

Model standard deviation, $\sigma_{i,\mathrm{Model}}$, characterizes model uncertainty. Since zero-mean noise uncertainty ($\sigma_{i,\mathrm{SS}}$) and model uncertainties ($\sigma_{i,\mathrm{Model}}$) amplify the variability of residuals independently, it is reasonable to assume that no joint effect exists between the two uncertainties. Therefore, the covariance between the two uncertainties ($\sigma_{i,\mathrm{SS}} \cdot \sigma_{i,\mathrm{Model}}$) is zero, and $\sigma_{i,\mathrm{NF}}$ will be a squared sum of $\sigma_{i,\mathrm{SS}}$ and $\sigma_{i,\mathrm{Model}}$ as shown below. By combining the equation with Table 1, $\sigma_{i,\mathrm{Model}}$ can be estimated in Table 2. From the evaluated uncertainty, the no fault threshold is determined in section IV.

IV. DETERMINATION OF NO FAULT THRESHOLD

In this section, confidence intervals – the thresholds of the uncertainties evaluated in previous section – will be determined for required credibility.

A. *Confidence interval, k_1, for the steady-state uncertainty*

Since we use measurements and standard deviations in a preset moving window, their distribution depends on the characteristics of the moving window. When n no-fault data are sampled Gaussian with standard deviation, σ_i, the t can be defined below, where μ_i is the current mean of the moving window of n samples. In such a case, t follows a Student's t-distribution with $n-1$ degrees of freedom. When we set $1-\alpha$ probability that the two values are equal ($x_i = \mu_i$), the confidence interval, $k_1 = t_{\alpha/2,n-1}$, is described as below where $t_{\alpha/2,n-1}$ is a two-sided confidence interval.

$$P\left(|x_i - \mu_i| < t_{\alpha/2,n-1}\frac{\sigma_i}{\sqrt{n}}\right) = 1-\alpha \quad (6)$$

With a $1-\alpha = 99$ % confidence, $t_{0.005,9} = 3.25$ which is larger than Gaussian distribution of 2.58. Table 3 shows the values of $k_1 = t_{\alpha/2,9}$. For 99 % confidence (or credibility) level, k_1 is 3.25.

TABLE III. TWO-SIDED CONFIDENCE INTERVALS WITH DEGREES OF FREEDOM OF FOUR AND NINE

$1-\alpha$ (%)	80.0	90.0	95.0	99.0
$\alpha/2$ (%)	10.0	5.0	2.5	0.5
$t_{\alpha/2,4}$ [1]	1.533	2.132	2.776	4.604
$k_1 = t_{\alpha/2,9}$ [2]	1.383	1.833	2.262	3.250

[1] 5 sample moving window
[2] 10 sample moving window

B. *Confidence interval, k_2, for model uncertainty*

The distribution of the T_{sh} residual using MPR model applied to the NFSS data is a Gaussian. However, residuals near zero are distributed narrower than a Gaussian. At high residual values where $|r(T_{sh})| > 1.67$°C (3.0°F), a Gaussian assumption underestimates the probability. From the Gaussian approach, 99 % of data fall within the range of ±0.6°C (±1.08°F), but no-fault test data have a wider range of ±0.78°C (±1.41°F) to cover 99 % of all data.

C. *Confidence interval, k_3, for lack of measurement repeatability*

Repetitive measurements of a random variable will follow a Gaussian distribution, thus, under similar measurement conditions; repetitively measured feature residuals will also follow a Gaussian distribution. Table 5 shows the confidence interval with regard to the confidence level for a Gaussian distribution at various confidence levels. For example, with 99 % credibility, k_3 equals 2.576. From the confidence intervals k_1, k_2, and k_3 obtained above, Table 5 is calculated for the feature thresholds with 50 %, 95 % and 99 % credibility for the moving window size of 10 samples.

TABLE IV. TWO-SIDED CONFIDENCE INTERVAL OF THE SEVEN FEATURES FOR THE 3RD ORDER MPR MODEL (TEMPERATURE IN °C)

$1-\alpha$ (%)		75.0	97.5	99.5
$k_2 = t_{\alpha/2,n-1}$	T_{sh}	1.00	2.26	2.96
	T_{sc}	0.93	2.22	3.37
	T_E	1.10	2.06	2.65
	T_D	1.15	1.96	2.63
	T_C	1.03	2.03	3.03
	ΔT_{CA}	1.14	1.95	2.64
	ΔT_{EA}	0.95	2.16	3.22

TABLE V. FEATURE THRESHOLDS AT DIFFERENT CONFIDENCE LEVELS FOR 10 SAMPLES (TEMPERATURE IN °C)

Threshold of the features	T_{sh}	T_{sc}	T_E	T_D	T_C	ΔT_{CA}	ΔT_{EA}
50 % credibility, $\varepsilon_{i,0.50}$	0.130	0.134	0.092	0.243	0.082	0.064	0.086
95 % credibility, $\varepsilon_{i,0.95}$	0.496	0.411	0.323	0.755	0.237	0.187	0.271
99 % credibility, $\varepsilon_{i,0.99}$	0.735	0.574	0.424	0.983	0.313	0.248	0.373

V. CONCLUSION

In this study, we developed no fault reference model of vapor compression heat pump by machine learning process with statistical evaluations. Characteristic variables were assumed to behave independently, and uncertainties were estimated in three different ways; steady-state uncertainty, repeatability uncertainty, and reference model uncertainty. From the analysis, we obtained each uncertainty and thresholds depending on the credibility. Distribution of residuals was unique compared to typical Gaussian or student t-distribution, especially larger residuals. To reduce uncertainty that may be occurred by the large residuals, it is necessary to increase threshold values to minimize false detection. From the study, a reference model of the heat pump system was obtained very handful and convenient way with an acceptable accuracy.

ACKNOWLEDGEMENTS

This paper is supported by Korea Evaluation Institute of Industrial Technology (KEIT) (No. 10063187) funded from Ministry of Trade, Industry and Energy of Republic of Korea, and authors appreciate their support.

REFERENCES

[1] J. Proctor, "Residential and small commercial central air conditioning; Rated efficiency isn't automatic," ASHRAE Winter Meeting, Jan. 26, Anaheim, CA., 2004

[2] M. S. Breuker and J. E. Braun, "Evaluating the performance of a fault detection and diagnostic system for vapor compression equipment," Int. J. of HVAC&R Research, vol. 4, no. 4, pp. 401-425, 1998.

[3] T. M. Rossi, "Detection, diagnosis, and evaluation of faults in vapor compression cycle equipment," Ph.D. Dissertation, Purdue Univ., West Lafayette, IN, USA, 1995.

[4] A. S. Glass, P. Gruber, M. Roos, and J. Tödtli, "Qualitative model-based fault detection in air-handling units," IEEE Control Systems Magazine, vol. 15, no. 4, pp. 11-22, 1995.

[5] H. Li, "A decoupling-based unified fault detection and diagnosis approach for packaged air conditioners," Ph.D. Dissertation, Purdue Univ., West Lafayette, IN, USA, 2004.

[6] M. Kim, W. V. Payne, P. A. Domanski, and C. J. L. Hermes, "Performance of a residential heat pump operating in the cooling mode with single faults imposed," NISTIR 7350, National Institute of Standards and Technology, Gaithersburg, MD, USA, 2006.

Human-Centric Internet of Things. Problems and Challenges

Ekaterina D. Kazimirova
AO Kaspersky Lab
Moscow, Russia
e-mail: Ekaterina.Kazimirova@kaspersky.com

Abstract — **The paper analyzes the Internet of Things from the perspective of designing a new ecosystem for humans. Both the opportunities and the threats are analyzed. It is concluded that Internet of Things platforms will eventually integrate all aspects of human life, creating a new information environment that will help people to achieve maximum self-fulfillment and significantly greater life expectancy.**

Keywords* - *Internet of Things; Industrial Internet of Things; neuromorphic computing; affective computing.

I. INTRODUCTION

Technology is rapidly changing our lives. The evolvement of the Internet of Things (IoT) is a major new technology trend that is changing the principles on which the relationship between people and things has been based for hundreds of years. It is creating a new environment, where people are surrounded by "living" things. Like any radically new environment, it has both opportunities and dangers in store for us. Naturally, we cannot identify all the benefits and risks of the various development scenarios from the current observation point, but we should certainly try, because this will help to crystalize the principles on which the Internet of Things platforms that are now emerging should be based. Tomorrow, these platforms will be our new habitat. In this paper, we look at some of the problems and issues associated with the Internet of Things as a new ecosystem.

Our idea is that, in order for a secure and truly useful human-centric Internet of Things to be built, IoT platforms should from the outset be developed to integrate the most important areas of human life, to include a comprehensive set of features related to caring for people's health and supporting them in their self-development and leisure, rather than simply resolving individual problems (that is, making it more convenient to control specific sets of things).

In this paper, we look at the current state of the Internet of Things, as well as its development prospects, from different viewpoints, including that of security. This is an extensive subject area and we do not undertake to address all the issues. This article is an attempt to outline the problem and the main approaches for addressing it.

The paper is structured as follows. In Section II, we discuss the Internet of Things as a new environment, and in Section III, briefly discuss IoT and IIoT security. Conclusions and future work are indicated in Section IV.

II. INTERNET OF THINGS AS A NEW ENVIRONMENT

A. Internet of Things Today

Although the Internet of Things is a universally recognized global trend, it has not yet evolved as a generally accepted practice, nor as a unified set of technologies, methods and approaches, nor as a new environment for people to live in. Humanity may be able to break through the new technological barrier but is as yet unable to see what is beyond the line of the horizon.

For now, it is clear that:

- Things will have built-in microchips or RFID tags.
- Things will connect to humans via the Internet.
- People will use mobile apps to control things remotely, such as turning off a forgotten iron from the office.
- Hopefully, things will be able to adapt to people's needs [1].

The first multifunctional personal assistants have the potential to evolve into fully-fledged advisors to humans, to the point of playing a role in forming their life strategies (existing intelligent personal electronic assistants include Amazon Echo [2], Google Assistant [3], and Azuma Hikari produced by Vinclu Inc [4]). These are only the first signs of global changes in the information environment.

B. Internet of Things as a Dream

Many amazing phenomena that people only used to dream about and describe in tales have come to pass – such as the magic bowl of water or crystal ball reflecting things that are happening far away, which has come to life as television and the Internet; the magic flying carpet from oriental stories, which has become the airplane, etc. Note that in fairy tales, things could talk and interact with people in various other ways, helping them or interfering with their plans. It is possible that we have now approached one of the last "fairy-tale" technological barriers – that is, lifelike things that can speak and understand speech, and interact with people in other ways. The right conditions for breaking through that barrier will soon be in place, including the emerging Internet of Things, speech recognition and affective computing.

C. Internet of Things as a New Ecosystem

Such gadgets as smart power outlets, irons, backpacks, etc. are already available on the market. However, it is no coincidence that the European Commission's strategy is based on the human-centric Internet of Things [5]: things should not just have some attributes of intelligence and remote monitoring support (e.g., checking from the office whether the TV set at home is off) – they should eventually make up a new ecosystem centered around humans, who are surrounded by "living", self-aware and context-oriented things. We believe that the role of things in such an ecosystem will go beyond satisfying the simple needs of humans – intelligent things will also become people's advisers, monitor their physiological condition, suggest solutions and scenarios of successful actions (which reminds us of Ariadne's thread from the Ancient Greek myth).

Importantly, things and robots, which are also a form of things (i.e., various artificial personal assistants), are already becoming capable of displaying emotions themselves and, in the near future, will be able to detect emotions in humans – based on their tone of voice, facial expressions, skin reactions, etc. While so far people have been the only sentient and cognizant creatures around, in the future the very environment in which they live will be cognitive and capable of making decisions on its own. We believe that this functionality will be implemented gradually in the process of building IoT platforms.

Note that monitoring the psycho-emotional and physiological status of people has the potential to extend human life: by avoiding functional overload, we can optimize the activity of our organisms and reduce their wear and health risks.

Creating a friendly environment can also be seen as an independent task: imagine walking along the platform waiting for your train, with the pillars smiling at you as you pass them.

D. Changing the Technological Landscape

From the technology viewpoint, there are several major objectives, the primary of which is to create a technological platform that would enable a human-centric Internet of Things to be built.

Consumer IoT platforms should integrate various facets of life – people's need for comfort, emotional support, finding a work and leisure balance, caring for their health. With the help of smart personal assistants, people may be able to optimize not only their everyday affairs, but also their life strategies. Cognitive technologies involved in the dialog between people and machines will help individuals to compensate their cognitive shortcomings and achieve maximum self-fulfillment.

Neuromorphic computing [6][7] is seen as an important element of the computing base for such platforms, since a) it is the intelligence implemented in a thing that makes it truly intelligent, and b) the digitization of everything will result in skyrocketing volumes of data that will need to be handled, and it is best to process part of the data locally (using embedded microchips), rather than in the cloud.

Naturally, information security will be of crucial importance for such systems.

III. SECURITY

The problem of protecting information in IoT must be addressed in an entirely new way, since this is about creating and protecting an ecosystem that will accumulate all kinds of diverse information about people.

In fact, it would be fair to say that people themselves will be integrated into information flows. Clearly, it is essential to maintain the security of data on their health, behavior, future plans and emotional state. Even today, experts emphasize the importance of safeguarding information stored and processed by IoT devices – such as medical data [8]. As technology evolves, such information sometimes becomes too accessible. The new IoT reality and new technologies that provide protection for that reality should develop hand-in-hand.

For Industrial Internet of Things (IIoT), on the contrary, the nearly complete absence of people from industrial processes (humanless technologies) will be an important factor. It remains to be determined in what measure and form humans should be involved in automated industrial processes and the control of their safety and security.

IV. CONCLUSIONS AND FUTURE WORK

The Internet of Things is not simply a range of comforts but a new ecosystem that should be centered around people.

Going forward, different categories of the Internet of Things will be increasingly connected, shaping an integral environment, the essence of which will be in creating a living and thinking space around humans. It should be designed to ensure that people do not simply live in comfort but reach maximum self-fulfillment and the longest lifespan possible.

In the process of building this living and thinking space we are going to face new challenges:

- How can people avoid being lost in the world of things: if the environment becomes more intelligent than its users, how can they keep it under their control?
- How will things interact with each other - what should be the main principles of device-to-device communication?
- How autonomous will those smart things be in making decisions? Should they be allowed to make decisions proactively? How can we make sure that they will behave the way they should?

We believe that further research should be focused on finding answers to these fundamental questions.

Problems associated with protecting the IoT and IIoT ecosystems are different in some essential ways. While in the former case, protection is needed for extremely personalized information flows, in the latter, it is humanless industrial zones that will need to be protected.

ACKNOWLEDGMENTS

The author is grateful to Andrey Lavrentyev, Michael Gusev and Evgeny Volovich for fruitful discussions.

REFERENCES

[1] N. Gershenfeld, R. Krikorian, and D. Cohen, "The Internet of Things," Scientific American, vol. 291, Issue 4, pp. 76–81, Oct. 2004.

[2] What is Amazon Alexa? Available from: https://developer.amazon.com/alexa 2017.06.28

[3] Meet your Google Assistant. Available from: https://assistant.google.com/ 2017.06.28

[4] Azuma Hikari. Official Site. Available from: http://gatebox.ai/hikari/en/ 2017.06.28

[5] Public Report from the Workshop on the Exploitation of Neuromorphic Computing Technologies, Brussels, Feb 2017. Available from: http://ec.europa.eu/newsroom/document.cfm?doc_id=43537 p. 13 2017.06.19

[6] The issues of the "Workshop on the Exploitation of Neuromorphic Computing Technologies" of European Commission. Available from: https://ec.europa.eu/digital-single-market/en/news/workshop-exploitation-neuromorphic-computing-technologies 2017.06.24

[7] S. Furber and K. Meier "Neuromorphic Computing in the Human Brain Project", The issues of Innovation Workshop Exploitation of Neuromorphic Computing Technologies Feb. 2017, Brussels. Available from: http://ec.europa.eu/information_society/newsroom/image/document/2017-8/1_furber_steve_and_meier_karlheinz_CDA4E45F-EF31-6FBF-1642BB9BAB97CEF4_43088.pdf 2017.06.19

[8] S. Lozhkin "Hospitals are under attack in 2016" Available from: https://securelist.com/hospitals-are-under-attack-in-2016/74249/ 2017.06.19

Life Cycle Agent
Beyond Intelligent Manufacturing

Leo van Moergestel, Erik Puik,
Daniël Telgen, Feiko Wielsma, Geoffrey Mastenbroek,
Robbin van den Berg, Arnoud den Haring
Institute for ICT
HU Utrecht University of Applied Sciences
Utrecht, the Netherlands
Email: leo.vanmoergestel@hu.nl

John-Jules Meyer
Intelligent systems group
Utrecht University
Utrecht, the Netherlands
Alan Turing Institute Almere, The Netherlands
Email: J.J.C.Meyer@uu.nl

***Abstract*—In this paper, a model is proposed where a software agent will be tied to a product during all parts of its life-cycle. This agent will enhance the possibilities of the product itself but will also play a role in collecting important data from the device that can be used by the manufacturer, as well as the end user. The software agent will be the basis for the device to participate in the Internet of Things (IoT) concept. The motivation to use agent technology, the architecture as well as the implementation in two different products are presented.**

Keywords–Agent technology; Internet of Things; Lifecyle agent

I. INTRODUCTION

Today, Information technology plays a major role in manufacturing as well as in other aspects of our modern society. In manufacturing the trend is towards low-cost agile manufacturing of small batch sizes or even one product according to enduser requirements. This is also known as Industry 4.0 [1] or cyber physical systems [2]. Recycling is also an important issue that should have attention starting at the design and manufacturing phase. In our daily life, more and more devices are connected to the Internet thus creating the Internet of Things (IoT). In this paper, a concept is presented where a software entity will be responsible for a certain product in all phases of its life cycle. This software entity starts by manufacturing the product and will collect data during the manufacturing phase. Next, the software entity will be tied to or even embedded in the product, making it a part of the IoT during all phases of its life cycle. For most products, the usage phase has the longest duration. It turns out that this phase can also play a role to adapt the production. When a manufacturer has a lot of data available about the usage of a product, the manufacturing process itself can benefit. This paper will describe the concept of the software entity and the architecture used to implement the concept. The focus will be on the usage phase and two cases are elaborated where a complex device will collect usage data as well as open the possibility to be remotely monitored and controlled.

The rest of this paper is organised as follows. Section II is dedicated to the related work and definitions. In Section III, the motivation for the chosen technology and the advantages will be discussed followed by Section IV presenting two specific cases where the concept, architecture and implementation will be explained. Section V about future work and a conclusion will end the paper.

II. RELATED WORK AND DEFINITIONS

The concept of using a software entity to guide a product through its life cycle was first published by Moergestel [3]. The software entity used was a so called software agent. Nowadays, the concept of an agent is already widely known in the field of information technology. Unfortunately, there are several definitions, so we give here the definition as stated by Wooldridge [4], that will be used in this paper:

Definition: *An agent is an encapsulated computer system that is situated in some environment and that is capable of flexible, autonomous action in that environment in order to meet its design objectives.*

For reasons explained in the next section, we will stick to the concept of an agent and for this paper we have a special purpose for the software agent in mind: the life cycle agent.

Definition: *a life cycle agent is a software entity that is the representative of a product in all phases of its life cycle.*

For more complex products having an environment where such an agent can run, as the actual implementation a twin agent system is proposed, where one agent lives in the product itself and another one in cyberspace. These agents will synchronise to keep the knowledge on both systems equal and up-to-date.

Every product goes through a sequence of phases as depicted in Figure 1. Starting with design, the product will be manufactured and distributed to reach the actual user. This user will use the product, perhaps hand it over to another user. During this usage phase repair and maintenance play a role. Finally the product will come to the end of its life and parts of it will be recycled.

Figure 1. Different phases in the life cycle

The manufacturing starts by the agent itself. It will control the production as described in [5]. This approach is also used by Bussmann [6]. Agent-based manufacturing is also described by Paoluci and Sacile [7]. The difference with the solutions for manufacturing so far is that in our concept [5], the agent controlling the production will stay alive and embed itself in the product, becoming the life cycle agent. If embedding is not possible, the agent will live remote and keep contact with the product to send and receive information. It should be clear that a certain complexity of the product is assumed. The product should have sensors for measuring things of interest and it should be capable to communicate this to the outside world, either continuously or on demand.

Monitoring systems that check and collect data during the usage phase, are widely used nowadays. An Aircraft is constantly monitored during the flight. These monitoring systems are specially designed for the aircraft involved [8]. The information collected is used for safety, preventive maintenance as well as redesign. So the purpose of monitoring is comparable to the agent-based concept presented. A term used in the transport industry is Health and Usage Monitoring System (HUMS) [9]. This system helps to ensure availability, reliability and safety of vehicles. An overview of health monitoring is given in [10]. These monitoring systems are specially designed for monitoring purposes and rarely used in other parts of the life cycle. Monitoring for medical and human health is also an interesting and important aspect. An example of an application is this area is given by Otto [11].

III. Technology used and its advantages

In this section, the choice for agent technology is motivated. Another part of this chapter presents an overview of the benefits of the model for different stakeholders.

A. Agent technology

The reason why an agent is proposed is based on some important characteristics of agents:

- autonomy; no user intervention is required. A device can operate on its own.
- communicating; devices need to communicate with the external world.
- reactive: this property will make the device work as expected.
- pro-active: this might be a property that will make the device smart.
- mobile: an agent can move from one platform to another.
- learning: this is also a property that makes a device smart
- adapting: the device can adapt itself to different situations
- reasoning: an advanced property for making the device smart
- cooperative (important in a multiagent approach).

All these properties fit well within the concept of a smart software entity to guide and represent a product and making it a part of the IoT.

When agent-based product guidance is used, two possibilities arise:

1) one single agent is developed to guide the product during its whole life cycle. This agent might have a backup or counterpart outside the device living in cyberspace.
2) a multiagent approach is used, where different agents operate at different phases but where information exchange between these agents is possible.

Without pretending to give an exhaustive overview, we will now describe some advantages of using agents in the life cycle of a product.

B. Advantages

To investigate the benefits of the approach proposed, the advantages and possibilities for different stakeholders will be presented.

1) manufacturer: Though the life cycle agent concept was introduced as a tool to implement agile manufacturing for batch size equal to one, the concept can be used for all types of products having a certain complexity and the capability to register data from sensors installed in the product itself. For the manufacturing phase, the concept is the enabler for agile production of small quantities as described in [12]. It will result in logging the production data for every single product. However, in case of a batch production the logging could be specific for the whole batch and shared by all products belonging to that production batch.

By using the feedback during usage, the manufacturing process itself and the product can be optimized, because of the availability of usage information. Over the air (OTA) updates of product software can be performed within the proposed model. The mean time between failure (MTBF) of subparts of the system will become a well-known factor because of the information collected during usage. Finally the end-user can be specifically advised by the manufacturer about a replacement of a product, knowing the type of usage by that specific end-user.

2) distributer: Logistic systems can benefit from the fact that the product involved is already "smart" by having a software agent available. If the device is capable of using its sensors during transport, the possibility arises to check that transport has been done under acceptable conditions (temperature, shock, time involved etc.). This might be helpful because in many situations the distributor is responsible for damage during transport.

3) end-user: When a device is connected to the internet, several possibilities that can benefit the end-user arise. First, the device can be monitored and controlled by the end-user using a device like a smart phone, tablet or any other system having a web browser. By collecting the usage that is made the device can optimise itself to the usage of a specific end-user. Preventive maintenance and over the air updates can also benefit the user.

4) environment: Because the usage, MTBF and wear of several subparts is available as well as the maintenance and replacement of subsystems, during the process of recycling, subparts can be reused based on these data. This makes it possible to reuse materials as well because during the manufacturing phase, data about the materials used are collected by the life cycle agent. All these possibilities will reduce the amount of waste.

IV. Usage phase cases

Two different types of devices are shown as proof of concept. The first one is an autonomous robot vacuum cleaner. The second one is a radio device for playing internet audio streams. Though different there are also similarities. In both cases the device contains the local agent. In case of the internet radio, the hardware where the agent resides is also the hardware that controls the device itself. In the case of the vacuum cleaner, the agent has its own specific hardware that is only connected to the system to get information about the internal controls. Both cases use a Raspberry-Pi as the agent platform. The reason is the low price and extensive documentation available.

A. *Generic and specific*

The approach used was to build a generic system, that can be used for a wide range of devices, while extra software will be added to adapt to the specific properties of a device.

1) Functional requirements: When the needs for both manufacturer and user in the use phase are considered, the following list applies:

- the manufacturer needs data about the usage of the products
- the manufacturer needs data about component failures
- the user wants to remotely control and monitor the product.
- the user wants a generic system with similarities among different products

These needs resulted in the following functional requirements:

- interface to collect information about the usage of a product
- connection with the cloud, to prevent that data will be lost in case a product is completely destroyed.
- Easy configuration for both the user as well as the manufacturer
- Agent-based to fit in the concept of the life cycle agent. The advantages and reason to use agent technology are already explained in the previous section.

2) overview: Figure 2 shows an overview of the architecture proposed. As seen in the figure, there are actually two agents involved for every device. One residing in the device, while the other is living in the cloud. The reason for this is that in situations where the agent in the device is completely destroyed, the cloud agents still has all the information available. A collection of cloud agents store their data in a database that is accessible to the manufacturer. An API will open the possibility for the end-user to interact with the device.

3) Technical requirements: For the implementation Jade has been used. Some important properties of jade are: Jade [13] was used as a platform for the Multiagent System (MAS). The reasons for choosing Jade are:

- the system is a multiagent-based system. Jade provides most of the requirements we need for our application like platform independence and inter agent communication;
- Jade is Java-based. Java is a versatile and powerful programming language;
- because Jade is Java-based it also has a low learning curve for Java programmers;
- the life cycle agents should be capable to negotiate to reach their goals. Jade offers possibilities for agents to negotiate. If we need extra capabilities, the Jade platform can easily be upgraded to an environment that is especially designed for BDI agents like 2APL [14] or Jadex [[13]]. Both 2APL as well as Jadex are based on Jade but have a more steep learning curve for Java developers;
- agents can migrate, terminate or new agents can appear.

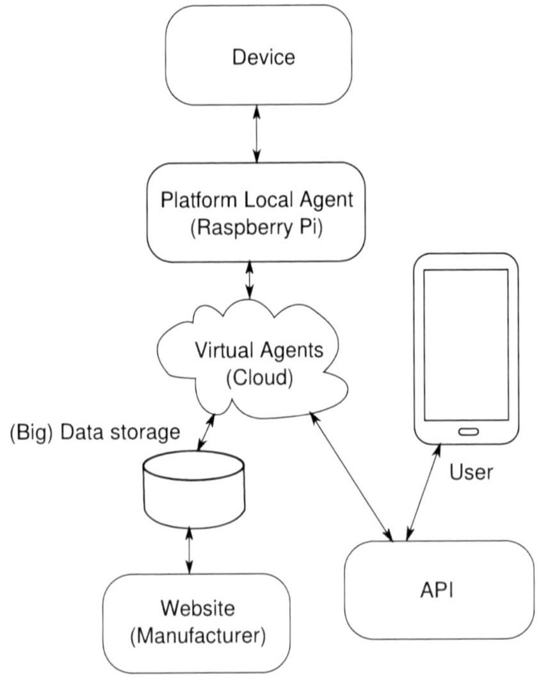

Figure 2. Architecture overview

The Jade runtime environment implements message-based communication between agents running on different platforms connected by a network. In Figure 3, the Jade platform environment is depicted.

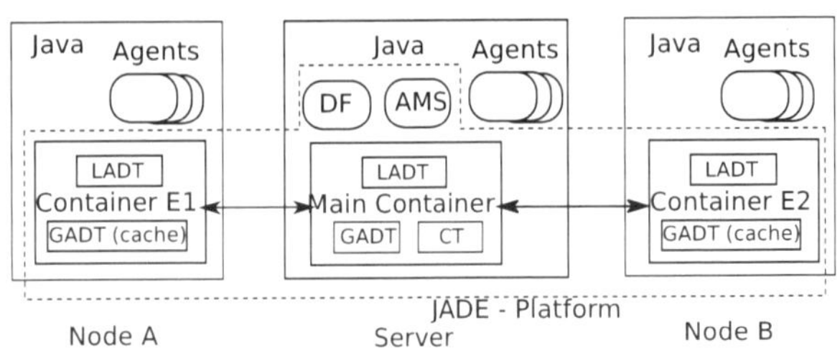

Figure 3. The Jade platform

The Jade platform itself is in this figure surrounded by a dashed line. It consists of the following components:

- A main container with connections to remote containers (in our case Node A and Node B, representing for example other computer platforms running Java);
- A container table (CT) residing in the main container, which is the registry of the object references and

transport addresses of all container nodes composing the platform;

- A global agent descriptor table (GADT), which is the registry of all agents present in the platform, including their status and location. This table resides in the main container and there are cached entries in the other containers;
- All containers have a local agent descriptor table (LADT), describing the local agents in the container;
- The main container also hosts two special agents AMS and DF, that provide the agent management and the yellow page service (Directory Facilitator) where agents can register their services or search for available services.

Several requirements justified this choice.

- Open source, so the further development and integration with other sofwtare developments would be possible, without dependence on developers of closed software.
- Based on a standard widely accepted programming language, making the adoption by third parties easy.
- Jade has been designed as a platform for a distributed multiagent system. This is exactly the type of multiagent system that is needed in our case.

4) Software architecture: The generic system has a modular setup. The main modules of the system are depicted in Figure 4 (LCA stands for Life Cycle Agent). LCADevice is the module where the life cycle agent residing in the device is created, while LCACloud is the module for the agent living in cyberspace. LCAWebAPI contains a REST API (REpresentational State Transfer Application Programming Interface) [15] that enables message transfer (by HTTP requests) to the JADE platform that has been used for the implementation (see the subsection Technical Requirements). All messages used by the system use the same concept and are available to all modules by LCAMessage.

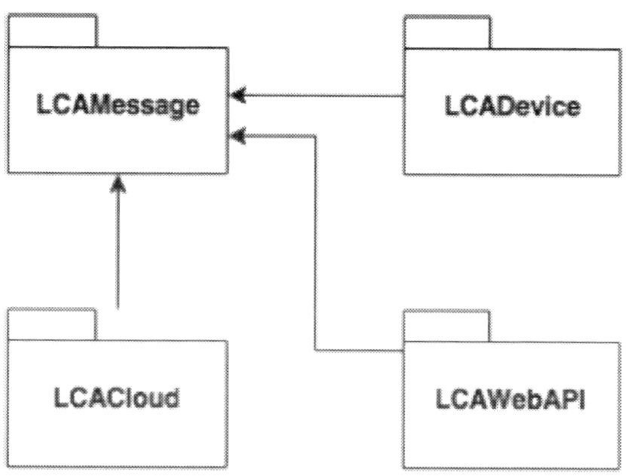

Figure 4. Modules used

B. case vacuum cleaner

The model used in this experiment was a Roomba vacuum cleaner. This brand had been chosen because of the availability of an Open Interface (OI). A document is available where this OI is described [16]. By using this interface most of the sensors and actuators can be used. A simple serial interface makes the connection to the device. A Raspberry-Pi was added to the Roomba to enable a JADE runtime environment for the agent and for establishing a WiFi connection.

1) sensors and actuators: The sensors can give information if there are walls or holes in the floor near the device. The amount of current used by the motor is available. A raise can signal a wearing-out of the brushes. The buttons on the device can be read. The distance travelled in millimetres since the previous request can be read. Voltage and current from the battery as well as the capacity and maximum capacity are available. Bumper sensors are also available. Apart from the sensors there are actuators.

- The motors driving the wheels. Speed and turning can be controlled.
- Motors moving the brushes. The speed can be controlled by Pulse Width Modulation (PWM).
- Several LEDs are available on the device. The intensity is also controllable.
- The device contains a speaker for making sounds. Sounds can be loaded and played.

2) Roomba application: As a proof of concept, an application has been developed to monitor and control the vacuum cleaner by the end-user. The vacuum cleaner should be connected to the LifeCycleAgent platform as explained earlier in this paper. The following list of functionalities is available (see the start menu in Figure 5):

- user login;
- battery status (see figure 6);
- playing music;
- start cleaning;
- return to dock;
- remote control for driving the cleaner around.

Figure 5. Main menu for the user

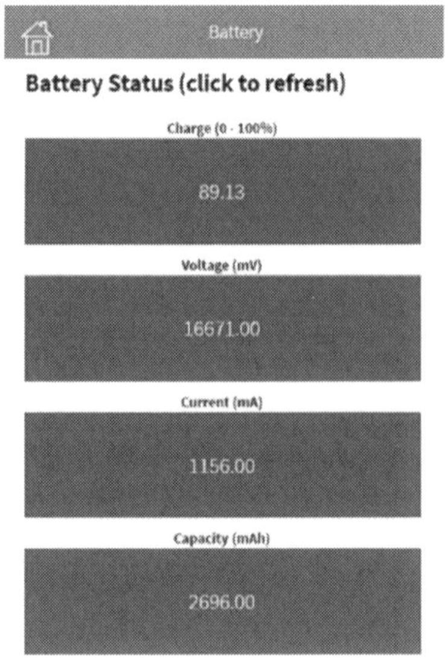

Figure 6. Battery status page

To make this implementation work, two device-specific software modules were developed. This is depicted in Figure 7.

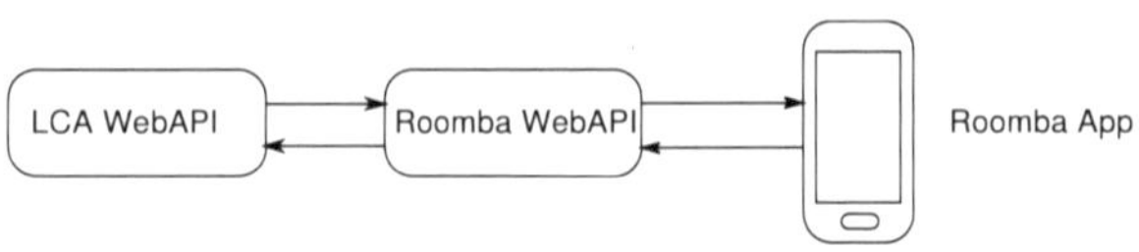

Figure 7. Architecture

The Roomba App will be installed on the smartphone or tablet and is the actual user interface as presented in Figures 5 and 6. Because this is a device-specific application, a second specific application has been added to control the communication between the Roomba App and de LCA WebAPI. Normally, these two parts should be supplied for every specific device.

C. case internet radio

In Figure 8 a blockscheme of the internet radio is shown. The core of the system is a Raspberry-Pi enhanced with a touchscreen and a powerful soundsystem that drives the speakers.

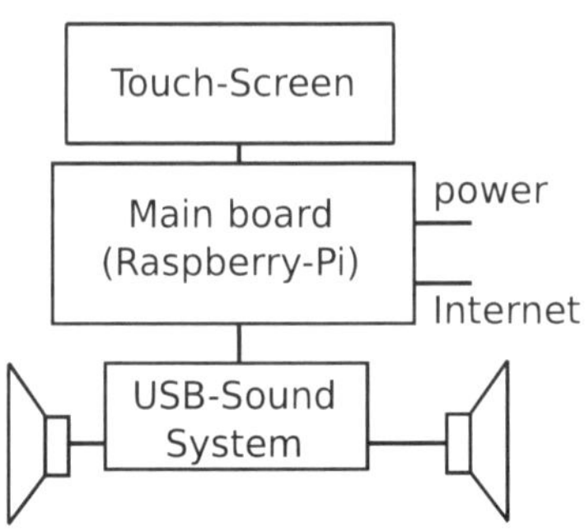

Figure 8. Block schematic

1) sensors: This is the list of input data available: The volume setting, currently chosen audio stream, play (yes/no), type of music chosen. Strictly speaking this information is not directly originating from a sensor, but it is data provided by the software entity that is the internet radio itself.

2) actuators: The actions that can be performed are:

- change the selected audio stream;
- change volume
- start playing
- stop playing
- pause playing

3) realisation: An application for remote control has not been completed yet, but the radio is integrated as a system in the life cycle agent platform, having its own virtual agent to synchronise with. The usage of the radio is monitored by the agent that lives inside the radio and the information is also available for the agent in the cloud.

The display is shown in Figure 9. The radio itself is shown in Figure 10.

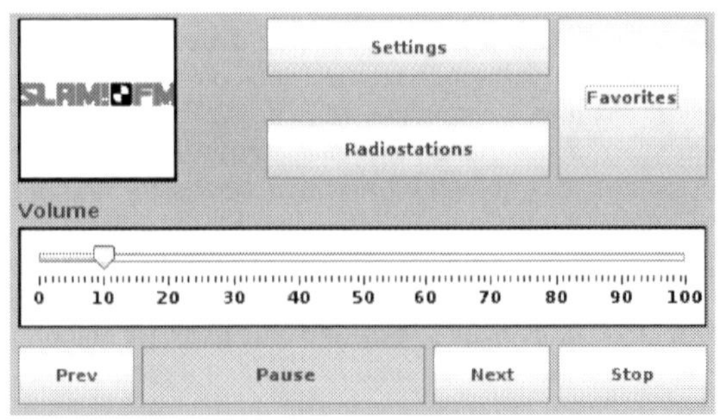

Figure 9. Display

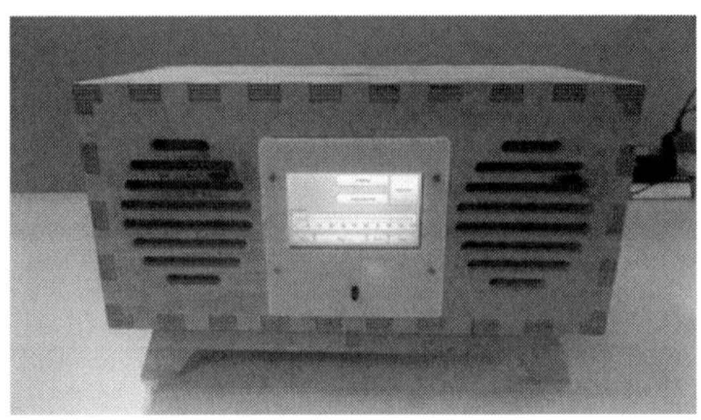

Figure 10. Radio

In Figure 10, a design is shown that was made by using a water jet cutter to make the different panels. To these panels several components are attached. The radio consists of six panels (front, back, top, bottom, left and right) with zero or more attachments. The end-user can select a shape, resulting in these six panels. This results in a toplevel XML-file where the radio is defined to consist of a these six panels in combination with actions describing how to assemble the radio using these panels. A simplified example of this XML-file that describes the components of the radio as well as the actions to be taken to construct it, looks like:

```
<Radio>
  <Source>
    six panels
  </Source>
  <Actions>
    assembly instructions
  </Actions>
</Radio>
```

Other XML-based information is added to refine the description, that is used to actually construct the radio.

V. FUTURE WORK

The manufacturing phase is still under development. Several production machines have been constructed. The flexible transport system is still under development. For the internet radio the user specified production is also under development. That means that a webinterface will be created where a user can specify his or her specific implementation of an internet radio. A list of so-called production steps (explaining what to do) and materials (what to use) should be the result of this design phase. This would be the input of an agent that will guide the manufacturing and will become the life cycle agent as presented in this paper. The first step in that direction will be to replace the production machine agents by real humans. These human agents will be instructed by the life cycle agent during the manufacturing phase to actually make the product. Meanwhile the recycling phase is studied by implementing a marketplace for devices to buy and sell parts for maintenance and repair. In all these situations we try to stick to the same multiagent-based architecture, so migration from one phase to another should be easy.

A special focus should be on the ethical aspects of the approach proposed in this paper. When information is collected during the usage phase, all kind of questions arise, like who owns this information. Who should have access to this information and so on. An end-user owning a device might have concerns about his or her privacy and should be capable to decide who should have access about the usage data of the device.

VI. CONCLUSION

In this paper, the concept of a life cycle agent has been introduced. The motivation for using agent technology was that this fits all the requirements that the system proposed should have. The multiagent architecture of the distributed system has been presented. To test this architecture in the use phase the system has been implemented. By using two different cases the generic and specific parts of the architecture became clear. The system worked as expected and can be further developed.

REFERENCES

[1] M. Brettel, N. Friederichsen, M. Keller, and M. Rosenberg, "How virtualization, decentralization and network building change the manufacturing landscape: An industry 4.0 perspective," International Journal of Mechanical, Aerospace, Industrial, Mechatronic and Manufacturing Engineering, vol. 8, no. 1, 2014, pp. 37–44.

[2] R. Rajkumar, I. Lee, Insup, S. L., and J. Stankovic, "Cyber-physical systems: The next computing revolution," Proceedings of the 47th Design Automation Conference (DAC), Anaheim, California, 2010, pp. 731–736.

[3] L. v. Moergestel, J.-J. Meyer, E. Puik, and D. Telgen, "The role of agents in the lifecycle of a product," CMD 2010 proceedings, 2010, pp. 28–32.

[4] M. Wooldridge, An Introduction to MultiAgent Systems, Second Edition. Sussex, UK: Wiley, 2009.

[5] L. v. Moergestel, J.-J. Meyer, E. Puik, and D. Telgen, "Decentralized autonomous-agent-based infrastructure for agile multiparallel manufacturing," Proceedings of the International Symposium on Autonomous Distributed Systems (ISADS 2011) Kobe, Japan, 2011, pp. 281–288.

[6] S. Bussmann, N. Jennings, and M. Wooldridge, Multiagent Systems for Manufacturing Control. Berlin Heidelberg: Springer-Verlag, 2004.

[7] M. Paolucci and R. Sacile, Agent-based manufacturing and control systems : new agile manufacturing solutions for achieving peak performance. Boca Raton, Fla.: CRC Press, 2005.

[8] URL, HindSight-Eurocontrol Publications. at http://www.skybrary.aero/index.php/HindSight_-_EUROCONTROL, june, 2017.

[9] D. He, S. Wu, and E. Bechhoefer, Use of physics-based approach to enhance HUMS prognostic capability, 2007, vol. 1, pp. 354–361.

[10] H. Sohn, C. R. Farrar, F. M. Hemez, D. D. Shunk, D. W. Stinemates, B. R. Nadler, and J. J. Czarnecki, "A review of structural health monitoring literature: 1996–2001," Los Alamos National Laboratory, 2003, pp. 1–7.

[11] C. Otto, A. Milenkovic, C. Sanders, and E. Jovanov, "System architecture of a wireless body area sensor network for ubiquitous health monitoring," Journal of mobile multimedia, vol. 1, no. 4, 2006, pp. 307–326.

[12] L. v. Moergestel, J.-J. Meyer, E. Puik, and D. Telgen, "Implementation of manufacturing as a service: A pull-driven agent-based manufacturing grid," Proceedings of the 11th International Conference on ICT in Education, Research and Industrial Applications (ICTERI 2015), Lviv, Ukraine, 2015, pp. 172–187.

[13] N. Bordini, M. Dastani, J. Dix, and A. E. F. Seghrouchni, Multi-Agent Programming. Springer, 2005.

[14] M. Dastani, "2apl: a practical agent programming language," Autonomous Agents and Multi-Agent Systems, vol. 16, no. 3, 2008, pp. 214–248.

[15] R. Fielding, "Architectural styles and the design of network-based software architectures," Ph.D. dissertation, University of California, Irvine, 2000.

[16] URL, pdf file name iRobot_ Roomba_ 500_ Open_ Interface_spec.pdf. at http://www.irobot.lv/uploaded_files/File, june, 2017.

A Marketplace for Cyber-Physical Production Systems: Architecture and Key Enablers

Susana Aguiar, Rui Pinto, João Reis, Gil Gonçalves

Department of Informatics Engineering
Faculty of Engineering, University of Porto
Porto, Portugal
Email: {saguiar, rpinto, jpcreis, gil}@fe.up.pt

Abstract—**With the Industry 4.0, which can be referred to as the fourth industrial revolution, the concept of Smart Factories has emerged into the spotlight. This new trend in automation and manufacturing encompasses a wide range of technologies such as Cyber-Physical Systems (CPS), the Internet of Things (IoT), and Cloud computing. The conjunction of these technologies creates new opportunities at all levels, such as technological, economical, and societal. In this paper, an architecture that combines results from two European R&D projects is presented. The aim of the proposed architecture it to allow a step forward in utilizing all the advantages of the Industry 4.0 concept and the technological advances. The ultimate goal of the proposed architecture is to allow the existence of a flow of information from the physical equipment in the shop-floor up to an on-line Marketplace, and to allow a safe and reliable way of using all the information.**

Keywords*–*Smart factories; Intelligent Production systems; Industry 4.0; Cyber-physical systems; Marketplace.

I. INTRODUCTION

Today, sensors can be found in just about anything, from home appliances, mobile phones, cars to complex health equipment or industrial equipment. These sensors continuously produce enormous amounts of data concerning some type of event. All these different available sensors provide heterogeneous raw data, which is provided at different formats and with no common semantics to describe its meaning. Sheth, Henson, and Sahoo [1] described this paradigm as "too much data and not enough knowledge".

This paradigm is being leveraged by the development of components and systems called Smart Components. Smart Components in manufacturing are defined as components that incorporate functions of self-description, communication, sensing, and control in order to cooperate with other smart components, analyze a situation, make decisions based on the available data, and modify their behavior through feedback [2].

Over the past few years, many projects have been dedicated to these issues. Among those projects there are two in particularly that have been focused on bringing knowledge to all the collected data, in industrial environments: the ReBorn - Innovative Reuse of modular knowledge Based devices and technologies for Old, Renewed and New factories project, and the SelSus - Health Monitoring and Life-Long Capability Management for SELf-SUStaining Manufacturing Systems project.

The ReBorn project [3] was a project funded under THEME FoF.NMP.2013-2 - Innovative re-use of modular equipment based on integrated factory design until August of 2016. The vision of ReBorn was to demonstrate strategies and technologies that support a new paradigm for the re-use of production equipment in factories. This re-use will give new life to decommissioned production systems and equipment, helping them to be reborn in new production lines. Such new strategies will contribute to sustainable, resource-friendly and green manufacturing and, at the same time, deliver economic and competitive advantages for the manufacturing sector.

The developments made in ReBorn helped production equipment to extend its life cycle, contributing to economic and environmental sustainability of production systems [4] [5]. The concept of modular production equipment may also be re-used between different production systems, after servicing and upgrading. This new business paradigm will move from an equipment-based business to a value added business, where equipment servicing and equipment knowledge are main drivers.

The SelSus project [6] is a project also funded by the European Commission under the Seventh Framework Program for Research and Technological Development, until August of 2017. The vision of SelSus is to create a new paradigm for highly effective, self-healing production resources and systems to maximize their performance over longer life times through highly targeted and timely repair, renovation and upgrading through the use of the Smart Component concept as a SelComp (SelSus Component). These next generation machines, fixtures and tools with embed extended sensory capabilities and smart materials combined with advanced Information and Communications Technology (ICT) for self-diagnosis enabling them to become self-aware and supporting self-healing production systems. Distributed diagnostic and predictive repair and renovation models will be embedded into smart devices to early prognosis failure modes and component degradations. Self-aware devices will built on synergetic relationships with their human operators and maintenance personnel through continuous pro-active communication to achieve real self-healing systems. This will drastically improve the resilience and long term sustainability of highly complex manufacturing facilities to foreseen and unforeseen disturbances and deteriorations thereby minimizing energy and resource consumption and waste.

The current work consists on an architecture that enables the connection between Wireless Sensor Networks (WSNs) in a manufacture context with an open marketplace. This architecture intends on bridging the gap between the results achieved in both ReBorn and SelSus projects, namelly the ReBorn Marketplace and the Selsus Dashboard.

This paper is organized in four more sections. In Section II, a brief overview of related work is presented. Section III presents the previous results that are the basis for the work proposed in this paper, and in Section IV the proposed architecture to be implemented is described. Finally, Section V concludes the paper by exposing some final remarks and the next steps for future work are identified.

II. Related Work

Nowadays, sensors and actuators have become more affordable and available, which contributed to the wide adoption of WSNs solutions, used for monitoring of physical and environmental conditions into several applications.

WSNs are an emerging technology that exhibits a great potential and that can play an important role in many applications. It is becoming common to use WSNs in a variety of applications areas such as environmental monitoring, military, or industrial fields, specially since data gathering is one of the pillars for the implementation of IoT concepts. However, since they typically contain small sensor devices, WSNs present some constraints, such as limitations on the memory, computation, energy, and scalability [7]. To take full advantage of the WSNs potentialities an infrastructure that is powerful, scalable, and secure must be implemented.

Llanes *et al.* [8] presented a survey of the main approaches that have been developed to deal with all the raw data collected by sensors. Sensors continuously collect data regarding a given event and send it to a gateway, which usually needs a specific protocol to process the received raw data. The problem is that the various sensor manufacturers provide different communication protocols that use different message formats, so there is not an universal technology that can receive raw sensor data and support every message type for processing further the received information. In the survey, several solutions are described, as well the strengths and limitations of each one. Also, an attempt was made by Gil *et al.* [9] to provide an Universal Gateway in order to mitigate this problem. Shen *et al.* [10] provided an overview of recent developments of agent technology applied to manufacturing enterprises, which include enterprise collaboration regarding supply chain management and virtual enterprises, manufacturing process planning and scheduling, shop floor control, and also holonic manufacturing as an implementation methodology.

There have been other studies on how to manage the physical sensors. Sensor Modeling Language (SensorML) [11] intends to provide standard models in a XML encoding for physical sensors description and measurement processes. It is being used by the international non profit organization Open Geospatial Consortium (OGC), which is committed on making quality open standards for the global geospatial community.

As mentioned before, sensors from different manufactures use different communication protocols, which makes it difficult to share sensors and its information between applications. Shneidman *et al.* [12] presented an infrastructure called Hourglass, which addresses the need for a software infrastructure that enables the rapid development and deployment of applications that use data from several, heterogeneous sensor networks. Yuriyama & Kushida [13] propose a new infrastructure called Sensor-Cloud infrastructure, which can manage physical sensors on an IT infrastructure. The proposed Sensor-Cloud Infrastructure virtualizes a physical sensor as a virtual entity in the Cloud.

Several research work has been performed regarding this new paradigm of connecting and virtualizing sensors in Cloud infrastructures for data processing. Yan *et al.* [14] propose a cloud-based production system, across distributed data centers, which integrates several web and Cloud computing technologies. Yang *et al.* [15] propose a full connection model of product design and manufacturing in an IoT-enabled Cloud manufacturing environment, which uses the social networks to enable the connection of multiple parties. Zhang *et al.* [16] describes the Cloud Manufacturing (CMfg), defined for solving the bottlenecks in the data and manufacturing applications. Alam & Saddik [17] present and describe a digital twin architecture reference model for the cloud-based CPS, named C2PS. Neto *et al.* [18] presented the first steps in the development of a framework that takes advantage of several technologies like UPnP, OSGi, and iPOJO, which addresses some of the challenges needed to enable a Sensor Cloud in the shop floor.

Alamri *et al.* [19] provides a survey of some of the most relevant work related to Sensor-Cloud infrastructure, its definition, architecture, and applications. Moano *et al.* [20] analyse how the IoT can be used in the manufacturing industry, by proposing a metamodel for integrating the Internet of Things, Social Networks, Cloud, and Industry 4.0.

With the increase of the number of devices connected to the Internet, having centralized Cloud services will become unsustainable. This is leading to new paradigms, such as Fog or Edge computing [21] [22].

A huge requirement that is slowing the advances and the wide use of the technologies described previously is the security and data privacy. The security and privacy issues over the IoT have been addressed by several authors [23]–[29], which propose new approaches of securing and enable reliability on sensor data [30] [7]. Nevertheless, there is still a lot of work to be done in areas such as cryptographic mechanisms, data, identity, and privacy management, as well as defining trusted architectures.

III. Previous Results

The work proposed in this paper, arises from the idea of combining some of the results accomplished in the ReBorn and SelSus projects. In both projects, the achieved results are based on the concept of a Smart Component, which has different designation in each project, namely VERSON in ReBorn and SelComp [31] in SelSus. A Smart Component, as mentioned before, is an intelligent agent-based representation of industrial equipment in manufacturing environment, which enables both complex machines and sensor & actuators of added value functionalities, such as self-description capabilities and standardized communication skills. These are useful for inter-device collaboration and process optimization, based on analyses of collected environmental and context data, for proper decision making regarding actuation and equipment behavior modification.

In the following sections, a brief overview of the ReBorn and SelSus projects is presented as well as the results that are used for the proposed architecture, namelly the ReBorn Marketplace and SelSus Dashboard.

A. ReBorn Marketplace

As mention before, the ReBorn main goal was to demonstrate strategies and technologies that support a new paradigm for the re-use of production equipment in factories (Figure 1).

This new paradigm builds on self-aware and knowledge-based equipment that needs functionalities to collect and manage information regarding their capabilities and their evolution

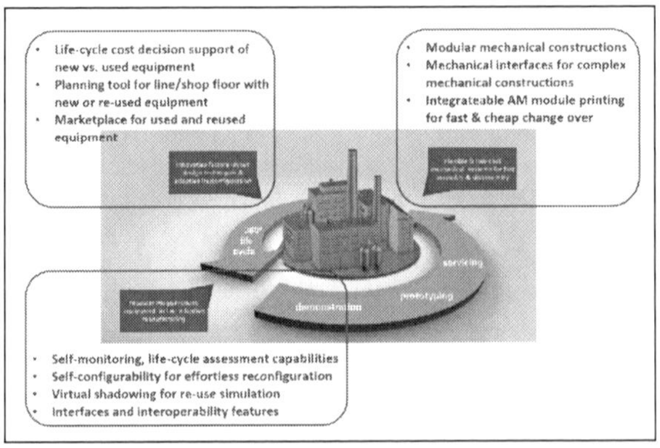

Figure 1. ReBorn re-use approaches

over time, maintenance, upgrade or refurbishment operations over its lifetime and information of use and wear. To enable this, versatile and modular, task-driven plug&produce devices, with built-in capabilities for self-assessment and optimal re-use were implemented, along with strategies for their re-use and models for factory layout design and adaptive configuration.

These new technologies were demonstrated in the context of intelligent repair, upgrade and re-use of equipment, the re-design of factory layouts and flexible & adaptable production on shop floor within several industrial demonstration scenarios. This demonstration scenarios include a flexible pick&place machine, a multi-purpose on demand 3D printing module, a condition monitoring and virtual programming, a modular and self-configuring servo press, and tools for planning and assessment as presented in Figure 2. Having ReBorn technology available, significant reduced the efforts when setting-up and ramping-up production systems, enabling a significant step towards 100% re-use of industrial equipment.

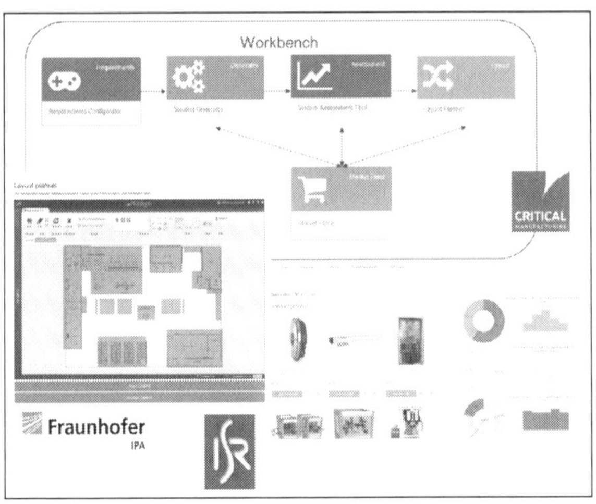

Figure 2. Tools for planning and assessment

One of the resulting technologies of the ReBorn project is the Marketplace represented in Figure 3. This tool is a platform that allows equipment owners and buyers to have a common ground to communicate. The ReBorn Marketplace [5] offers its services in an online platform format, as a Platform as a System (PaaS). PaaS enables the creation of an evolving market between actors, which would be difficult to reach without this platform. PaaS comprises different participant groups, making a multi-sided market possible.

Figure 3. Marketplace

The ReBorn Marketplace is a n-sided market, with service providers on one end and service consumers on the other. This will attract service suppliers in order to respond to the demand side of the platform. The demand side, in the Marketplace, is comprised of any potential end-user to the platform offerings. Service consumers comprise the Marketplace participants, which mainly relate to the ReBorn Marketplace service offerings. The Marketplace service suppliers can normally be instantiated by any entity capable of offering its services to the platform while altogether adding value to the platforms base proposition. Service suppliers are Original Equipment Manufacturer (OEM) who provide mainly machines and components, as well as equipment information, functionalities (software), and operations. Entities capable of providing complementing services to the platform, in order to co-create value, are labeled as complementors. Complementors can be, for instance, independent software developers that provide additional equipment functionalities.

Figure 4 provides a high level overview of the ReBorn Marketplace architecture. The Marketplace has all the basic functionalities such as management of clients, vendors, and products; general administration of the Marketplace; and services related to payment methods. Additionally to these basic functionalities, for the ReBorn Marketplace it was necessary to developed modules that provide the ability to communicate and manage the VERSONs, one being the Plugin Manager. The Plugin Manager main functionality is to allow the management of the application content of each equipment smart component, it is an easy and simple way of allowing the upgrade of the smart component software. The Plugin Manager allows the integration of new technologies and functionalities in industrial equipment on the fly. It will be extended in the new architecture.

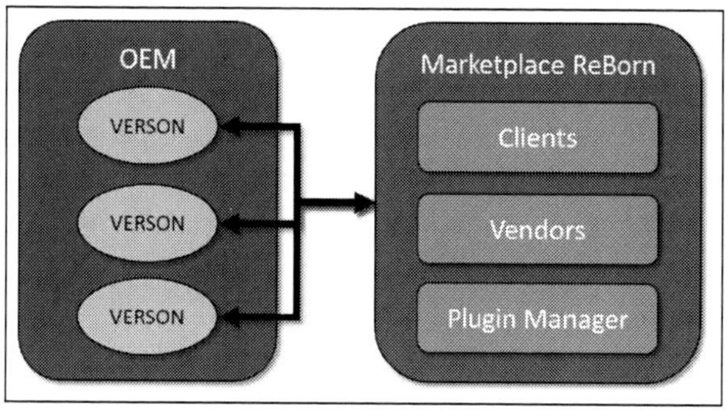

Figure 4. Marketplace Architecture

B. *Selsus Sensor Cloud*

The SelSus vision will be achieved by the development of a new synergetic diagnostic and prognosis environment, which is fully aware of the condition and history of all the machine components within a system or factory and is in constant knowledge enriched dialog with their human personnel. In Figure 5 the overall project architecture is presented.

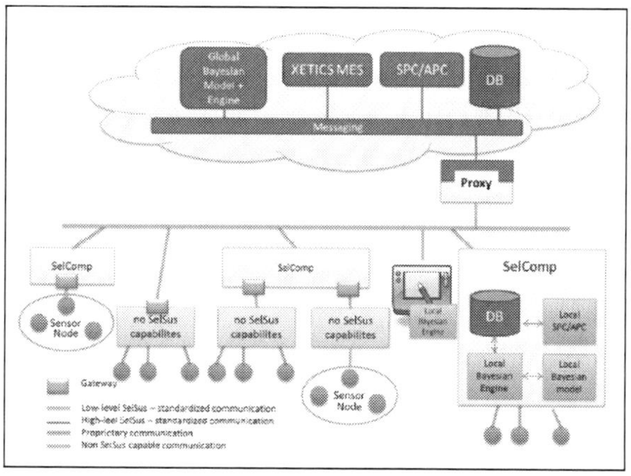

Figure 5. SelSus Architecture

One key area explored in the SelSus project is related with industrial WSNs and Cloud Systems that ranges from sensor integration, sensor data visualization, statistical processing and access, where sensors, external to the process, used for machine monitoring are introduced at the shop-floor level [32].

Sensor information is considered one key element for machine behavior modeling and process optimization, due to the possibility of gathering not only data from machine parametrization (variables that control the process) but also from the observable impact of this parametrization in the final quality of the product. Moreover, this type of information builds knowledge that, despite allowing an immediate perception of the process conditions, it can be used in a myriad of applications. These applications range from predictive maintenance where a failure of a certain machine can be predicted within an interval of confidence, to the optimization of a certain process to minimize the cost without jeopardizing the product quality, and even learning if a process is drifting from what was defined in the design phase.

The concept of the Smart Component in SelSus [32] is applicable to both machine and WSNs, and is a virtual representation of these shop-floor components. This means that different Smart Components, where one represents a machine and the other a WSN, are both uniquely identified in the Cloud that is able to receive inter-device data. This way, it is possible to visualize and analyze independently the information from each component or correlate data information from a group of different Smart Components.

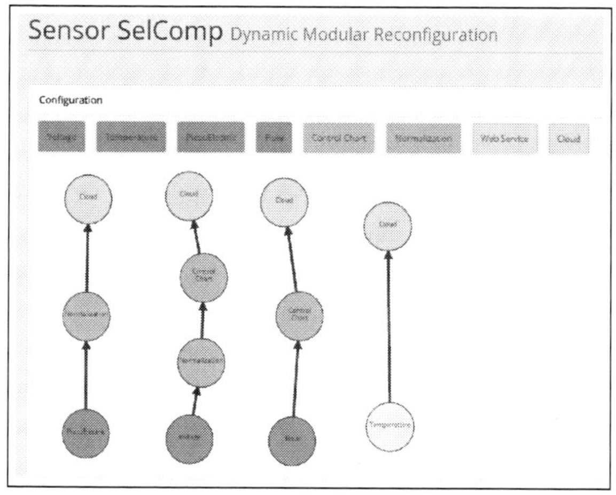

Figure 6. SelSus Dashboard

The SelSus Sensor Cloud, as seen in Figure 6, is a graphical tool that enables the user to dynamically change the configuration, reconfiguration, of a Smart Component. This configuration is drawn by using a directed acyclic graph, composed by three different types of nodes: 1) Interfaces or End Nodes (Web Service and Cloud); 2) Modules (Control Chart and Normalization); 3) Sensors (e.g., Voltage, Temperature, PiezoEletric, and Flow). Currently, there are two available Interfaces or End Nodes: Cloud and Web Service. These are called End Nodes because are the nodes that can only receive information. The Cloud node means that sensor or processed information can be sent to the Cloud, and Web Service means that the same information can be sent to an external entity.

The SelSus Sensor Cloud is used for data acquisition, storage, processing, visualization and access purposes. This type of solution was chosen due to the necessity of easy collection of data from multiple components, quick visualization of manufacturing process dynamics, statistical processing for monitoring purposes, and information exchange to other external applications.

IV. PROPOSED ARCHITECTURE

The ReBorn Marketplace already has several services implemented and running. One of these services is the ability of the equipment Smart Component communicate data directly to the Marketplace. This information is stored by the Marketplace and can be used by other external applications.

On the other side, the SelSus Sensor Cloud allows the user to reconfigure the methods used to process the sensor data locally at the SelComp level, even before the raw data from the components is synchronized with the System Level.

One of these methods allows the user to graphically develop an interpreter of raw sensor data packets at the gateway level for automatic data acquisition. The SelSus Dashboard also provides a Statistical Analysis section to enable some of the potentialities of using different data analytics and machine learning algorithms to analyze machine and sensor data, available at the Sensor Cloud level, which can be used in the reconfiguration process of the Smart Component.

The proposed architecture consists on connecting the ReBorn Marketplace with the SelSus Dashboard, extending the functionalities of both tools. By taking advantage of the already developed applications, the efforts can be applied to the development of the missing bridge between the two projects and the new needed functionalities. Figure 7 presents the overall architecture of how to combine the developments from both projects, ReBorn and SelSus.

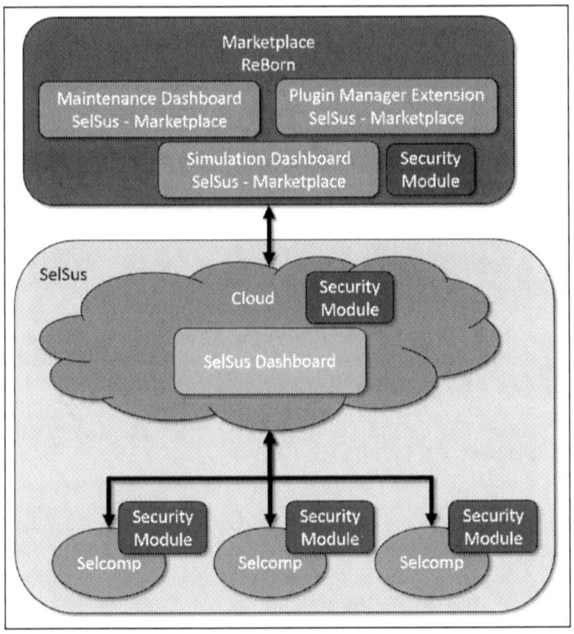

Figure 7. Proposed Architecture

As it can be seen, there are several blocks that compose the architecture shown in Figure 7. These blocks can be divided into three main blocks: (1) SelSus developments (SelComp and SelSus Dashboard); (2) ReBorn developments (ReBorn Marketplace); and (3) new developments necessary to bring the two tools together (Maintenance Dashboard, Simulation Dashboard, Plugin Manager Extension, and Security Module). All these blocks will be described in the following sections.

In order to implement this new architecture, new components and functionalities will have to be developed and integrated with the already existing tools. As shown in Figure 7, the Maintenance Dashboard, Simulation Dashboard, Plugin Manager Extension, and Security Module will be implemented.

Most of the functionalities and components will be added to the Marketplace side. Some of these modules were already developed in SelSus and will be extended to be used in the Marketplace, namely the Maintenance Dashboard and the Simulation Dashboard. These modules enable trading software and services in the Marketplace, extending the ability to sell, buy, or rent equipment.

The Maintenance Dashboard's main goal is to allow for an easier planning of the maintenance scheduling of a company. As mentioned before, the Marketplace can receive information from the equipment's Smart Components, which is stored in the Marketplace. This information is useful in order to compare collected metrics from different equipments, which can be used to aid OEM to provide maintenance services to their customers.

Assuming that an OEM, besides selling equipment for several customers at different countries, is also providing maintenance services, which usually cover annual inspections of the equipment in the costumer facilities, the information stored in the Marketplace reveals to be very important. The OEM is able to better use their resources as well as save money by optimizing the traveling that is needed by the maintenance engineer, taking into consideration the actual status of the equipment. This also permits a more active preventive maintenance, allowing the generation and simulation of several possible maintenance routes, based on the equipment metrics and in the current context and environment where the equipment is located.

The Simulation Dashboard aims at simplifying the process of developing new functions that can be sold in the Marketplace and uploaded to the Smart Components. This Simulation Dashboard module will facilitate the design of new functionalities, metric calculations, and treatment of raw data of the Smart Components. The user will be able to design a new functionality and simulate it, in order to check if the behavior of the Smart Component is the desired one. The new functionality can then be stored in the Marketplace for selling.

The existing Plugin Manager will be extended in order to also manage the download of new functionalities, instead of being limited to Smart Components software updates. The extended Plugin Manager will be able to manage the downloads of all software, both functionalities and software versions of the Smart Component.

One of the issues, nowadays, referenced by the industry that hinders the wide use of the full functionalities of todays technologies is the lack of security as well as the lack of privacy. For that purpose, a Security Module will be implemented, in order to reinforce the system security, by adding privacy to every communications performed between the different tools.

As shown in Figure 7, the idea is to be able to have a Security Module in all the layers of the architecture. This Security Module will be configurable, in order to adapt to the needs of each layer and each OEM. The Security Module will have two main functionalities, namely privacy and authentication. This will be accomplished through the use of an encryption algorithm, which will use a public key encryption algorithm, in order to provide means of data encryption.

The communication between an OEM and the Marketplace is performed over the Internet, which is well known to be insecure if users are not authenticated and data exchange is encrypted. Other simpler encryption algorithms, such as symmetric keys, might also be considered to be implemented. The Security Module will have the ability to be updated with new methods, much like the Smart Component through the Dashboard.

V. CONCLUSION

Nowadays, sensors are widely available, mostly because they are becoming increasingly more powerful, diverse, and cheaper. With the Industry 4.0 the concept of Smart Factories emerged. At the core of this concept is the use of sensors to collect data. This collected data is then processed using data analytics algorithms, to be used for many different purposes such as monitoring or predictive maintenance. Over the last few years, a lot of research has been dedicated to this topic. Two such projects are the ReBorn and Selsus projects.

This paper proposes a new architecture that combines both ReBorn and SelSus results, namelly the ReBorn Marketplace and the SeSuls Dashboard. The idea is to use the results and developments already accomplished and take them a step forward. With the implementation of the described architecture, a flow of information will exist from the equipment at the shop-floor, up to the Marketplace and back. This will allow to take advantages of all the current technological advances, and allow a safe and reliable way of using all the available information.

REFERENCES

[1] A. Sheth, C. Henson, and S. S. Sahoo, "Semantic sensor web," IEEE Internet computing, vol. 12, no. 4, 2008, pp. 78–83.

[2] "Review of standardization opportunities in smart industrial components," URL: http://publica.fraunhofer.de/starweb/servlet.starweb?path=epub.web&search=N-413239 [accessed: 2017-05-10].

[3] "ReBorn Project web site," URL: http://www.reborn-eu-project.org/ [accessed: 2017-05-10].

[4] S. Aguiar, R. Pinto, J. Reis, and G. Gonçalves, "Life-cycle approach to extend equipment re-use in flexible manufacturing," in INTELLI 2016, The Fifth International Conference on Intelligent Systems and Applications. IARIA, 2016, pp. 148–153.

[5] R. Fonseca, S. Aguiar, M. Peschl, and G. Gonçalves, "The reborn marketplace: an application store for industrial smart components," in INTELLI 2016, The Fifth International Conference on Intelligent Systems and Applications. IARIA, 2016, pp. 136–141.

[6] "SelSus Project web site," URL: http://www.selsus.eu/ [accessed: 2017-05-10].

[7] F. Banaie and S. A. H. Seno, "A cloud-based architecture for secure and reliable service provisioning in wireless sensor network," in Computer and Knowledge Engineering (ICCKE), 2014 4th International eConference on. IEEE, 2014, pp. 96–101.

[8] K. R. Llanes, M. A. Casanova, and N. M. Lemus, "From sensor data streams to linked streaming data: a survey of main approaches," Journal of Information and Data Management, vol. 7, no. 2, 2017, pp. 130–140.

[9] G. Gonçalves, J. Reis, R. Pinto, M. Alves, and J. Correia, "A step forward on intelligent factories: A smart sensor-oriented approach," in Emerging Technology and Factory Automation (ETFA), 2014 IEEE. IEEE, 2014, pp. 1–8.

[10] W. Shen, Q. Hao, H. J. Yoon, and D. H. Norrie, "Applications of agent-based systems in intelligent manufacturing: An updated review," Advanced engineering INFORMATICS, vol. 20, no. 4, 2006, pp. 415–431.

[11] "Sensor ML," URL: http://www.ogcnetwork.net/SensorML [accessed: 2017-05-10].

[12] J. Shneidman, P. Pietzuch, J. Ledlie, M. Roussopoulos, M. Seltzer, and M. Welsh, "Hourglass: An infrastructure for connecting sensor networks and applications," Tech. Rep., 2004.

[13] M. Yuriyama and T. Kushida, "Sensor-cloud infrastructure-physical sensor management with virtualized sensors on cloud computing," in Network-Based Information Systems (NBiS), 2010 13th International Conference on. IEEE, 2010, pp. 1–8.

[14] J. Yan, Y. Ma, L. Wang, K.-K. R. Choo, and W. Jie, "A cloud-based remote sensing data production system," Future Generation Computer Systems, 2017, pp. 1–13.

[15] C. Yang, S. Lan, W. Shen, G. Q. Huang, X. Wang, and T. Lin, "Towards product customization and personalization in iot-enabled cloud manufacturing," Cluster Computing, 2017, pp. 1–14.

[16] L. Zhang, Y. Luo, F. Tao, B. H. Li, L. Ren, X. Zhang, H. Guo, Y. Cheng, A. Hu, and Y. Liu, "Cloud manufacturing: a new manufacturing paradigm," Enterprise Information Systems, vol. 8, no. 2, 2014, pp. 167–187.

[17] K. M. Alam and A. El Saddik, "C2ps: A digital twin architecture reference model for the cloud-based cyber-physical systems," IEEE Access, vol. 5, 2017, pp. 2050–2062.

[18] L. Neto, J. Reis, D. Guimarães, and G. Gonçalves, "Sensor cloud: Smartcomponent framework for reconfigurable diagnostics in intelligent manufacturing environments," in Industrial Informatics (INDIN), 2015 IEEE 13th International Conference on. IEEE, 2015, pp. 1706–1711.

[19] A. Alamri, W. S. Ansari, M. M. Hassan, M. S. Hossain, A. Alelaiwi, and M. A. Hossain, "A survey on sensor-cloud: architecture, applications, and approaches," International Journal of Distributed Sensor Networks, vol. 9, no. 2, 2013, pp. 1–18.

[20] J. I. R. Molano, J. M. C. Lovelle, C. E. Montenegro, J. J. R. Granados, and R. G. Crespo, "Metamodel for integration of internet of things, social networks, the cloud and industry 4.0," Journal of Ambient Intelligence and Humanized Computing, 2017, pp. 1–15.

[21] B. Varghese, N. Wang, D. S. Nikolopoulos, and R. Buyya, "Feasibility of fog computing," CoRR, 2017, pp. 1–8.

[22] M. Satyanarayanan, "The emergence of edge computing," Computer, vol. 50, no. 1, 2017, pp. 30–39.

[23] R. Roman, P. Najera, and J. Lopez, "Securing the internet of things," Computer, vol. 44, no. 9, 2011, pp. 51–58.

[24] Q. Jing, A. V. Vasilakos, J. Wan, J. Lu, and D. Qiu, "Security of the internet of things: perspectives and challenges," Wireless Networks, vol. 20, no. 8, 2014, pp. 2481–2501.

[25] A. Sajid, H. Abbas, and K. Saleem, "Cloud-assisted iot-based scada systems security: A review of the state of the art and future challenges," IEEE Access, vol. 4, 2016, pp. 1375–1384.

[26] S. Sicari, A. Rizzardi, L. A. Grieco, and A. Coen-Porisini, "Security, privacy and trust in internet of things: The road ahead," Computer Networks, vol. 76, 2015, pp. 146–164.

[27] X. Lu, Q. Li, Z. Qu, and P. Hui, "Privacy information security classification study in internet of things," in Identification, Information and Knowledge in the Internet of Things (IIKI), 2014 International Conference on. IEEE, 2014, pp. 162–165.

[28] A. Alcaide, E. Palomar, J. Montero-Castillo, and A. Ribagorda, "Anonymous authentication for privacy-preserving iot target-driven applications," Computers & Security, vol. 37, 2013, pp. 111–123.

[29] A. Puliafito, A. Celesti, M. Villari, and M. Fazio, "Towards the integration between iot and cloud computing: an approach for the secure self-configuration of embedded devices," International Journal of Distributed Sensor Networks, 2015, pp. 1–9.

[30] J.-X. Hu, C.-L. Chen, C.-L. Fan, and K.-h. Wang, "An intelligent and secure health monitoring scheme using iot sensor based on cloud computing," Journal of Sensors, vol. 2017, 2017, pp. 1–11.

[31] L. Neto, J. Reis, R. Silva, and G. Gonçalves, "Sensor selcomp, a smart component for the industrial sensor cloud of the future," in Proceedings of the 2017 IEEE International Conference on Industrial Technology. IEEE, 2017, pp. 1256–121.

[32] "SelSus - White paper on sensor cloud," URL: http://www.selsus.eu/fileadmin/mount/documents/SelSus_-_D3.5_-_White_paper_on_sensor_clouds.pdf [accessed: 2017-05-10].

A New Approach in System Integration in Smart Grids

J.I. Guerrero, Enrique Personal, and Carlos León
Department of Electronic Technology
University of Seville
Seville, Spain
e-mail: juaguealo@us.es, epersonal@us.es, cleon@us.es

Abstract—**The emergent technologies related to Smart Grids provide new scenarios with new challenges. Specifically, the deployment of Smart Grid management infrastructures involves very hard scheduling, very high economic investment, and a lot of resources. Moreover, the traditional systems are based on proprietary architectures, which make more difficult the deployment process. The solution proposed in this paper makes easier the integration process of modern and old systems, in two levels, at level of metadata and data with the Heterogeneous Data Source Integration System, and at level of web services with the Web Service Integration System. Both systems are based on advanced analytics techniques, like Web Service Mining, Process Mining, Metadata Mining, Decision Support Systems, etc. Additionally, this paper establishes a test environment for the simulation of the deployment projects, called Simulation Engine. The proposed solution performed a successful integration and increased the efficiency of infrastructure in more than 30%, increasing in each iteration.**

Keywords- heterogeneous data source integration; web service mining; metadata mining; data mining.

I. INTRODUCTION

The emergent technologies related to Smart Grid (SG) are providing a new scope of functionalities and possibilities for management the power grid and increasing the available services for clients and companies. Moreover, SGs are changing the current scenario of energy markets (due to: the renewable penetration, the electricity batteries, the electric vehicles, etc.), in which the companies manage the energy in different ways. Traditionally, the energy was an utility, but, in the SG scenario, energy has turned into goods, with which the companies commercialize it.

Additionally, the SG ecosystem compounds a great quantity of systems with different standard functionalities. Some of these systems are only aggregators of data or services, to make them available for other systems. Other systems have specific functionalities, like: Energy Management System (EMS), Distributed Management System (DMS), Customer Information System (CIS), Meter Data Management System (MDMS), etc. Moreover, these systems could integrate or implement advanced functionalities at different levels of SG, for example: Building Management System (BMS), Vehicle to Grid Management System (V2GMS), Electrical Lighting Management System (ELMS), etc. Each of these systems has different needs, requires different information and services, and have different user roles (with different user interfaces).

Although, there are several technologies that provide the possibility to integrate different systems: MultiSpeak, Enterprise Service Busses (ESBs), etc. and these systems are usually accepted by standards, the main problem of these technologies is: the success of integration process is based on the compliance of several restrictions or adaptations by different systems. Currently, the systems are developed to come to terms with restrictions of these technologies. However, the deployment of the new systems related to SGs, needs several intermediate steps, that compounds the integration of traditional systems with modern systems. This integration should be in service and data contexts.

Additionally, several organizations are working on the description of Smart Grid Architecture Methodology (SGAM). Although several organizations have different models, it is possible to shape each other, providing an interpretation or comparison between them. For example, GridWise Architecture Council (GWAC) defines an interoperability stack; The Open Group's Architecture Framework (TOGAF) provides the Architecture Development Method (ADM); the European Standardization Organizations (ESO) like the European Committee for Standardization (CEN), European Committee for Electrotechnical Standardization (CENELEC), and the European Telecommunications Standards Institute (ETSI) provides an SGAM aligned to M/490 reference architecture, etc. National Institute of Standards and Technology (NIST) provides the equivalences between these different models. These methodologies provide a general vision of SG ecosystem, and it is strongly recommended to take into account in the integration process, in order to identify the different levels or layers.

Thus, in the SG ecosystems may be different types of systems with different information. The development of new systems should consider the information from old systems, in order to take advantage from the combination of an old and new information. But this process is very complex, and requires long developments and deployments. In this sense, the present paper proposes an automatic system to integrate all information and services from different systems, making available their resources to other systems in SG ecosystem.

In Section II, a bibliographic review is included. In Section III, a general architecture of proposed solution is described. In Section IV, the Heterogeneous Data Source

Integration System (HDSIS) is described. In Section V, the Web Service Integration System (WSIS) is proposed, with a description of all its modules. In Section VI, the experimental results are described. Finally, in Section VII, the conclusion section is included.

II. BIBLIOGRAPHIC REVIEW

In this case, there are two technologies related with the proposed paper, the integration of heterogeneous data sources and the integration of the system at the service level.

In the HDSIS case, there are a lot of studies and researches related to heterogeneous data integration based on, for instance, XML [1], Lucene and XQuery [2]. In the same way, heterogeneous data integration has been applied on many areas, such as Livestock Products Traceability [3], safety production [4], management information systems [5], medical information [6], and web environments [7].

There are also examples of the application of data mining mixed with Heterogeneous Data Source Integration (HDSI). These types of solutions increase the capability of solution to adapt it to different and heterogeneous data sources. [8]proposes a framework of a self-Adaptive Heterogeneous Data Integration System (AHDIS), based on ontology, semantic similarity, web service and XML techniques, which can be regulated dynamically. [9] uses On-Line Analytical Processing (OLAP) and data mining to illustrate the advantages for the relational algebra of adding the metadata type attribute and the transpose operator.

In the integration of the system at the service level case, there are several technologies based on the definition of different interfaces and standards, but the Web Service Mining (WSM) [10] is used in this paper. There are also several solutions based on process mining [11], pattern usage discovery [12], hypergraph-based matrix representation with a service set mining algorithm [13], constraint satisfaction [14], semantics-based methods [15], customer value analysis [16], frequent composite algorithm [17], Heterogeneous Feature Selection [18], etc.

III. GENERAL ARCHITECTURE

The proposed solution is based on the merging of two previously published solutions:

- A solution for HDSI [19]. This solution provides the integration from different relational database or data source, providing a new data model based on information standards, and providing models for the main parameters identified in data, according to the results of the application of metadata mining and a decision support system.
- A solution for integration of web services in SG ecosystem [20]. This solution based on WSM and Swarm Intelligence, provides a way to automatically integrate the Web Service (WS) interfaces from all authorized systems, creating and configuring new WSs based on the usage of previously existing WSs.

Both solutions have been integrated, and some modules were updated to interconnect each other. Thus, the proposed solution, shown in Figure 1, provides a solution to integrate information and services, which offers the possibility to create new WSs or information based on the integration process.

Although some of the proposed modules have been previously published, several of them have been updated in order to adapt the architecture, providing additional basic and advanced functionalities. The updates and new functionalities are described below.

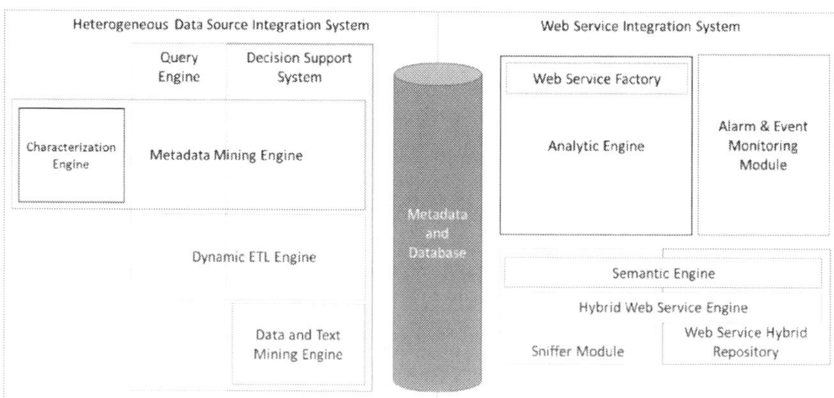

Figure 1. General Architecture.

IV. HETEROGENEOUS DATA SOURCE INTEGRATION SYSTEM

The HDSIS has several modules, mainly described in [19]. This system is based on the usage of a Decision Support System (DSS) and a Query Engine (QE), which supports different processes of Metadata Mining, Data Mining, and Text Mining.

QE is an extended library, which provides connection interfaces to different databases or data sources, allowing advanced SQL queries. Decision Support System (DSS) is implemented as a framework, which allows to manage rules, applying them to the different data sources.

Metadata Mining Engine (MDME) has several stages. In a first step, the metadata is extracted from each data source. In the second step, the Characterization Engine characterizes columns, tables, relationships and data sources, calculating several indicators or coefficients. The indicators or coefficients are used to classify the metadata, checking the coherence, the quality, and some other features of data and metadata. Finally, all the generated information is stored in order to integrate all metadata and data.

The Dynamic ETL (Extract, Translate, and Load) Engine (DETLE) implements an ETL with extended functionalities. This module was enhanced since the publication of the other papers. Nevertheless, this module has been modified in order to create specific ETL based on the information from Analytic Engine of WSIS to create specific and theme-oriented data warehouse, with star or snowflake structure. Initially, DETLE was a module which creates a new relational database based on information standard from International Electrotechnical Committee (IEC) or Distributed Management Task Force (DMTF) or, even, data warehouse with star or snowflake structure, according to the information from MDME. Specifically, in this new proposed solution, the DETLE has new functionalities that can generate a new ETL based on information from Analytic Engine (WSIS) and from WSs usage, or can create a new ETL according to a requested model for a specific parameter in any data source integrated in the system. This new functionality has increased the intercommunication with other modules, like Data and Text Mining Engine (DTME).

The DTME has increased their functionalities, too. Currently, this module implements an automatic modelling tool, which can model based on the information from MDME or based on information from WSIS. So, for example, a client can request by using a WS call a creation of a data warehouse for a specific parameter. When this call is fired the system retrieves all information related with this parameter (metadata and data) and tries to release the best data mining or/and text mining model, creating a data warehouse to feed it. The client can modify or update the model, or even, model again.

The HDSIS has provided additional services for the WSIS, which are included in Web Service Hybrid Repository (WSHR).

V. WEB SERVICE INTEGRATION SYSTEM

The WSIS is based on WSM and Process Mining. The first version of this WSIS was previously published in [20]. However, there are new functionalities and some modules have been merged, and others have been updated with new functionalities. In this way, the Sniffer Module integrates functionalities related with monitoring and discovering of new WSs. Traditionally, this task was made by an Ant Colony Optimization (ACO) technique. Currently, this functionality is integrated in Hybrid Web Service Engine (HWSE) and Semantic Engine.

The Analytic Engine analyzes the WS traffic based on WSM, in order to identify the sequences of WSs and their feasible relation to alarm or events in the ecosystem. Using the Web Service Factory (WSF), the Analytic Engine can create new WS with aggregated behavior of sequences of WS. Although the aggregation of WSs can be made by different ways, the proposed solution groups WS according to several features: the semantical interpretation of WS sequences, the number of invocation of the same WS sequence, and the feasible variations in a WS sequence.

The Alarm and Event Monitoring Module provides information about the external events and alarms generated in low level systems. The low level systems usually work in real time, representing from Internet of Things (IoT) devices to Intelligent Electronic Devices (IEDs).

A. *The Web Service Hybrid Repository and the Semantic Engine.*

The WSHR implements a WS repository. Additionally, this module gathers all request or notification WSs in different systems.

The Sniffer Module monitors the channel and performs the task of service discovering.

The HWSE parses all WSs. This engine provided compatibility with different Service Oriented Architectures (SOA). HWSE is a bidirectional module. When is a request WS or a sniffed WS, and it has been generated by the external system, the WS message is gathered by the corresponding module (Sniffer module or WSHR) and analyzed by HWSE and, finally, by Semantic Engine, registering all information in the internal database. If the message is generated by WSIS the message makes the inverse route, it is constructed by Semantic Engine, translated to JSON (JavaScript Object Notation) or XML (eXtended Marked Language), and sent by the corresponding module. The details of both modules are shown in Figure 2.

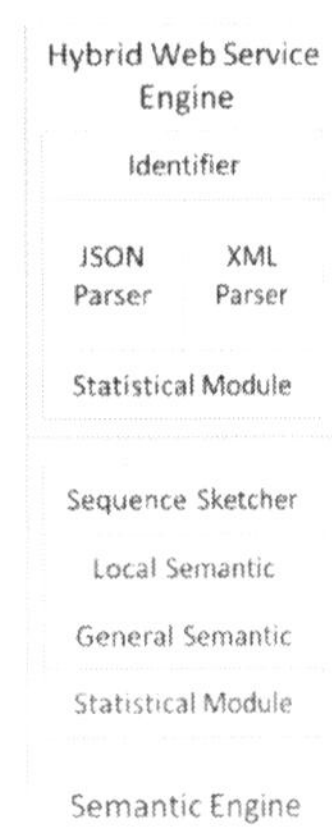

Figure 2. Hybrid Web Service Engine and Semantic Engine details.

The HWSE has different modules (Figure 2). Identifier module identifies the language of the message. According to this identification, the message is parsed by JSON or XML parser. Finally, the parsed message is enriched with additional information about statistics related to other messages or other systems. When this engine treats a message from the WSIS the modules make the inverse function.

The Semantic Engine has several modules (Figure 2), too. When the messages come from external systems, after they are treated by HWSE, they are sent to the Sequence Sketcher. This module establishes a relation in sequence call of different WS based on application of Process Mining techniques. Local Semantic is a module based on fuzzy logic, which extracts the semantic related to different parts of the message. After this step, General Semantic establishes the relation to other messages, and possible future messages. Th module is based on fuzzy and time series. Finally, in Statistical Module, several statistics and results from previous modules are registered in the WSIS database.

When the message come from the internal systems, they are treated in a reverse way. At the end, the Sequence Sketcher sends the message to HWSE. Thus, all messages in the channel are registered by the WSIS.

VI. Experimental Results

The proposed solution was tested in a little cluster of computers, with different features and functionalities. Although, the proposed solution can work in distributed environments, in this case, the proposed solution was integrated in a unique computer.

The cluster was implemented with four servers. The first server has an Intel i7 (3GHz), 16GB RAM and GTX750 (2GB and 640 CUDA cores). The second server has an Intel Xeon E5 (2GHz), 64GB RAM and Quadro K1200 (4GB and 512 CUDA cores). The third and fourth servers have the same configuration: i5 (2.7GHz) and 8 GB RAM. The two first servers are virtualized, and the rest of them are not virtualized, because they have low performance features.

A. General Description of the Test Environment

The proposed solution is integrated in a simulated ecosystem. In this way, several systems are simulated:

- EMS. This system simulates the generation of information related with the demand response and the energy flow management. The internal database follows the IEC standards implemented in a relational database for the Energy Management Systems. The demand response information is randomly generated limited to different intervals. Moreover, when the system detects that the random information is near to the end of proposed intervals generates alarms or events. This system has available several WS related to reporting activities, and several request/response WS that implements commands about consumption and generation.
- Commercial System. This system randomly generates information about consumption. This generation is based on the real consumption curves, from the residential and industrial consumers. The system generates random information for 3400 residential and 50 industrial customers, although these parameters are configurable. The information is stored in a relational database with a non-standard structured, based on real database structure. This system integrates several WS of subscription/notification type, in order to notify the billing process, and request/response services to provide different information for reporting activities.
- Electric Vehicle Charging Infrastructure Management (EVCIM). This system implements several procedures to generate random information about consumption in different points of power grid. The original system is implemented with 6 charging stations, with a maximum power of 50 kW. The information is stored in a relational database without any information standard structure. There is not implemented any simulation system for routes and fleet management, only simulates the impact of information generated to manage the electric vehicles charging.
- DMS. This system stores information about the power grid infrastructure. The system simulates a segment of generic distribution grid. This segment is based on the IEEE 34 Node Test Feeder ([21]). The system stored all information based on International Electrotechnical Committee (IEC) Common Information Model (CIM), extended to allow the acquisition of information from the specific protection modules, which are randomly generated. The main services available in this system are requests/responses retrieving the information from the server and generating alarms and events.
- Photovoltaic Generation Management System (PVGMS). This system implements a simulated photovoltaic generation station, with 1.5 MWh. The data about generation is randomly generated, based on the model generated from real information of photovoltaic farm. This system has several responses/requests WS oriented to retrieve information from the server. Additionally, this system can receive different commands to manage the load on power grid.

The interconnection of these systems are implemented based on an ESB. Two ESB have been tested: Mule and TIBCO. The proposed architecture is shown in Figure 3.

B. Simulation Engine

The Simulation Engine is the external system, which orchestrates the simulation. The Simulation Engine has programmed several simulation sequences related to:

- Normal operation. The request of different WS is related to the normal operation of power grid. In this sense, the DMS, EMS and Commercial System are the systems with a high number of request/response WS, although there are mainly a lot of subscription/notification WS. PVGMS and EVCIM receive commands and generate notifications about the generated information in each system.
- Fault in a specific feeder node. This case is characterized by a very high level of request WS without response, and additionally, the generation of several alarms and events from the simulated external systems.
- Billing period. In this case, the Commercial System increases its activity, with a lot of notification WSs.

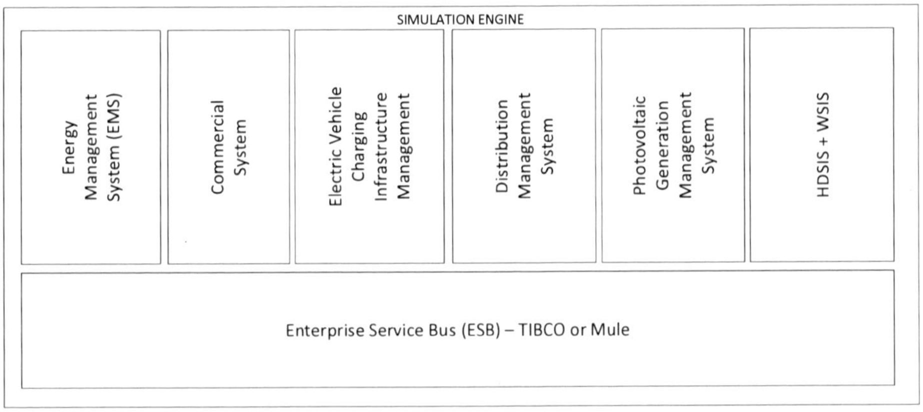

Figure 3. Architecture of simulation infrastructure.

- Massive electric vehicle charging period. In this case, the Commercial System, the PVGMS and the EVCIM generate a lot of notification WSs, and EMS and DMS generate a lot of request WSs and commands.
- Mixed mode. In this case, a combination of two of the previously described cases are combined, generating alternative scenarios, which could provide variations in the detected WS sequences because of the interference of both cases.

The Simulation Engine randomly runs each of these behavior patterns, until 100 patterns are performed. This parameter is configurable. The system converges to the best solution in each iteration, making variations of WS definition.

Although, these sequences are programming according to standards in the Simulation Engine, the proposed solution has not any information about it. The proposed solution only gathers information from ESB.

C. *Simulation Results*

In the first stage of the system, the HDSIS makes the integration of all available metadata in different systems, providing 47 new WS, which provided access to the old and new information, generated by different models created by DTME. The data access is based on WS call that deals with metadata to address the data target. In this case, due to the lack of disk space, the integration was performed at metadata level. This is a configurable option in HDSIS.

The Simulation Results show that after performing of 10 patterns, the proposed solution has reduced the number of calls in 20.62%, and the response time in 17.6%. The proposed solution increased the efficiency in 32.09%. After the running the 10th pattern, the system can increase the efficiency with a low rate of variation between 0.2% and 8.92% per each 10 performed patterns. After the 10th pattern, the WSHR has increased the available WS in 6 new WS, aggregated from existing WSs.

After several iterations of simulation process, the increase of efficiency rate depends on the regularity of WS usage and the semantic coherence of response. It is very difficult to simulate all contingencies and scenarios of this type of ecosystems. However, the implementation of simulation infrastructure and the simulation processes performed for the project have provided several requirements and modules to establish a basic Simulation Engine for this type of system.

VII. CONCLUSION

The integration of different systems in a SG ecosystem is one of the most important topics in Smart City, one of the most important way to make a good integration is the standardization of different process related to SG. However, this process is still running and the current distribution system cannot afford them to discard the old system (with all information stored) and start with a new system and with new specifications. The distribution companies have to define hard deployment plans that allow the implementation and integration of the modern architectures with the traditional ones.

The proposed solution is a novel approach to achieve this goal, making easier the deployment processes of old and new systems in a SG ecosystem. The new systems are integrated, providing new information and services, which could be available for other components or systems in the SG. This integration is performed at data level with an HDSIS and WS level with a WSIS, increasing the global efficiency than 30%.

Additionally, a Simulation Engine has been designed and tested, providing a test environment for this type of deployments, which, in the real case, requires a lot of hardware and software resources.

ACKNOWLEDGMENT

The authors are also appreciative of the backing of the SIIAM project (Reference Number: TEC2013-40767-R), which is funded by the Ministry of Economy and Competitiveness of Spain.

REFERENCES

[1] X. Fengguang, H. Xie, and K. Liqun, "Research and implementation of heterogeneous data integration based on XML," 9th International Conference on Electronic Measurement Instruments, 2009. ICEMI '09, Beijing, 2009, pp. 4-711-4-715.

[2] L. Tianyuan, S. Meina, and Z. Xiaoqi, "Research of massive heterogeneous data integration based on Lucene and XQuery," in 2010 IEEE 2nd Symposium on Web Society (SWS), Beijing, 2010, pp. 648-652.

[3] X. d Chen and J. z Liu, "Research on Heterogeneous Data Integration in the Livestock Products Traceability System," in International Conference on New Trends in Information and Service Science, 2009. NISS '09, Beijing, 2009, pp. 969-972.

[4] X. b Han, F. Tian, and F. b Wu, "Research on Heterogeneous Data Integration in the Safety Production and Management of Coal-Mining," in 2009 First International Workshop on Database Technology and Applications, Wuhan, Hubei, 2009, pp. 87-90.

[5] W. Hailing and H. Yujie, "Research on heterogeneous data integration of management information system," in 2012 International Conference on Computational Problem-Solving (ICCP), Leshan, 2012, pp. 477-480.

[6] Y. Shi, X. Liu, Y. Xu, and Z. Ji, "Semantic-based data integration model applied to heterogeneous medical information system," in 2010 The 2nd International Conference on Computer and Automation Engineering (ICCAE), vol. 2, Singapore, 2010, pp. 624-628.

[7] H. Fan and H. Gui, "Study on Heterogeneous Data Integration Issues in Web Environments," in International Conference on Wireless Communications, Networking and Mobile Computing, 2007. WiCom 2007, Shanghai, 2007, pp. 3755-3758.

[8] Y. Cao, Y. Chen, and B. Jiang, "A Study on Self-adaptive Heterogeneous Data Integration Systems," in Research and Practical Issues of Enterprise Information Systems II, L. D. Xu, A. M. Tjoa, and S. S. Chaudhry, Eds. Springer US, 2007, pp. 65–74.

[9] T. H. Merrett, "Attribute Metadata for Relational OLAP and Data Mining," in Database Programming Languages, G. Ghelli and G. Grahne, Eds. Springer Berlin Heidelberg, 2001, pp. 97–118.

[10] G. Zheng and A. Bouguettaya, Web Service Mining: Application to Discoveries of Biological Pathways. Boston, MA: Springer Science+Business Media, LLC, 2010. p. 152.

[11] W. v d Aalst, "Service Mining: Using Process Mining to Discover, Check, and Improve Service Behavior," IEEE Trans. Serv. Comput., vol. 6, no. 4, pp. 525–535, pp. 525–535, Oct. 2013.

[12] Q. A. Liang, J. y Chung, S. Miller, and Y. Ouyang, "Service Pattern Discovery of Web Service Mining in Web Service Registry-Repository," in 2006 IEEE International Conference on e-Business Engineering (ICEBE'06), Shanghai, 2006, pp. 286-293.

[13] A. Zhao, X. Wang, K. Ren, and Y. Qiu, "Semantic Message Link Based Service Set Mining for Service Composition," in Fifth International Conference on Semantics, Knowledge and Grid, 2009. SKG 2009, Zhuhai, 2009, pp. 338-341.

[14] Q. A. Liang, S. Miller, and J. Y. Chung, "Service mining for Web service composition," in IRI -2005 IEEE International Conference on Information Reuse and Integration, Conf. 2005, 2005, pp. 470-475.

[15] H. Luo, L. Liu, and Y. Sun, "Semantics-Based Service Mining Method in Wireless Sensor Networks," in 2011 Seventh International Conference on Mobile Ad-hoc and Sensor Networks (MSN), Beijing, 2011, pp. 115-121.

[16] W. Hu and Y. Hui, "Service-mining Based on Customer Value Analysis," in 2007 International Conference on Management Science and Engineering, Harbin, 2007, pp. 109-114.

[17] H. Meng, L. Wu, T. Zhang, G. Chen, and D. Li, "Mining Frequent Composite Service Patterns," in 2008 Seventh International Conference on Grid and Cooperative Computing, Shenzhen, 2008, pp. 713-718.

[18] L. Chen, Q. Yu, P. S. Yu, and J. Wu, "WS-HFS: A Heterogeneous Feature Selection Framework for Web Services Mining," in 2015 IEEE International Conference on Web Services (ICWS), New York, NY, 2015, pp. 193-200.

[19] J. I. Guerrero, A. García, E. Personal, J. Luque, and C. León, "Heterogeneous data source integration for smart grid ecosystems based on metadata mining," Expert Syst. Appl., vol. 79, pp. 254–268, pp. 254–268, Aug. 2017.

[20] J. I. Guerrero, E. Personal, A. Parejo, A. García, and C. León, "Forecasting the Needs of Users and Systems - A New Approach to Web Service Mining," in The Fifth International Conference on Intelligent Systems and Applications, Barcelona, Spain, 2016, pp. 95-99.

[21] W. H. Kersting, "Radial distribution test feeders," in 2001 IEEE Power Engineering Society Winter Meeting. Conference Proceedings (Cat. No.01CH37194), vol. 6, no. 3, 1991, pp. 975-985.

Data Analysis for Early Fault Detection

On-line monitoring approach for heat exchanger in solar-thermal plant

Javier M. Mora-Merchan, Enrique Personal, Antonio Parejo, Antonio García, Carlos León
Electronic Technology Department
Escuela Politécnica Superior, University of Seville,
Seville, Spain
e-mail: jmmora@us.es

Abstract—**Nowadays, the reliability and robustness levels required for production systems are growing. These demands make philosophies, such as predictive maintenance essential in modern industry, among which the energy sector stands out. In this sense, this paper proposes an on-line monitoring system based on data mining models, which provides a useful tool to identify operation anomalies easily, being able to identify and prevent possible future failures. This approach has been applied successfully in a real case, where a performance analysis for the cooling systems of a solar-thermal power plant was implemented.**

Keywords-Predictive maintenance; fault detection; solar plant; data analysis.

I. INTRODUCTION

Nowadays, it is easy to see that the presence of continuous and more critical processes is growing in the industrial ambience. As their names suggest, these types of processes must run uninterruptedly and demand more in their reliability levels. Obviously, these demands require special treatment beyond a reactive or preventive maintenance. These needs are directly translated into an increment on the number of on-line monitoring or analysis systems, following what is known as a Predictive Maintenance (PdM) [1] philosophy. Specifically, PdM consists of a defect inspection strategy to prevent future problems using data analysis and identifying indicators for its detection.

The use of time series analysis to improve a process reliability is not a new approach [2][3]. However, the sensor number in processes, as well as their analytical capacity have grown systematically in the last years. An example of this evolution can be clearly seen in the energy industry, where machine learning and data mining analysis approaches are applied as useful tools to improve this service.

Specifically, these techniques have been applied by energy utilities at different levels, as can be seen in [4], where their authors propose methodologies based on data mining analysis, for maintaining the elements of smart grid distribution networks (cables, joints, manholes, and transformers), forecasting their failure probability. Specifically for cables isolation analysis, we can find [5], which proposes a partial discharge analysis, using the combination of wavelet packet transform analysis and a probabilistic neural network. Related to power transformers maintenance, [6] proposes a smart fault diagnostic approach combining five well-known methods based on dissolved gas studies, using several Artificial Neural Networks (ANNs) for their individual classification analysis and one more for the combination of their results.

Nevertheless, it is in the maintenance analysis of power generation systems where the application of intelligent approaches is more present in the last few years. As an example, [7] introduces an analysis framework for maintenance management of wind turbines, based on the characterization of correct operation settings, using ANNs. This framework directly obtains the information from the Supervisory Control and Data Acquisition (SCADA) system, combining it with an alarm and warning analysis. This approach allows the system to model the normal behavior of the gearbox bearing temperature. This estimation makes it possible to forecast possible damage in a gearbox earlier than traditional vibration-based approaches [8].

As can be observed above in the previously cited articles, most of the efforts are focused on the prediction of failures in the gearbox of wind generators that are the typical elements with greater cost and difficult substitution in them. However, there exist a multitude of elements in a generation plant, and without which its target could not be carried out either. This is what happens with the fluid condenser and cooling tower, essential in the refrigeration system of a solar-thermal power plant, and whose operation must also be monitored.

In this sense, this paper describes a Condition Monitoring System (CMS) to identify anomalies in the operation of both subsystems. For this, different approaches based on data mining have been evaluated to implement their operation models, determining the best option and validating their use for this purpose.

Specifically, the presented paper has been divided as follows; Section II describes the different necessary stages to make up a process model (data filtering, main variables identification, modeling technique election, etc.). After this, an on-line monitoring approach based on these models is described in Section III. Once the modeling and monitoring approaches have been described, Section IV performs a real application of them over some elements of a solar-thermal power plant. Finally, Section V lays out the conclusion of this work.

II. PROCESS MODEL GENERATION

As can be seen in next sections, the proposed analysis will be applied on a solar-thermal application. However, this CMS approach can be applied in the characterization of more applications or environments for a performance or a PdM analysis. In this sense, this approach proposes a monitoring system that analyzes the correct behavior of a process comparing it to one or more (if different modes of operation are identified) pre-estimated operating models, all of them based on data mining. Obviously, a correct estimation of these models will be essential for a valid operation of this monitoring system. Due to this, the modeling task will be described in detail, dividing it into four stages:

A. *Extraction of historical data*

This stage consists of the extraction of historical data of the process, which should contain measurements and event logs (typically collected from the process SCADA). Obviously, the length and granularity of this historical data must be adequate and contain a representative sample of the behavior in the plant under study.

B. *Identification of operating modes*

In this stage, the data are split up according to the different operation modes, in which the plant was operating. From this division, the next stages of this section (Data filtering and Models implementation) will be performed with each of these sets independently.

C. *Data filtering*

Unfortunately, it is very common to find anomalies in historical data. Due to this, before starting the modeling process, it is necessary to carry out an integrity analysis over them. These analyzes usually require a preliminary visual inspection, later choosing the most appropriate statistical method. A typical approach to this end (when normal behavior follows a normal distribution), is the use of interquartile distance criterion, which allows the filter process to determine a limit to separate the outlier data from those are considered as correct.

D. *Models implementation*

Once the data has been separated for each operation mode and the anomalies have been eliminated for each one, the following step will be to make the process models up.

However, not all the information acquired from the SCADA (direct measurement, cross-effects between them and their non-linear effects) has the same effect over the parameter to be modeled, may not even be relevant. Therefore, to simplify the model, a sensitivity analysis based on Akaike Information Criterion (AIC) [9] has been carried out over the data. This process makes it possible to identify those variables without relevance, discarding them from the initial input set, simplifying the final input set of the model.

After selecting these relevant variables, the next step is to make up a model with a better fit. In this sense, up to five different modeling data mining techniques are proposed for this task, such as:

1) Linear model [10]

In this approach, it consists of estimating the coefficients (β_i) that represent the weight of each input (X_i), which try to fix the behavior of Y, following (1). This approach raises the drawback of not being able to model non-linear behavior. However, it is traditionally a good option for a large number of cases.

$$Y = \beta_1 \cdot X_1 + \beta_2 \cdot X_2 + \ldots + \beta_n \cdot X_n \tag{1}$$

2) Linear model with quadratic and cubic terms [11]

This model is really an extension of the previous approach, incorporating also the quadratic ($\beta_{2,i}$) and cubic ($\beta_{3,i}$) terms of the model inputs (X_i). Equation (2) represents this type of model, making it possible to incorporate possible non-linear effects implicit in the process behavior.

$$\begin{aligned} Y = \beta_{1,1} \cdot X_1 + \beta_{2,1} \cdot X_1^2 + \beta_{3,1} \cdot X_1^3 + \ldots \\ \ldots + \beta_{1,n} \cdot X_n + \beta_{2,n} \cdot X_n^2 + \beta_{3,n} \cdot X_n^3 \end{aligned} \tag{2}$$

3) Linear model with second order combinations [11]

This model considers multiple interactions between variables up to the second degree, the relationship now being expressed by (3). This expression makes it possible to model the possible cross-interaction between the inputs (X_i).

$$\begin{aligned} Y = \beta_{1,1} \cdot X_1^2 + \ldots + \beta_{1,i} \cdot X_1 \cdot X_i + \ldots + \beta_{1,n} \cdot X_1 \cdot X_n + \ldots \\ \ldots \\ \ldots + \beta_{n,1} \cdot X_n \cdot X_1 + \ldots + \beta_{n,i} \cdot X_n \cdot X_i + \ldots + \beta_{n,n} \cdot X_n^2 \end{aligned} \tag{3}$$

4) Decision Tree [12]

A decision tree is a regression model represented as a binary tree. Each node contains a condition and the data traverses the tree according to the conditions that they fulfill. The leaves (nodes without descendants) include the regression formula to apply to each data that reaches it.

Therefore, a tree does not generate a linear model but a piecewise linear model.

5) Random Forest [13]

This last alternative consists of a classification and regression model based on a group of decision trees and a voting system.

Finally, all of these techniques are evaluated, only the best of them will be chosen for the monitoring systems.

III. MONITORING SYSTEM

The modeling process is a complex task that typically involves a lot of data and requires a high computation cost. However, this process is only done once (as off-line task), or with low periodicity to obtain models that reflect some possible changes in the process.

Conversely, on the on-line monitoring system, the pre-estimated model is faced with the direct measurements of the parameter to be evaluated, using this error normalized by its standard deviation as a performance indicator of the correct operation (see Figure 1).

This tool allows the user to identify anomalous trends easily, using standard deviation analysis, identified by the following color code:

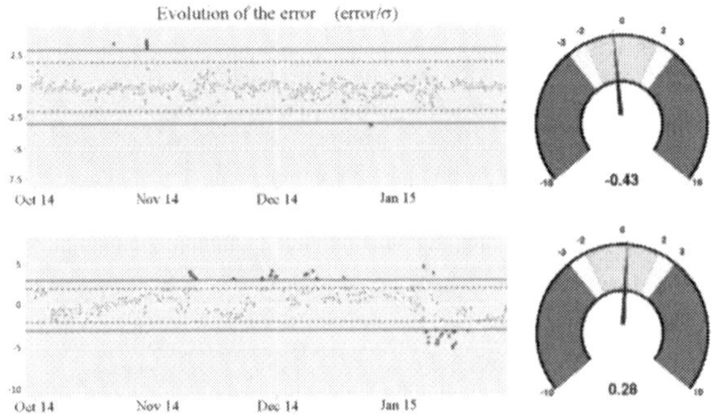

Figure 1. Monitoring interface of the proposed solution.

- *Correct operation* (green points). Cases whose predictions do not differ by more than 2σ.
- *Warning* (yellow points). Cases whose predictions have an error between 2σ and 3σ.
- *Offlimit* (red points). Cases whose predictions exceed 3σ.
- *Out* (black points). Cases whose distances exceed 10σ.

This analysis is able to anticipate a possible failure. For example *warning points*, although still in the normal data range, require greater observation to estimate if the system has a tendency to leave such margins. *Offlimit points* may represent a clear anomaly case (and a possible failure cause). And *Out points,* which are clearly out of the model and are operation modes completely out of training. These points should be studied separately to find possible failures.

IV. Study Case

Once the proposed approach to monitoring and PdM has been described, this section shows its application over a solar power plant based on heliostats.

As a brief description, this type of power plant uses mobile mirrors (or heliostats) that are oriented reflecting and concentrating sunlight toward a specific spot (typically located on a tower). This concentrated radiation generates heat energy that will be converted into motion through a turbine and various fluid circuits (with molten salts and fluids like water). Later, this rotating energy will be converted to electricity through a power generator (as can be seen in the Figure 2).

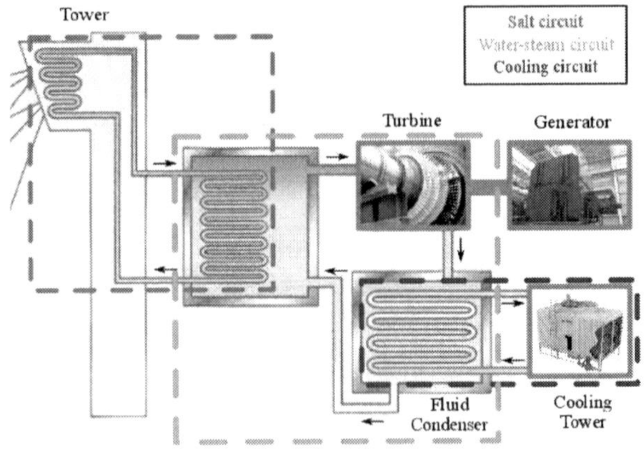

Figure 3. Basic schema of the heat exchange processes.

Thus, neither the power generation levels nor critical operations were analyzed for this example. Actually, the proposed analysis consists of monitoring two elements of the cooling system; the fluid condenser and the cooling tower. Specifically, the fluid condenser is the first stage of the cooling system, and it is responsible for carrying out the heat exchange between the water-steam and the cooling circuits (see Figure 3). The next element, the cooling tower is the part of the cooling process where the water of this circuit is cooled down in other heat exchangers, to be finally poured into a water tank.

Regardless of the temperature ranges in which both process operate, both have the same target (reduce the temperature of the fluid that is flowing through it). In this sense, a good indicator to evaluate this target fulfillment could be the difference between the input and output (thermal jump) of each one. Due to this, both processes have been analyzed, following in both the same approach (obviously varying the input data set for each).

The available information and its reliance for each process is summarized in Table I, which has provided up to 522,664 observations (one year of data approximately). Each of them was divided into two operation modes (day and night modes), as can be seen in the example shown in Figure

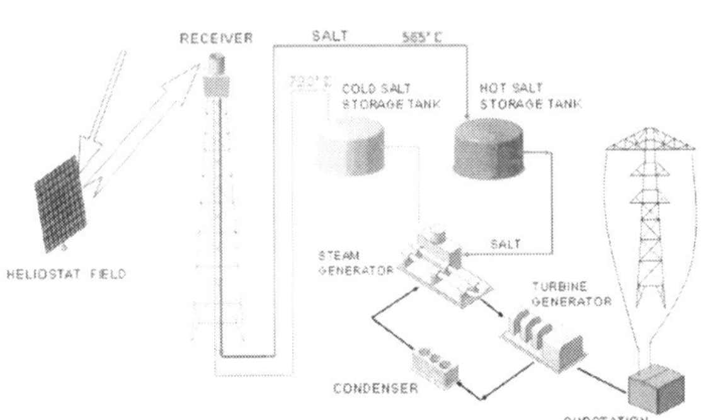

Figure 2. Solar flow basic shema [14].

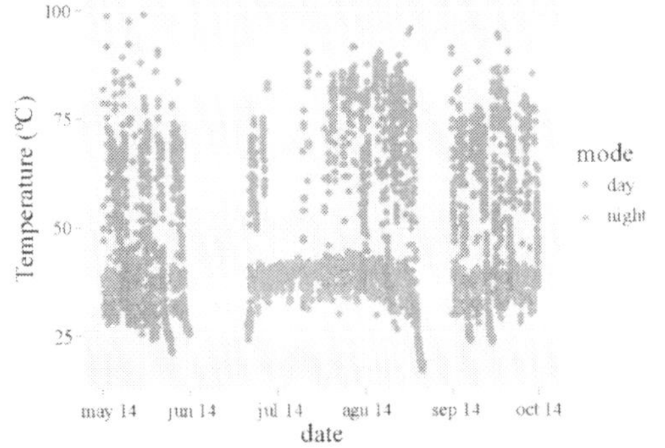

Figure 4. Condenser input temperature (in day and night modes).

TABLE I. COMPLETE SET OF INPUT PARAMETERS

Available measurements	Relev.*
Temperature at steam input in the fluid condenser	
Pressure at steam input in the fluid condenser	(1)
Level at steam input in the fluid condenser	
Temperature at cooling water input in the fluid condenser	(2)
Pressure at cooling water input in the fluid condenser	(1)
Temperature at cooling water output in the fluid condenser	(2)
Pressure at cooling water output in the fluid condenser	(1),(2)
Flow of the input cooling water in the fluid condenser	
Motor current of the cooling tower	(2)
Temperature of water tank	
Level of water tank	
pH of water tank	
Ambient temperature	
Relative humidity	
Atmospheric pressure	
Active power generated	(1)

* Note: (1) relevant for the fluid condenser model, (2) relevant for the cooling tower model.

4. Thus, following the previously described AIC selection method, it is possible to identify four relevant variables for each model (see details in Table I). From this information, and applying the procedures described in previous sections, it is possible to infer up to four system models (one for each subsystem and each mode), necessary for the proposed monitoring.

As can be seen in Table II, Table IV, Table VI and Table VIII, the best evaluated techniques in the four cases is the random forest, using an implementation with five trees.

In this sense, a cross-validation technique was proposed to validate each model. This test allows each method to show how well they function and how good they are.

TABLE II. COMPARISON BETWEEN MODELING METHODS (FLUID CONDENSER, DAY MODE)

Method	σ (°C)
Linear model	1.488
Model with quadratic and cubic terms	1.309
Second order cross model	1.313
Decision tree	1.364
Random forest (five trees)	**0.598**

TABLE III. OBTAINED RESULTS WITH SELECTED MODEL (FLUID CONDENSER, DAY MODE)

Category	Percentage of cross-validation subset (%)	Percentage of complete filtered set (%)	Percentage of complete set (%)
Correct	95.36	95.57	89.37
Warning	2.54	2.51	6.23
Offlimit	2.01	1.83	4.30
Out	0.09	0.09	0.10

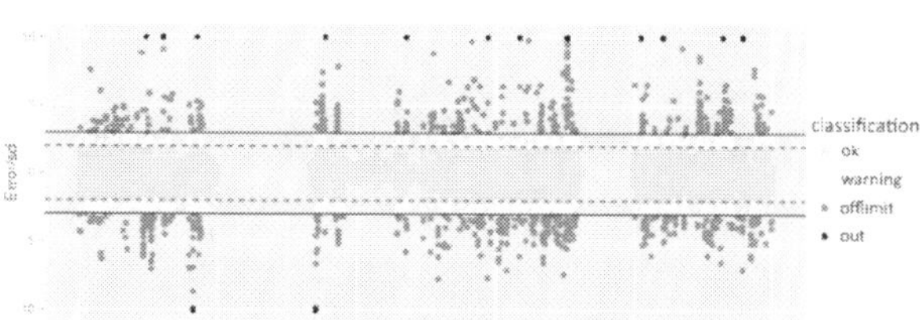

Figure 5. Distribution for complete set of filtered historical data with selected model (fluid condenser, day mode).

TABLE IV. COMPARISON BETWEEN MODELING METHODS (FLUID CONDENSER, NIGHT MODE)

Method	σ (°C)
Linear model	1.497
Model with quadratic and cubic terms	1.403
Second order cross model	1.454
Decision tree	1.360
Random forest (five trees)	**0.635**

TABLE V. OBTAINED RESULTS WITH SELECTED MODEL AND UNFILTERED DATA (FLUID CONDENSER, NIGHT MODE)

Category	Correct	Warning	Offlimit	Out
Percentage (%)	95.50	2.48	1.94	0.08

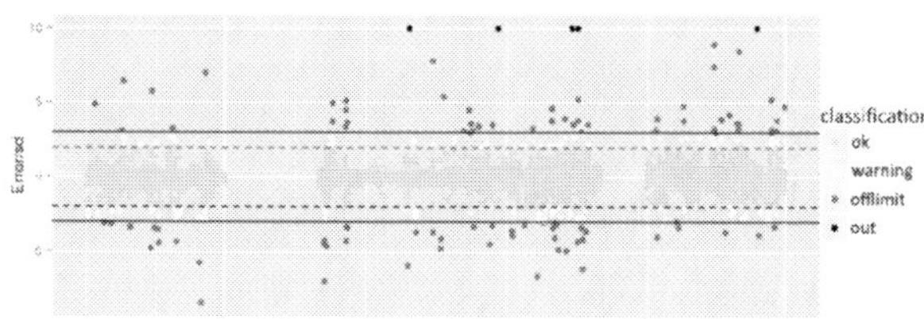

Figure 6. Distribution for complete set of unfiltered historical data with selected model (fluid condenser, night mode).

On the one hand, once the more adequate technique has been chosen, a fluid condenser model raises a standard deviation of 0.61589°C in day mode and 0.62475°C in night mode. Additionally, on the other hand, the cooling tower model raises a standard deviation of 0.38035°C in day mode and 0.62475°C in night mode. Therefore, it is possible to conclude that these proposed models are a valid estimation for the studied subsystems. This conclusion is also validated

TABLE VI. COMPARISON BETWEEN MODELING METHODS (COOLING TOWER, DAY MODE)

Method	σ (°C)
Linear model	0.940
Model with quadratic and cubic terms	0.906
Second order cross model	0.717
Decision tree	1.269
Random forest (five trees)	**0.380**

TABLE VII. OBTAINED RESULTS WITH SELECTED MODEL (COOLING TOWER, DAY MODE)

Category	Percentage of cross-validation subset (%)	Percentage of complete filtered set (%)	Percentage of complete set (%)
Correct	94.70	94.96	84.87
Warning	3.21	3.06	5.88
Offlimit	2.06	1.96	8.61
Out	0.03	0.02	0.64

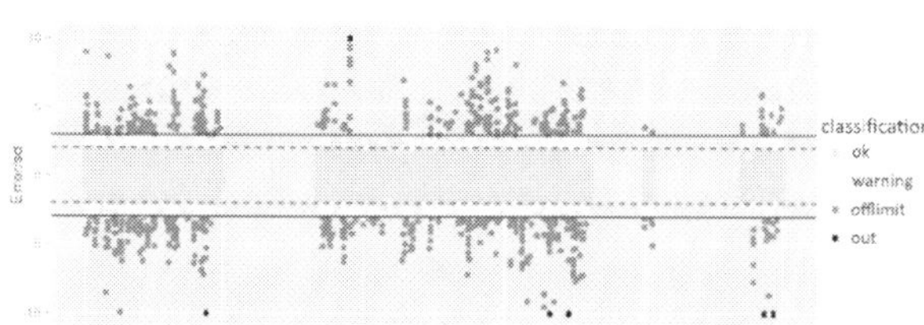

Figure 7. Distribution for complete set of filtered historical data with selected model (Cooling tower, day mode).

TABLE VIII. COMPARISON BETWEEN MODELING METHODS (COOLING TOWER, NIGHT MODE)

Method	σ (ºC)
Linear model	0.965
Model with quadratic and cubic terms	0.952
Second order cross model	1.281
Decision tree	1.376
Random forest (five trees)	**0.422**

TABLE IX. OBTAINED RESULTS WITH SELECTED MODEL AND UNFILTERED DATA (COOLING TOWER, NIGHT MODE)

Category	Correct	Warning	Offlimit	Out
Percentage (%)	94.92	3.09	1.96	0.03

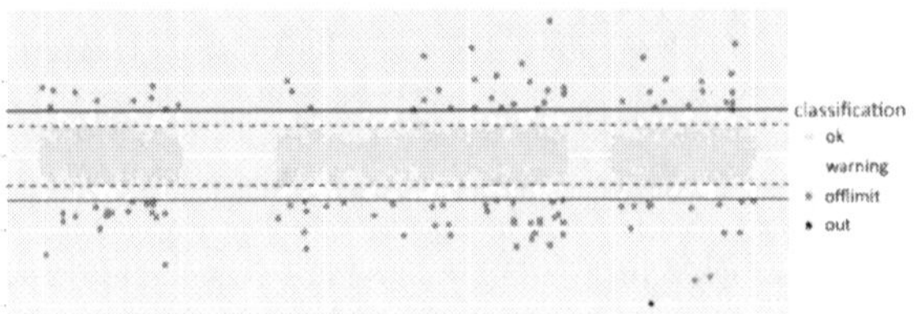

Figure 8. Distribution for complete set of unfiltered historical data with selected model (Cooling tower, night mode).

by Table III, Table V, Table VII and Table IX, and also from Figure 5 to Figure 8 that show the distribution of the error between real an estimated historical data.

V. CONCLUSIONS

As was commented in this paper, the accuracy requirements of current systems have grown enormously in the last few years. This evolution makes the monitoring and on-line analysis (such as PdM) essential in the production systems, among which the energy industry stands out.

In this sense, a PdM approach based on data mining techniques is proposed in this paper. This approach brings up a comparison between the real performance of a plant and an estimation (based on a model) of it, identifying a possible deviation from it as an anomaly, which could lead to future failure.

This approach has been evaluated over the cooling subsystems of real solar-thermal power plant. In this way, the analysis of this application made possible to validate its usefulness, comparing different modeling techniques and identifying the more appropriate of them for this application.

ACKNOWLEDGMENT

This research has been supported by the Ministry of Economy and Competitiveness of Spain through the SIIAM project (Reference Number: TEC2013-40767-R).

REFERENCES

[1] H. M. Hashemian and W. C. Bean, "State-of-the-Art Predictive Maintenance Techniques*," *IEEE Transactions on Instrumentation and Measurement*, vol. 60, no. 10, pp. 3480–3492, Oct. 2011.

[2] H. Lu, W. J. Kolarik, and S. S. Lu, "Real-time performance reliability prediction," *IEEE Transactions on Reliability*, vol. 50, no. 4, pp. 353–357, Dec. 2001.

[3] D. B. Durocher and G. R. Feldmeier, "Predictive versus preventive maintenance," *IEEE Industry Applications Magazine*, vol. 10, no. 5, pp. 12–21, 2004.

[4] C. Rudin *et al.*, "Machine Learning for the New York City Power Grid," *IEEE Transactions on Pattern Analysis and Machine Intelligence*, vol. 34, no. 2, pp. 328–345, Feb. 2012.

[5] D. Evagorou *et al.*, "Feature extraction of partial discharge signals using the wavelet packet transform and classification with a probabilistic neural network," *IET Science, Measurement Technology*, vol. 4, no. 3, pp. 177–192, May 2010.

[6] S. S. M. Ghoneim, I. B. M. Taha, and N. I. Elkalashy, "Integrated ANN-based proactive fault diagnostic scheme for power transformers using dissolved gas analysis," *IEEE Transactions on Dielectrics and Electrical Insulation*, vol. 23, no. 3, pp. 1838–1845, Jun. 2016.

[7] P. Bangalore and L. B. Tjernberg, "An Artificial Neural Network Approach for Early Fault Detection of Gearbox Bearings," *IEEE Transactions on Smart Grid*, vol. 6, no. 2, pp. 980–987, Mar. 2015.

[8] A. Zaher, S. D. J. McArthur, D. G. Infield, and Y. Patel, "Online wind turbine fault detection through automated SCADA data analysis," *Wind Energy*, vol. 12, no. 6, pp. 574–593, 2009.

[9] J. M. Chambers, *Statistical Models in S; Chapter 6: Generalized linear models*, 1st ed. Chapman and Hall/CRC, 1991.

[10] J. M. Chambers, *Statistical Models in S; Chapter 4: Linear Models*, 1st ed. Chapman and Hall/CRC, 1991.

[11] D. C. Montgomery, E. A. Peck, and G. G. Vining, *Introduction to linear regression analysis*. John Wiley & Sons, 2015.

[12] T. Therneau, B. Atkinson, and B. Ripley, *Recursive Partitioning and Regression Trees*. 2017.

[13] A. Liaw and M. Wiener, "Classification and Regression by randomForest," *R News*, vol. 2, no. 3, pp. 18–22, 2002.

[14] J. I. B. J.I. Ortega and F. M. Tellez, "Central Receiver System Solar Power Plant Using Molten Salt as Heat Transfer Fluid," *Journal of Solar Energy Engineering*, vol. 130, no. 2, pp. 1-6, 2008.

An Intelligent Help-Desk Framework for Effective Troubleshooting

Miguel Ángel Leal , Antonio Martín, Jorge Ropero, Julio Barbancho, Carlos León
Department of Electronic Technology
University of Seville
Seville, Spain
e-mail: maleal@us.es, toni@us.es, jropero@dte.us.es, jbarbancho@us.es, cleon@us.es.

Abstract— **Nowadays, technological infrastructure requires an intelligent virtual environment based on decision processes. These processes allow the coordination of individual elements and the tasks that connect them. Thus, incident resolution must be efficient and effective to achieve maximum productivity. In this paper, we present the design and implementation of an intelligent decision-support system applied in technology infrastructure at the University of Seville (Spain). We have used a Case Based Reasoning (CBR) methodology and an ontology to develop an intelligent system for supporting expert diagnosis and intelligent management of incidents. This is an innovative and interdisciplinary approach to knowledge management in problem-solving processes that are related to environmental issues. Our system provides an automatic semantic indexing for the generating of question/answer pairs, a case based reasoning technique for finding similar questions, and an integration of external information sources via ontologies. A real ontology-based question/answer platform named ExpertSOS is presented as a proof of concept. The intelligent diagnosis platform is able to identify and isolate the most likely cause of infrastructure failure in case of a faulty operation.**

Keywords-Case Based Reasoning; Helpdesk; Artificial Intelligence; Fuzzy Logic; Ontology.

I. INTRODUCTION

Today, troubleshooting intelligent management is viewed as one of the fastest growing areas of research, while new applications are developed in decision-support systems. Some of the challenges on these systems depend on the integration of intelligent systems in existing conventional systems. Many researchers are working on these topics, but none of them have focused on normalizing the management of knowledge.

In this work, we study a technology infrastructure troubleshooting maintenance centre at the University of Seville (Spain). This paper shows how semantic web and artificial intelligent technologies can be utilized in help-desk systems from the point of view of the content indexer. We also describe an inteligent decision-based semantic service named ExpertSOS. This is an example of how to apply a semantic technique for extracting troubleshooting knowledge. Clients may send trouble symptoms or questions to the system. Then, the system provides an expert answer to these questions. Moreover, this work proposes a method to efficiently search for the expert information on an Intelligent Decision Support System (IDSS) with multiple independent information sources.

Typical work in related fields includes intelligent agents. Ottosen et al. [1] suggest a heuristic model that simulates real-world troubleshooting system. Chu et al. [2] describe how data mining technologies can be used to build a rule-based system for customer service automatically. Cebi et al. [3] propose an expert system to help shipboard personnel solving ship auxiliary machinery troubleshooting. Zahedi et al. [4] investigate fuzzy troubleshooting of a complex crude oil desalination plant. Sierra et al. [5] describe a maintenance system for a microsatellite. Abdul-Wahab et al. [6] describe a fuzzy logic-based technique to design real-time troubleshooting advice.

Although there have been great advances in intelligent troubleshooting management, very few studies investigate the use of hybrid techniques to integrate the acquired knowledge from management experience based on Case Based Reasoning (CBR) engines and ontologies. This paper presents the integration of several computational intelligence techniques in ontology search and CBR. This way, a real-time intelligent assistant has been developed to automatically find patterns for the incidents and possible solutions from the stored cases in the system knowledge database. We present a method to efficiently retrieve knowledge from an intelligent decision support system (IDSS) with a semantic source. We have designed and developed an intelligent decision support environment named ExpertSOS to assist the customer service center of a large University within the technological infrastructure. In the following sections, we review the CBR framework and its features for implementing the reasoning process over ontologies. Section 2 presents a general overview about the technology infrastructure at the University of Seville, analyzing its failures and discovering the needs that push us toward new intelligent help desk paradigms. Section 3 analyzes ontology requirements and proposes the design criteria to guide the development of ontologies for knowledge-sharing purposes. Section 4 examines the design and development of the intelligent ExpertSOS platform, while Section 5 presents the Graphic User Interface (GUI). Section 6 shows tests and results. Finally, Section 7 shows the main conclusions of our work.

II. GENERAL OVERVIEW

The historic University of Seville (UoS) is one of the top-ranked universities in Spain. The UoS has a present student body of over 75,000, 4,500 teaching staff, and 2,500 administrative staff. UoS provides a robust infrastructure utilizing state-of-the-art technologies, with 1,200 wireless access points, 55,000 laptops, and 25,000 PCs distributed in the more than 30 buildings. In this scenario, UoS information systems and technology infrastructure must respond to the requirements of the community by providing additional quality functionalities. The Service of Information and Communication (SIC) of the UoS is responsible for Information Technology issues and offers technical services to the university. SIC offers a range of technical services for the university community, which include the architecture, installation, administration, and maintenance of servers; back end services, such as monitoring, updating, patches, security, data integrity assurance, and license management; computer network maintenance, including the backbone campus network, student hosting, and wireless networking. Moreover, SIC provides services such as e-mail, file storage, online courses, etc., and is responsible for maintaining all administrative applications. Due to the wide variety of technical services, resources and software that can be found, SIC has got a team of highly-trained technicians (45 workers) in the different university campus buildings. This group performs a varied set of tasks, assisting the university community with a wide range of services. The list includes, but is not limited to maintenance and monitoring resources, installation of computer equipment, security, monitoring hardware requirement assessment, virus and malware removal, hardware installation and troubleshooting, software troubleshooting, network connection issues, data recovery services, etc.

Derived from the various devices, heterogeneity and different group of programs can be found in this infrastructure, and given the lack of the standardization, the numerous devices and resources cause different types of diagnostic information when an incident occurs. Thus, the UoS installed a help desk platform named TSOS (Technical SOS). TSOS was designed to support and answer calls from customers and find the answer to their problems. A call center was responsible for receiving reports on faulty machines, or inquiries from their customers. When a problem is reported, a TSOS service engineer suggests a series of "checkpoints" to the technicians to solve the reported problem. Such suggestions are based on past experience or extracted from a customer service database. The database contains previous service records that are identical or similar to the current one. When an online session cannot solve the problem, the service center will dispatch the service engineers to the customer's site as soon as possible, in order to carry out an onsite repair. This traditional tool has limited functionalities. Three major problems are identified:

1) Choosing the appropriate index terms for a question–answer pair is often time consuming and difficult.

2) There are different conventions in indexing. As many people are taking part on it, the content is eventually unbalanced. For example, a technician may use a few general index terms to describe an answer, whereas another one may use a larger amount of specific terms.

3) No system gathers the experience gained during the actions. Thus, this information is not available to the other technicians.

With the advent of technology, it is now feasible to provide effective and efficient help desk service over a global platform to meet the technicians' requirements. Thus, we present a method to efficiently retrieve knowledge from an Intelligent Decision Support System (IDSS) with a semantic source. The IDSS plays a significant role, offering a wide range of realistic possibilities for assistance with incidents. Instead of asking for the help of a desk technician, or searching through the Internet for an answer, with the intelligent help desk system, the technician just must describe the problem and the agent may automatically search the appropriate knowledge bases. Finally, the system presents a consolidated answer, being the most likely in the first place. An intelligent help desk can help finding and filtering information. The IDSS can handle complex problems, applying domain-specific expertise to assess the consequences of executing its recommendation [7]. In addition, the decisions supported by the IDSS tend to be more consistent, and better managed in terms of managing uncertainty in the outcome.

A. System architecture

Our objective is to design an effective intelligent system with an ontology mapping mechanism for troubleshoot computing environment. ExpertSOS is a research tool built to explore the possibilities and the potential of introducing ontologies into decision-support systems. With ExpertSOS, it is possible to capture, understand and describe the knowledge on troubleshooting in a technology infrastructure. This intelligent system, running on a server, is programmed using PHP/MySql, it captures the domain expert knowledge in Troubleshooting FAQ (Frequently Asked Questions) process into the knowledge base. ExpertSOS is an integrated tool within an incident management system.

Based on these characteristics, we have created an intelligent decision system named ExpertSOS for providing automated decision analysis assistance in the management of failures. The system allows technicians and engineers to quickly gather information and process it in several ways, in order to make an intelligent diagnosis and arrive at an efficient solution. This is achieved by using intelligent and knowledge-based methods. The system architecture is shown in Figure 1.

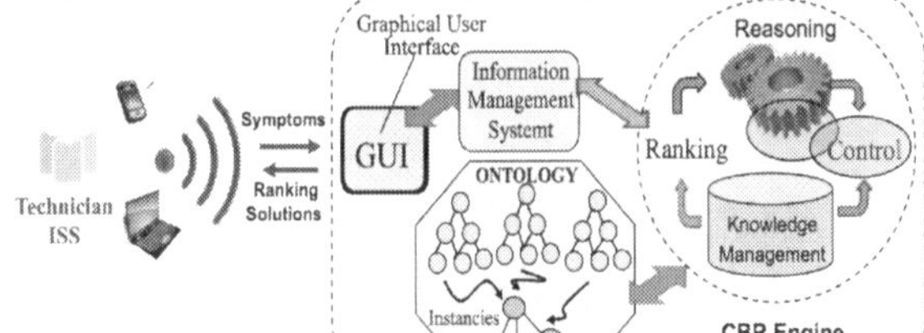

Figure 1. System Architecture.

The elements of the system are the following:

– A user interface: for queries and case knowledge acquisition. This module is mainly for acquiring case-related knowledge so as to build up and maintain databases such as the case library, the ontology library, the similarity matrix library and the global vocabulary library [8].

– A CBR engine: When users input case attributes, this processes the computing algorithm and prompts with similar cases for reference.

– A case knowledge sharing converter: the major function of this module is to offer standards for the translation and the mapping of domain knowledge elements.

III. ONTOLOGY DESIGN AND DEVELOPMENT

The effectiveness of fault management is heavily dependent on the algorithms that are available for diagnosing and determining the source of a problem. Knowledge management is concerned with the representation, organization, acquisition, creation, use, and evolution of knowledge in its many forms. Nowadays, there are different techniques commonly used to manage the knowledge, such as topology analysis, rule-based method, decision tree, dependency graphs, code book technique, Bayesian logic approach, neural networks, etc. However, these techniques find it difficult to catch the semantic meanings of the user requests and the cases stored in the knowledge base. For this purpose, it is necessary to include capabilities to capture the semantic meanings of the managed information and data [9].

In this work, we use a hybrid technique, which consists of a CBR system and ontology. Our IDSS architecture operates through ontologies for knowledge acquisition to allow learning and reasoning. This higher level of understanding can be achieved through processing of the information based on semantics, which is not possible by considering a document as a bag of words. Semantic technologies are usually based on ontologies and play a central role in semantic applications by providing a shared knowledge about the objects in real world. Ontologies are specifications of concepts and relations among them and provide a powerful way to organize information. Ontologies promote reusability and interoperability among different modules and their main goal is to support the interchange of information [10]. This work follows an iterative development process in the ontology-engineering phase and defines the ontologies needed to be used together with the current application.

B. *Case type attribute*

In order to make an ontology-based intelligent retrieval, we need to build a case knowledge base with inheritance structure.

We developed these ontologies in Ontology Web Language (OWL), by building hierarchies of classes describing concepts and relating the classes to each other using properties. We also used the Resource Description Framework (RDF) to define the structure of the metadata, describing knowledge management of the incidents and the Semantic Web Rule Language (SWRL) to specify rules that validate the defined constraints. In order to express this model, we have created an ontology called OntoSOS, based on pairs Question–Answer (QA), and explicitly specifying the relationships between the ontology classes. The ontology and its sub-classes are established according to their taxonomies, as shown in Figure 2.

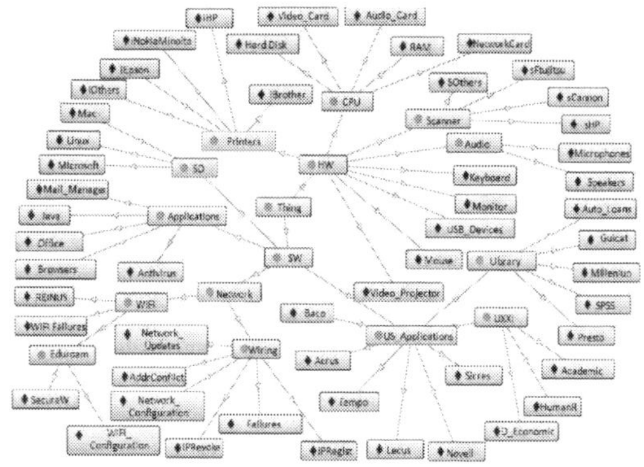

Figure 2. Ontology.

The ontology can be regarded as the quaternion OntoSOS:={technician_profile, object, symptom, action) where the profiles represent the technical kinds; the objects are the resources with the underlying problem or fault; symptoms are the indications that can be observed directly by the customer or the technician; finally, actions are associate operations to solve the problem.

C. *Creation of the ontology*

This work uses an ontology technique for representing information, so that CBR techniques can be used. The ontology-based architecture is made of a set of knowledge, an ontology of the domain, and intelligent access to the set of knowledge. For every request, the intelligent system searches into the cases stored in the knowledge base. The cases are grouped using a metadata language model. Retrieved cases are ranked using a semantic relevance method, and are summarized to generate optimal solutions.

First, we started with a core ontology including the basic concepts and a simple hierarchy. Then, we experimented with this ontology and fixed the issues in reasoning and searching. These steps were repeated until we ended up with a stable ontology containing 35 classes and 191 properties in the domain. When the model got large enough, we needed some tools to help for their management. Several tools may be used in this process, such as Protégé. Protégé is a software tool that supports the specification and maintenance of terminologies, ontologies, and knowledge bases. This framework is an ontology development environment that provides tools for authoring ontologies [11]. Protégé uses OWL and RDF as an ontology language to establish semantic relations. In Figure 3, we show a screenshot of the Protégé editor with a section of the ontology class hierarchy.

After the ontology is established, the case base is generated from a file store where each case is represented with RDF syntax. Knowledge for this system was taken from the expert domain through interviews and discussions. The dataset currently consists of over 7,200 QA pairs.

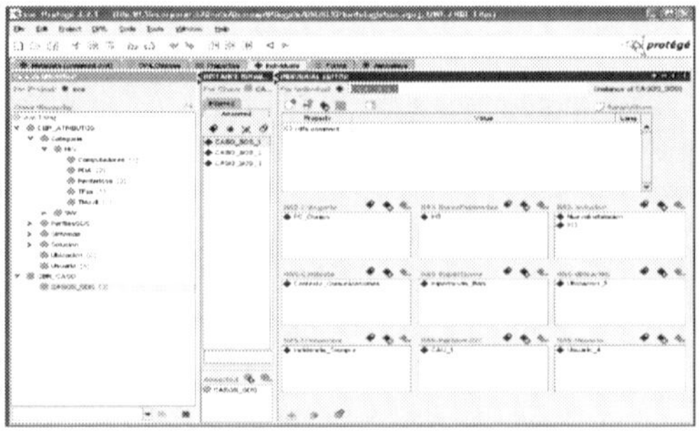

Figure 3. Prótegé Ontology Development

IV. INFERENCE ENGINE

We proposed CBR as a plausible approach to profit from the framework usage experience. When developing applications from a framework, knowledge about the way in which similar domain actions were previously implemented is very useful in order to deal with a new domain action. Thus, we developed a CBR system on framework usage experiences. CBR is a problem-solving paradigm that uses knowledge of relevant past experiences (cases).

These usage experiences explain, through a sequence of steps, how to implement concrete domain actions (incidents) using specific pieces of the framework. This knowledge acts as a prescriptive guide to the framework use and constituted the cases of our system.

Three basic tasks constitute the cycle of the CBR systems: the retrieval of the case that solves the most similar problem to the current one, the adaptation of the retrieved case when it does not exactly fit the current problem and the case learning.

In this study, we used the CBR object-oriented framework development environments jcolibri, that is conceived to help application designers to develop and quickly prototype CBR systems. Jcolibri is an object-oriented framework in Java, along with a number of supporting tools that is designed to facilitate the construction of CBR systems. Jcolibri has been designed as a wide spectrum framework able to support several types of CBR systems from the simple nearest neighbor approaches based on flat or simple structures to more complex Knowledge Intensive ones. Its broad coverage of methods used in case-based recommendation makes jcolibri specially suited for building this type of systems. A key feature of jcolibri authoring tools is the use of templates. In order to facilitate the development of systems, we have been investigating how to reuse templates that abstract past CBR systems. In order to test these ideas we have developed a case base of templates for building case-based recommender systems which effectiveness has been tested through empirical evaluation. Templates store the control flow of the CBR applications and include semantic annotations conceptualizing its behavior and expertise.

A common scenario in an intelligent help desk system is finding whether similar faults have been processed before. The intelligent diagnosis platform should be able to identify and isolate the most likely cause of infrastructure failure in case of a faulty operation. In an IDSS, a response can be defined as the activation, coordination, and management of the appropriate personnel, equipment, communication links, and user information. A potential user provides initial ideas, and possibly a description of the incident. The intelligent help system must retrieve the most likely existant cases, and a possible solution to the given incidents. The goal of the information retrieval (IR) system should be retrieving only those documents that satisfy the user needs, not a bunch of unnecessary data. To improve the efficiency of the system, an original rank algorithm has been developed. It consists of a combined method, which uses a metadata model and semantic matrix factorization to group the top-ranking cases into different categories, while reducing the impact of the general and common information contained in these cases. This method relates the similarity between strings and the calculated correlation belonging to the knowledge in the ontology, as shown in Figure 4.

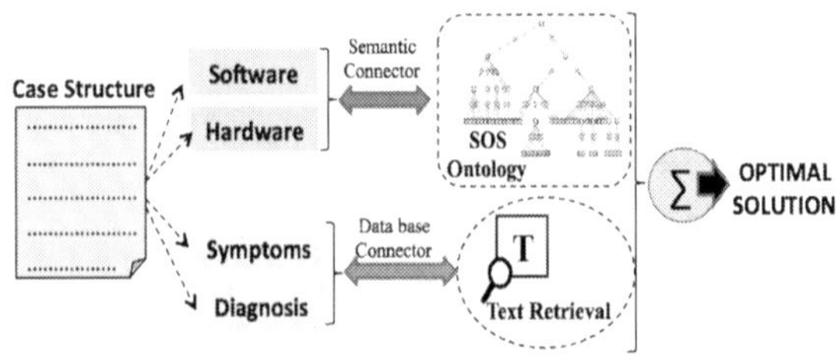

Figure 4. Knowledge Recovery scheme

The indexing algorithm provides an efficient way to search for possible solutions. The indices choice is important to retrieve the right case at the right time. ExpertSOS retrieves the cases stored in the knowledge base and ranks the retrieved cases by establishing a relevance method to the request using similarity measurement. The similarity between indications and the attributes is determined by calculating the weighted sum of the similarities between the values for each attribute.

V. GRAPHIC USER INTERFACE (GUI)

The acceptability of the system on the part of technicians depends to a great extent on the quality of the user interface component. The main goal of our GUI is to gauge the users' satisfaction and trust in the usage of a live help system. We use a simple and useful interface to achieve maximum usability and to reduce the number of ambiguous queries. Each service record consists of the customer account information and service details. A login system receives a set of credentials from the user, through single sign on (SSO) systems, which mostly use lightweight directory access protocol (LDAP) authentication. This way, technicians can interact with the system to fill in the gaps to retrieve the right troubleshooting cases. For this purpose, a keyword-based search service is available on the system, as can be seen in Figure 5.

Figure 5. Technical User Interface

Usually, a query is transformed into an internal form so that the system can interpret it. The raw query submitted by the user should be processed before searching. Several processing tasks can be involved, such as stop word elimination, stemming, and other application-specific tasks. Besides, the user must input the keywords in the user interface. The aim of the interface is to ease the interaction between the user and the system in a natural way. The preprocessor query module translates a query written in natural language into a high-level code. During the preprocessing stage, a query is splitted into keywords, constants, identifiers, operators, and other small pieces of text that the language defines (tokens). Syntactical analysis is the process of combining the tokens into well-formed expressions, statements, and programs. In ExpertSOS, the case-ranking module - the past cases - are ranked based on their semantic importance to the preprocessed input request. During the semantic analysis, the symptoms, values, and other required information about statements are recorded, checked, and transformed. Moreover, a domain-specific semantic dictionary to keep the synonyms has been designed. The required QA pairs should contain some knowledge about the queries and its related issues. Apart from searching and ranking the relevant cases, the system groups the top-ranking cases into categories. Finally, the cases are sorted according a score, so that the most relevant cases are presented to the user at the top of the retrieval list. The system must retrieve an object that contains the service engineer's description of the machine fault, and another object that indicates the suggested actions or services to be carried out. An example is shown in Figure 6.

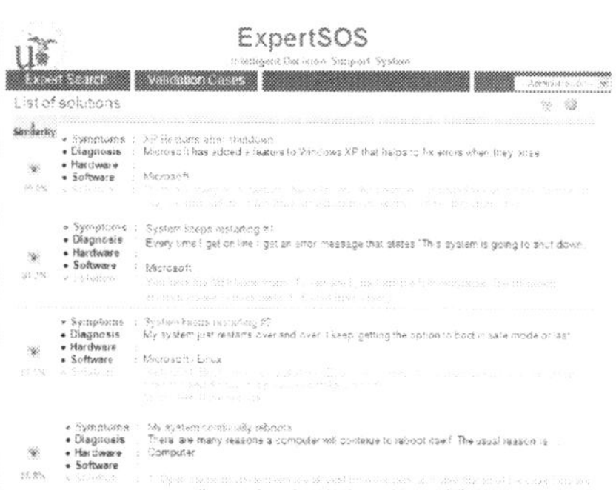

Figure 6. Search engine results

When the solution is generated, it is necessary to validate if that solution is correct. The answer contains a brief summary for each case as a reference solution to the technician. Changing the values that are proposed by the system to other values that are similar, is used to revise the correction of a solution. Each case contains a set of attributes concerning both the metadata and the knowledge. ExpertSOS provides the QA indexer with a list of possible index terms as ontological references. We used a computational-based retrieval system where numerical similarity functions are used to assess and order the cases regarding the query. With this aim, we first need to recover the similar cases from the knowledge base and then propose a new solution to solve the present problem in an efficient way. If the solution generated by the similar values is not better than the proposed one, then the chosen one is a good solution for the problem. Semantic algorithms are used to revise the correction of new solutions. After running those algorithms, the solutions can be accepted and added to the case base.

VI. PERFORMANCE TESTS

In order to compare the ExpertSOS efficiency with the traditional help desk system TSOS, we have compared the resolved incidents using ExpertSOS with those that had been resolved with the TSOS system. Figure 7 shows the total number of incidents across the years up to the end of 2014. We observe a negative trend in the number of incidents resolved using TSOS, while the number of incidents was increasing and how the ExpertSOS improves this negative trend with the implementation of an intelligent help desk system.

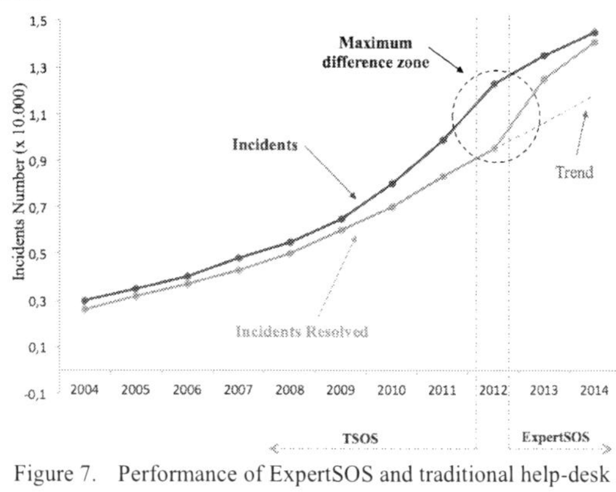

Figure 7. Performance of ExpertSOS and traditional help-desk

Thus, ExpertSOS, based on CBR and ontologies has proved to be cost effective. The benefits stemming from the use of semantic web technologies in the troubleshooting context can be recognized in the following services:

- ExpertSOS has proven to be effective in reducing troubleshooting time, secondary incidents, and environmental impacts.. Increasing speeds and capability during troubleshooting can decrease the incident response time and save over 12% in the daily performance of a service.

- Improved knowledge distribution: Knowledge is distributed in a better way and moved from the expert technicians to the novel technicians, improving the overall solving and dispatching capability.
- Composing new cases compliant to the requirements of a particular user out of the available resources and resource solution automatic interaction dynamically adapts to the features of the particular user.
- Higher service quality, higher customer satisfaction. Furthermore, knowledge can be maintained easily and directly used. This flexibility allows for a quick response to dynamic technological and standards fluctuations.
- Increased first time resolution: Technician groups can access to the right knowledge at the right time to solve incidents quickly and efficiently. Because of this, more productive human capacity in each line was achieved.

VII. CONCLUSIONS

The technology infrastructure of universities and institutions needs the integration of different methods and techniques for developing knowledge management systems. This way, the effectiveness of management activities is increased. There is a strong need to provide support for a whole range of technicians. Different technicians have different needs and skills. An intelligent semantic help desk has been developed to assist and advice new technicians or computer users, in order to diagnose problems in the technological infrastructure of a university. In this paper, we have used computational intelligence and ontologies techniques to integrate the knowledge of incident management in a troubleshooting system. ExpertSOS serves an educational user community, helping people with different skills. Ontologies are applied for extracting knowledge, building up an IDSS. Technicians send symptoms and queries to the system, which provides an expert answer about the question. This work focuses on three aspects to enhance knowledge retrieval: how to apply CBR to find existing similar QA-pairs for a newly submitted question; how to utilize relevant information services to support answers; and how to use semantic indexing to help choosing the appropriate index terms for QA pairs.

For this purpose, our platform is focused on providing expert solutions, delivering exceptional technician service, and creating a reliable infrastructure. We have used a CBR system structure to provide a systematic and analytical troubleshooting procedure. The intelligent help desk described in this work is capable of learning, generalizing, and self-organizing information, in order to find complex patterns and assist in decision support. The main contribution is the described approach for the integration of knowledge from different sources and metadata characterizations of the QA pair in a help desk system to achieve semantic interoperability. This method has a positive effect on technician interpersonal development, such as an enhanced sense of personal efficacy, and the development of technical skills.

The use of computational intelligence and ontologies as a knowledge representation formalism offers many advantages in Information Retrieval. Ontologies and CBR technologies provide a solid solution as an ontology gives an explicit definition of the shared concepts of a certain domain. In fact, the ontology constrains the set of possible mappings between queries and their answers.

Finally, the study analyzes the implementation results and evaluates the viability of our platform. The experimental results shows that the proposed approach can achieve high retrieval accuracy and can considerably improve efficiency compared to existing techniques used in typical customer service systems. ExpertSOS helps to save costs in eliminating the expensive telephone charges, and the number of onsite visits by service engineers.

REFERENCES

[1] T. J. Ottosen, and F. V. Jensen, "When to test? Troubleshooting with postponed system test, Expert System with Applications, vol. 38 (10), pp. 12142-12150, 2011.

[2] B. Chu, C. Lee, and C. Ho, "An ontology-supported database refurbishing technique and its application in mining actionable troubleshooting rules from real-life databases", Engineering Applications of Artificial Intelligence, vol. 21 (8), pp. 1430-1442, 2008.

[3] S. Cebi, M. Celik, C. Kahraman, and I. D. Er. "An expert system towards solving ship auxiliary machinery troubleshooting: SHIPAMTSOLVER," Expert Systems with Applications, vol. 36 (3), part 2, pp. 7219-7227, 2009.

[4] G. Zahedi, S. Saba, M. al-Otaibi, and K. Mohd-Yusof, "Trobleshooting of crude oil desalination plant using fuzzy expert system," Desalination. vol. 266 (1-3), pp. 162-170, 2011.

[5] E. A. Sierra, J. J. Quiroga, R. Fernández, and G. E. Monte, "An intelligent maintenance system for earth-based failure analysis and self-repairing of microsatellites," ActaAstronautica, vol. 55 (1), pp. 61-67, 2004.

[6] S. A. Abdul-Wahab, A. Elkamel, M. A. Al-Weshahi, and A. S. Al-Yahmadi, "Trobleshooting the brine heater of the MSF plat fuzzy-logic based expert system," Desalination. vol. 217 (1-3), pp. 100-117, 2017.

[7] O. A. Blanson, V. M. Sawirjo, C. A. van der Mast, M. A. Neerincx, and J. A. Lindenberg, "Computer assistant for remote collaborative troubleshooting of domestic medical instruments," Pervasive Computing Technologies for Healthcare, pp. 285-288, 2008.

[8] D. Wang, T. Li, S. Zhu, and Y. Gong, "iHelp: An Intelligent Online Helpdesk System," IEEE Transactions on Systems, Man, and Cybernetics, vol.41 (1), pp.173-182, 2011.

[9] F. George, Artificial Intelligence, Structures and Strategies for Complex Problem Solving, 4ª edition, Ed. Pearson, Education Limited, 2002.

[10] C. C. Huang, and S. H. Lin, "Sharing knowledge in a supply chain using the semantic web," Expert Systems with Applications, 37(4), pp. 3145–3161, 2010.

[11] A. Gomez-Perez, A. Corcho, and M. Fernandez-Lopez, "Ontological Engineering", Advanced Information and Knowledge Processing, Springer-Verlag London, 2003.

International Academy, Research, and Industry Association (IARIA)
412 Derby Way
Wilmington, DE 19810

ISBN 978-1-5108-5130-6

9 781510 851306

CURRAN ASSOCIATES INC.
proceedings.com

Eleventh International Conference on Adaptive and Self-Adaptive Systems and Applications (ADAPTIVE 2019)

Held at ComputationWorld 2019

Venice, Italy
5–9 May 2019

IARIA